Migration and Return in Modern African Literature

Rochester Studies in African History and the Diaspora

Toyin Falola, Series Editor
The Jacob and Frances Sanger Mossiker Chair in the Humanities
and University Distinguished Teaching Professor
University of Texas at Austin

Recent Titles

Transactional Culture in Colonial Dakar, 1902–44
Rachel M. Petrocelli

*African Migration and the Novel:
Exploring Race, Civil War, and Environmental Destruction*
Jack Taylor

The Global Ethiopian Diaspora: Migrations, Connections, and Belongings
Edited by Shimelis B. Gulema, Hewan Girma, and Mulugeta F. Dinbabo

Ransoming Prisoners in Precolonial Muslim Western Africa
Jennifer Lofkrantz

Coming of Age in the Afro-Latin American Novel: Blackness, Religion, Immigration
Bonnie S. Wasserman

Masquerade and Money in Urban Nigeria: The Case of Calabar
Jordan Fenton

West African Soldiers in Britain's Colonial Army, 1860–1960
Timothy Stapleton

Decolonizing African Studies: Knowledge Production, Agency, and Voice
Toyin Falola

Youth and Popular Culture in Africa: Media, Music, and Politics
Edited by Paul Ugor

A complete list of titles in the Rochester Studies in African History and the Diaspora
Series may be found on our website, www.urpress.com

Migration and Return in Modern African Literature

Black Bodies in White Spaces

Ernest Cole

UNIVERSITY OF ROCHESTER PRESS

Copyright © 2025 Ernest Cole

All rights reserved. Except as permitted under current legislation, no part of this work may be photocopied, stored in a retrieval system, published, performed in public, adapted, broadcast, transmitted, recorded, or reproduced in any form or by any means, without the prior permission of the copyright owner.

First published 2025

University of Rochester Press
668 Mt. Hope Avenue, Rochester, NY 14620, USA
www.urpress.com
and Boydell & Brewer Limited
PO Box 9, Woodbridge, Suffolk IP12 3DF, UK
www.boydellandbrewer.com

ISBN-13: 978-1-64825-112-2 (hardcover)
ISSN: 1092-5228

Library of Congress Cataloging-in-Publication Data

Names: Cole, Ernest, 1965– author.
Title: Migration and return in modern African literature : Black bodies in white spaces / Ernest Cole.
Other titles: Rochester studies in African history and the diaspora ; 100. 1092-5228
Description: Rochester : University of Rochester Press, 2025. | Series: Rochester studies in African history and the diaspora, 1092-5228 ; 100 | Includes bibliographical references and index. |
Identifiers: LCCN 2024046707 (print) | LCCN 2024046708 (ebook) | ISBN 9781648251122 (hardback) | ISBN 9781648251139 (paperback) | ISBN 9781805436188 (pdf) | ISBN 9781805436195 (epub)
Subjects: LCSH: African fiction (English)—History and criticism. | Emigration and immigration in literature. | Immigrants in literature. | Black people in literature.
Classification: LCC PR9340 .C645 2025 (print) | LCC PR9340 (ebook) | DDC 823.00996—dc23/eng/20241008
LC record available at https://lccn.loc.gov/2024046707
LC ebook record available at https://lccn.loc.gov/2024046708

A catalogue record for this title is available from the British Library.

In memory of Yaguine Koita and Fode Tunkara: two young lives cut short in the pursuit of the dream. May their souls rest in peace.

Contents

Acknowledgments	ix
Introduction	1
Part I: Flight	
1. Reasons for Departure	23
2. Unfulfilled Dreams	45
Part II: Arrival	
3. Disillusionment and Death	77
4. Psychological Depression	109
Part III: Return	
5. Challenges to Reintegration	133
6. The New Hybridity	152
7. Constructive Liminality	180
Conclusion	202
Bibliography	209
Index	217

Acknowledgments

Sincere gratitude and love to my three girls—Everetta, Ernesta, and Tunde—for their support throughout this process.

Introduction

The impetus for writing this book was the tragic story of Yaguine Koita and Fode Tounkara, two stowaways from the Republic of Guinea, West Africa, in 1999, who froze to death on a Sabena Airlines Airbus flying from Conakry to Brussels, and whose bodies were discovered in the airplane's right wheel bay, after several trips between the two cities. The death of these two young men raises several questions regarding the state of African societies that could apparently justify such risk—the threat to their lives—just to make it to Europe. It also points to the expectation of rewards that migrants hope to achieve in Western societies.

Over the past decade, there has been an upsurge of African migrants trying to reach Europe and North America and the risks they are prepared to take keep escalating at an alarming rate. Images of migrants dying crossing the Sahara Desert and drowning in the Mediterranean Sea have almost become daily occurrences in the media. The plight of these migrants is also depicted in literature, and significantly, the past ten years have seen a rise in literary and critical works dealing with African migration in the diaspora.

Contemporary African diaspora literature suggests that the horrors of crossing the Sahara and the Mediterranean are only the beginning of many barriers to cross, that is, for those migrants who make it alive to Europe and North America. The social and cultural barriers and economic and linguistic hurdles that await them often prove insurmountable. The novels selected for study in this book address the reasons for flight, the struggle upon arrival, and the decision to return to the migrant's homeland. I focus on the painful experience of alterity consequent on isolation, marginalization, and racism and the precarity that leads to psychological depression, insanity, and sometimes death for the characters in these novels. I further explore the possibility of the migrant returning home, even though this move is a complicated one.

I must contend from the outset that migration is a complex issue. It can be seen from many perspectives that are sometimes conflicting and even divisive. It has social and political ramifications, and this has added to the controversy surrounding it. In many Western societies today, the topic of migration is a political lightning rod that threatens to upset the fabric of those societies. For this study, however, I focus on the literary domain of migration.

2 &❧ INTRODUCTION

My analysis of the nine novels selected for study—*We Need New Names* (2013), *Open City* (2011), *The Other Crucifix* (2010), *Blue White Red* (1998), *Harare North* (2009), *Behold the Dreamers* (2016), *Ghana Must Go* (2013), *Americanah* (2013), and *So the Path Does Not Die* (2008)—reveals that while the pursuit of the dream can be a viable endeavor, it is accomplished at tremendous cost to the migrants, sometimes to their minds and bodies and in certain cases their lives. The racism that fosters exclusion and marginalization is not only a threat to the achievement of the dream; it also puts migrants in precarious positions that make the journey and the expected rewards from it questionable. For the African migrant, as this study reveals, racism in the West is both racialized and ethnicized. It is the othering of the African migrants that is meant to indicate their inferiority. This fosters discrimination and opens the migrant to vulnerabilities, even for those who are legal and are considered successful. Race and racism are barriers to acculturation and integration, and the migrant finds it increasingly difficult to achieve social and economic advancement.

Ava Landry's theorization on the implications for race and racism for the African migrant offers a critical lens to understand their plight and is instructive for my argument of return. In her essay, "Black Is Black Is Black? African Immigrant Acculturation in Chimamanda Ngozi Adichie's *Americanah* and Yaa Gyasi's *Homegoing*," she states:

> African migrants come to the United States with a variety of different cultural heritages and identities, but they must deal with Blackness as another status, or as their most salient social identity, in ways that are new, complex, and foreign. . . . The process of acculturation for African migrants consists of a unique, tense, and ever-present struggle between pre-migration ethnic identity and post-migration racial identity. . . . In racialized societies, such as the United States, superordinate races construct racial structures composed of relations, practices, and ideologies to create and maintain their differentiated possession of and access to material benefits. . . . African migrants not only come to realize that they are black but that their Blackness places them at the bottom of the racial hierarchy. They mediate this struggle by occupying the status of ethnicized Other.

I draw from Landry's theorization to foreground my argument of return. I agree with Landry that the Black bodies of African migrants are perceived and interpreted with bias in the West. Black bodies are racialized and ethnicized as other, and this underpins inferiority and fosters exclusion. Racial identity leads to a process of othering that prohibits acculturation. The Black bodies of African migrants become the canvas for deployment of social exclusion and discrimination. While Landry's theory offers me a lens through which to read the ethnicized status of the African migrant, I go further in my study to predicate return on the othering of the migrant by developing and articulating a hermeneutic that frames return as both an act of resistance to otherness and a basis of hope for success in their homeland. I recognize that return is fraught with difficulties and complications, but the novels selected for study present a sobering depiction of migrant experience in the West that provides some justification for return. My study also adds to the argument of return by exploring the decision to return not as a homogenization of migrant experiences or a teleological depiction of them. While I acknowledge the success of some migrants, such as in Benjamin Kwakye's *The Other Crucifix* (2010), my findings in analyzing the migrant experience in *Ghana Must Go* (2013), *Americanah* (2013), and *So the Path Does Not Die* (2008) demonstrate that success comes at a cost and that return to the homeland could be a better alternative to the racism in the West. I argue in the book that while the dream can be accomplished and can offer possibilities for socioeconomic transformation, such as in *We Need New Names* (2013), *Open City* (2011), and *The Other Crucifix* (2010), the suffering of migrants in *Blue White Red* (1998), *Harare North* (2004), and *Behold the Dreamers* (2016) shows the achievement of the dream at the cost of irreparable psychological damage and even death.

Since mobility is based on the migrant's dream of a better life in the West, Langston Hughes's poetry helps shed light on the irony of the dream and the psychological consequences of failing to achieve it. Historical evidence affirms that the experience of African Americans, their struggles for integration in spite of the promises of emancipation and freedom, depict the realities of being Black in America. This reality, evident in Jim Crow, indicates a barrier to black accomplishment of the dream.

For the purpose of analysis, I am drawn to two poems by Langston Hughes that distinctively shed light on the consequences of unrealized dreams. Since the expectation of success in the migrant's dream is critical to why they migrate in the first place, Hughes's poems provide a context for understanding the barriers to achievement of dreams and the psychological depression that follows. In "Harlem," he asks in the opening line the question, "What happens to a dream deferred?" and provides in the subsequent lines a series of possible options, framed as questions, that could result from a failed dream. These include drying up "like a raisin in the sun," festering "like a sore," stinking "like rotten meat," crusting over "like a syrupy sweet," or just exploding. In the other poem, "Dreams," Hughes advises the reader to hold fast on to dreams, if human aspirations are to be accomplished.

In both poems, Hughes spells out the ambivalence of dreams. There is the aspirational quality to dreams that motivates the dreamer striving to accomplish life's objectives; for without dreams, "Life is a barren field/ Frozen with snow." However, there is a destructive side to dreams and

4 &♦ INTRODUCTION

dreaming, especially in situations where dreams are not accomplished. In these instances, "Life is a broken-winged bird/That cannot fly." In addition, as the first poem denotes, unaccomplished dreams have the capacity to dry up, to fester and stink, and to sag like a heavy burden in the dreamer's consciousness, in both its physical and psychological manifestations. At worst, dreams have the capacity to explode, a clear indication of their potential for self-destruction.

In unpacking the multiple layers of such a highly complex phenomenon as migration, I begin with a definition of the migrant and his representation in African diaspora literature. I conceptualize the African migrant as the subject in the diaspora who, because of their racial and ethnic identity, are constantly dealing with the complications of home, belonging, and return. My study reveals that the process of negotiating the many white spaces in which they find themselves and the examination of the structures that exclude them from fully participating in those spaces are critical to understanding the challenges to African migration.

It must be noted that the journey of African migrants to the West did not start yesterday. A historical trajectory of African migration reveals that African mobilities started as a response to the disillusionment of postindependent African societies in the mid-1960s. By the turn of the twentieth century, many African nations gained independence from France, Britain, and in some cases, Portugal. These newly independent societies were filled with high hopes of success, and the pioneers who took over the reins of power after the departure of the colonialists made huge promises to their respective societies. However, within a very short time, it was clear that the honeymoon was over and the much bandied-about promises of success were marred by a reversal of expectations anchored in disillusionment and discontentment. The realities of corruption and postindependence disillusionment have been well depicted in the African novel, typical among which are Ayi Kwei Armah's *The Beautyful Ones Are Not Yet Born* (1968), Chinua Achebe's *A Man of the People* (1966), and Ngũgĩ wa Thiong'o's *Petals of Blood* (1977). Together, these novels present a depiction of the continent where progress is stymied by political corruption, nepotism, exploitation, and inefficiency in governmental circles. This period of decadence engendered the advent of the military in politics, a phase in development in the continent marked by usurpation of political power by the hands of soldiers, who initially promised a return to democracy but quickly degenerated into a quagmire of persuasive corruption and the destruction of the state. Chinua Achebe's *A Man of the People* (1966) and *Anthills of the Savannah* (1987) are among the novels that brutally depict the role of the military in politics in African societies.

By the 1980s, it was becoming apparent that with the level of corruption, oppression, and exploitation of the masses, Africans would need to look elsewhere if they were to accomplish their dreams of material and social improvement. Among the many pathways envisioned as necessary for the accomplishment of this aspiration was international migration. By the late 1980s, immigration to the West became desirable if social and economic mobility were to be achieved, and the figure of the "been-to," the African who has traveled abroad and returned with some evidence of success, was highly revered and became a symbol of motivation for the youth.

The figure of the been-to in African literature is not new. The evolution of the African migrant as the symbol of success, especially in meeting Western ideologies of progress, was celebrated. These migrants who returned home indeed had their own share of problems, especially in the ensuing conflict between traditionalism and modernism that arose because of exposure to Western culture but were largely perceived as successful. Chinua Achebe's *No Longer at Ease* addresses this ambivalence of the returned migrants and the struggle to reintegrate and reassimilate into their traditional societies. Ayi Kwei Armah's *Fragments* (1970) and Ama Ata Aidoo's *Dilemma of a Ghost* (1965) tell similar stories. Recently, critical works such as William Lawson's *The Western Scar: The Theme of the Been-to in West African Fiction* (1982) provide a critical lens and ideological constructs to read novels that follow on this phase of development in African literature.

The struggle of the been-to and the future of society were made precarious by the events of the 1990s on the continent. If the discontentment stemming from the reversal of expectations in postindependence was not enough motivation for migration, the violence, trauma, and dislocation that came with civil wars in this period are abundant evidence affirming the decision to migrate to the West. In response, new narratives of war and what has come to be known as "refugee literature" or "literature of migration" developed. Later narratives such as Chimamanda Ngozi Adichie's *Half of a Yellow Sun* and Ishmael Beah's *A Long Way Gone* record the gruesome realities of civil wars in Nigeria and Sierra Leone, respectively. The violence and death depicted in these novels are abundant evidence of justification for translocation by African migrants.

The postcolonial era has historically produced migratory narratives that explore stereotypical portraits of African migrants in Western societies and their resulting exclusion. However, in the last decade, Western perceptions of the phenomenon of migration have deteriorated considerably. At a time when African migrants are fleeing the continent for a variety of reasons—poverty, wars, persecution, political oppression, natural disasters from weather-related conditions—and are perceived as coming from destitute

6 ❧ INTRODUCTION

societies; attitudes to them in the migratory countries in the West have also changed. With this changed attitude comes not only a level of restriction codified in immigration laws but also a level of contempt and hostility previously unseen. This attitude of hostility puts migrants in dangerous situations that amplify alterity and expose the precarity in their lives abroad. While some migrants are able to return to their countries of origin, others no longer have a home to return to. They are forced to stay abroad in precarious situations.

In the past decade, a number of literary texts as well as criticism related to African diaspora literature have focused on redefining the genre and the parameters within which it can be evaluated. This body of literature has explored many themes in diaspora literature and reassessed the meaning of success. Aminatta Forna's *Happiness* (2018), Randolf Okonkwo's *This American Life Sef* (2016), and Okey Ndibe's *Never Look an American in the Eye* (2016) are among new diaspora novels that depict the shocking realities of life of the African migrant in Western societies. The writers of French Expressionism such as Fatou Diome, Alain Mabanckou, J. R. Essomba, Nathalie Etoke, and Aminata Sow Fall have also been exploring the dehumanizing conditions in which the African migrant lives in the West and the irony of the quest to succeed for many of them. Essomba's *Le Paradis du Nord* (1996), Etoke's *Un amour sans papiers* (1999), and Sow Fall's *Douceurs du bercail* (1998) are indicative of this perspective on migration. Fatou Diome's *Le Ventre de L'Atlantique* (2003) brilliantly illustrates the irony of the quest and the threats to humanity, life, and dignity of the migrant.

From the study of the selected novels in this book, I argue that contemporary migration experiences of African migrants interrogate the rationale for migration and the possibilities of success initially promised. I note that the challenges to success for the African migrant start with the quest itself, the journey to the West, and that this is one of many barriers the migrant would have to cross. The book interrogates the meaning of success associated with migration by pointing out the realities of racial discrimination, exclusion, and marginalization experienced in the narratives and pinpoint the dehumanizing conditions anchored in alterity and precarity that they have to confront. I emphasize that for many of them, even with those that can be described as successful, the literature reveals the irony of the quest. I postulate the concept of "constructive liminality" as the "new hybridity" and way forward for the returned migrants and the societies to which they returned. In this way, the book makes a specific claim and offers a unique contribution to African diaspora studies.

Over the past decade, several critical works have been written that explore migration in its historical, sociological, philosophical, and theoretical contexts. These works have focused on migratory experiences of African

INTRODUCTION & 7

migrants both in the United States and in Europe and the United Kingdom. Issues central to displacement, home, belonging, identity, and exclusion are given detailed treatment in them. A number of these works have made significant contributions to the study of African migration in the diaspora are in the literature review. I must state that the list is by no means exhaustive. However, this study offers the reader different contexts and perspectives to locate contemporary African migration, analyze its overarching themes, and engage different critical approaches to their analysis.

Maximillian Feldner, Peter Aspinal, Martha Chinouya, and John Arthur have explored migratory experiences of recent African migrants abroad and depictions of their homeland in their works. Feldner was instructive in his comprehensive treatment of Nigeria diaspora literature through examining the works of novelists Helon Habila, Chimamanda Ngozi Adichie, Chris Abani, Helen Oyeyemi, among others. John Arthur, Joseph Takougang, Thomas Owusu, and Thomas Yaw also focus on detailed examination of themes relating to the migrant's experience abroad. They point out the attempts of migrants to re-create African diaspora communities abroad, the relationship between migrants and the host communities, the role of identity (racial, cultural, and ethnic) in reception and acculturation, and the negotiation of spaces for belonging. Arthur et al. are critical to my analysis of African migratory experience in this book. My book is a departure from this approach in using spatial geographies to examine crucial themes such as liminality, identity, and belonging in my exploration of the migrant experience. However, while the literature review reveals the contention that spatial and geographic constructions are amenable—in that they are not static but, rather, dynamic—I argue in this work that those spaces are both restrictive and creative: they can be used as spaces for deploying racism and can also be used to engender acts of resistance to it. My theorization, for instance, adds another layer of complexity to the perspective of Arthur et al. for it interrogates integration and advocates return, even if such a move is not without its complications.

Helen Cousins, and Pauline Dodgson-Katiyo provide a solid canvas to anchor the theme of return in *African Literature Today 34 Diaspora and Returns in Fiction* (2016). The essays in this collection shed light on the tensions between home and abroad, location and dislocation, integration and return, while foregrounding possibilities of the migrant reclaiming home through a process of (re)negotiation of values. Abdoulaye Kane, Todd Leedy, and Christopher Zembe shift the focus from the migratory experience to the reasons for departure. Kane and Leedy use sociological frames of displacement in rural-urban migration to examine the experience of migrants abroad, while Zembe draws from the colonial and postcolonial histories of Zimbabwe to pinpoint the contributions of race and ethnicity

8 ❧ INTRODUCTION

in the construction of diasporic identities and the process of integration of Zimbabwean migrants in the United Kingdom. I use *Harare North* (2009) and *We Need New Names* (2013), two novels from Zimbabwe, to depict two phases in the migration process: departure and arrival. My study of *Harare North*, for instance, fills a specific gap in previous treatment of the arrival phase of migration: the process of psychological breakdown of the unnamed narrator and the representation of that process in the linguistic and textual structures of the novel. The reality of trauma and the corresponding process of mental breakdown are inscribed into the materiality of the novel in its textual composition evident in incomplete sentences, the fragmentary thoughts of the narrator, and the dreamlike quality of the narrative. The psychological breakdown of the narrator is the linguistic fragmentation of the novel.

Approaches to the study of African migration in the diaspora are not limited to flight and return and theorizations about them. The different approaches adopted by writers call attention to the complexity of the topic of migration. Christopher Foster ventures into Atlantic, postcolonial, and queer studies to engage global migration and its overarching themes of neoliberal globalization and nationalism. Toyin Falola, Niyi Afolabi, and Adérónké Adesanya explore artistic and creative expressions in Africa and the African diaspora to explore migration. A similar approach is adopted by Abimbola Adelakun and Falola in their exploration of how the artistic works in Africa and the diaspora create national and global contexts for depicting Black culture, a basis for examining a host of themes including anti-Black racism, xenophobia, ethnocentrism, migration, and transnational feminisms.

Leigh Raiford and Heike Raphael-Hernandez use an artistic and creative approach in visual culture to examine the meaning of the Black body displaced through mobilities. Focusing on how perceptions of the Black body are constructed in the diaspora, the authors examine the role of visual technologies in the creation of dominant images of Blackness and how perceptions of them and the discourse used to analyze them help us understand the connections between place, body, and identity. Pauline Uwakweh uses a feminist perspective to depict African migrant experience through transnational negotiations and female agency. Her book brings together the voices of eight transnational African diaspora women writers including three, Chimamanda Ngozi Adichie, Imbolo Mbue, and NoViolet Bulawayo, whose works were selected for study in this book. Uwakweh's analysis of reversed migration is useful to the argument of return that I make in this book, particularly in its emphasis on home and belonging. I must add that while Uwakweh's work was insightful for my study, my book uses a combination of theoretical, philosophical, and cultural constructs to explore African migration and return. It draws from spatial theory and cultural criticism to engage ideological

INTRODUCTION &** 9

constructs such as Afropolitanism in theorizing the connections between home and belonging, history and identity, culture and location.

Understanding the lived experience of African migrants in the diaspora is not limited to notions of alterity and precarity. Donald Carter has drawn our attention to the theory of anthropology of invisibility to develop an aesthetics of migration to examine notions of social rejection and representation in popular culture. I value Jopi Nyman for his analysis of cultural encounters and the construction of migrant subjects, showing how postcolonial studies can be related to migration. His treatment of Ishmael Beah's *A Long Way Gone* (2007) sheds light on politics, mobility, and displacement as motivation for flight in postcolonial Sierra Leone.

Isidore Okpewho, Carol Boyce Davies and Ali A. Mazrui; Robert Cancel and Winifred Woodhull; Toyin Falola; and Obioma Nnaemeka and Jennifer Thorington Springer all add to the critical framework and discursive praxis for critiquing African migration and have provided additional interpretive frames critical to my study. While Falola and Okpewho et al. focus on history in terms of slavery, modernity, and globalization, Nnaemeka and Thornton Springer focus on gender and race. For Cancel and Woodhull, the focus is on the relationship between African cultures past and present and their reformulations in diasporic communities. Francoise Kral is useful in framing perspectives around identity, disjunction, and liminality.

The theoretical framework for this study seeks to fill specific literary and theoretical gaps in current criticism on African diaspora literature. Broadly, the study foregrounds the argument that crossing borders offers a critical space for thematization of the experiences of the migrant, a reimagination of the homeland, and the construction of new structures to rethink nostalgia and return. It makes the claim that migration engenders dramatic shifts in conception of self and Other, home and abroad, identity and belonging that allow for the creation of a hermeneutic of return. In making a case for return, the book argues for a transition that synthesizes migrant experiences abroad with Indigenous systems and structures to develop a new hybridity for individual transformation and national development. In this way, it initiates a new perspective for exploring the limits and possibilities of migration using new perspectives, theoretical frames, and critical models to analyze border crossings, identity formation, and aesthetics of representation. It concludes that return offers the migrant an opportunity to plot new futures in the context of a new and hybridized sociocultural space by emphasizing a process of reintegration based on a synthesis of cultural values and the experience of the returned migrant.

A significant contribution of this study to contemporary criticism on African migration is my analysis of the concept of migration. I argue that

10 &♦ INTRODUCTION

migration is itself characterized by a sense of rootedness, uprootedness, and displacement, a fluidity that denies concrete and substantial manifestations of tangible realities. It is defined around parameters of temporality and mobility that allow for a deep sense of uncertainty and indeterminacy that promotes anxieties. With this ambiguity, if not ambivalence, comes the painful realization of a crippling dichotomy: a fluidity characterized by stasis, in essence, rootlessness that is fixed in time and space, instability and insecurity that are constant, ongoing, nontransformative, and endlessly encoded in time and place. Here lie the roots of the gesture to return: the need to break the fixed cycle of rootedness.

Sten P. Moslund has focused on the new meaning attached to migration and its connections to the human condition. He asserts that the human condition is no longer defined by traditional identity markers like nationality, origin, settlement, dwelling, roots, birthplace, or bloodlines. In *Migration Literature and Hybridity* (2010), he contends that the figure of the migrant gives us a contemporary understanding of what it means to be human and emphasizes the migrant as the borderline figure of a massive historical displacement: one who is supposed to be in a state of uprooted, nomadic, transnational, and transcultural fluidity.

Moslund's conception of migration interrogates notions of fixity and fragmentation in terms of identities and relations. With the premise of fluidity and mobilities that the world offers, and the state of flux in cultures and traditions that are evolving, Moslund posits that the migrant figure illuminates the long-concealed truth of human nature, exploring how movement is the norm rather than the exception and how we are fundamentally creatures of movement rather than settlement. In his contention, migration illustrates the human condition of restlessness and new mobile identity formation. This sense of new identity formation is echoed in the construct of Afropolitanism. Simon Gikandi's analysis, "On Afropolitanism" in *Negotiating Afropolitanism: Essays on Borders and Spaces in Contemporary African Literature and Folklore*, is critical to my argument of return migration.

In addition to Moslund, Andrew Nyongesa has argued for critical hybridity and challenges notions of fixity in his work *Cultural Hybridity and Fixity: Strategies of Resistance in Migration Literatures*. He posits cultural hybridity as a strategy of resistance and pathway to success for the African migrant. His contention decries the location of African identities with a fixed geographical space and affirms a global dimension to being African and a host of other identities. With this conception, the claim of rootedness is challenged, and migrants are much more than their traditional regionalities. The possibilities of cultural hybridity and identity transformation resist, subvert, and transcend fixity and the obstacles to integration and success.

INTRODUCTION ❧ 11

Moslund's characterization of migration literature is critical for the arguments that I advance in this book. He notes that the characters of migration literature invariably "cope with migration" in different ways: from the experience of migration and the uncertainties of displaced identities as destructive, agonizing, and painful, to the experience of migration as "productive, fascinating, and appealing." For Moslund, in general, the migration novel works from a perspective of rewriting identities in order to evoke their impure and heterogenous character. While this theorization has been useful, my study takes the conversation further by arguing that on the contrary, the literature reveals a different reality, one that contests heterogeneity, universalism, and globalization; dissolves multiculturalism, diversity, and inclusion; and interrogates belonging and integration. The experiences of the major characters depicted in these works demonstrate a spatial reality that excludes difference and occludes possibilities of transcultural understanding and cultural hybridity. The book argues that the contemporary migrant finds himself in a space that is othered and devalued, that excludes him from participating in mainstream society, and that denies him access to social and economic opportunities.

Cajetan Iheka and Jack Taylor's "Introduction: The Migration Turn in African Cultural Productions" addresses many of the issues explored in this monograph: the socioeconomic condition of Africans in their homeland that necessitated, at times, unorthodox means of escaping the continent; such social quandaries as poverty, wars, hunger, and disease; the experiences of "a new generation of African, born in colonized Africa and then children outside the continent or somewhere other than their place of natural origin on the continent," and the possibilities of return. The portrayal of the deliberating conundrums that prepare migrants to leave the continent, the experience of migrants abroad, their relationship to their homeland, and the negotiation of a possible return, be it physical or physiological, are the major concerns expressed by Iheka and Taylor. They further note that the "longing or yearning for return is often connected to migrants' exclusion or limited access to the social and economic resources of their new environment." They are in Brenda Cooper's analysis of the work of the new generation of writers in *A New Generation of Writers: Migration, Material Culture, and Language,* in which "exclusion is what migrant writers often depict when their protagonists find themselves perplexed in strange, hostile climates and settings, where they do not set the joke, understand the irony, the pun, or the analogy and where their accented English and their dress, food and manner, are not quite right." This is the experience of the in-between and as Iheka and Taylor contend, "To be sure, the precarious conundrum of the African migrant in these narratives (as well as those specifically selected for

12 ❧ INTRODUCTION

this study) complicated the privileged Afropolitan subjectively that Taiye Selasi celebrates in her descriptive article on the elite, immigrant, mobile African subject who is comfortable in New York and Nairobi, as well as in Los Angeles and Lagos." I agree with Iheka and Taylor in their contention that "Selasi's Africans of the world enjoy a certain privilege that most Africans do not boast of; it is no wonder her Afropolitanism has been critiqued for its exuberant materialism."

The significance of Iheka and Taylor's theorization on my work cannot be ignored. However, my analysis of the migrant experience makes an advance by not only exploring three phases of the experience (departure, arrival, and return) it does so on two significant levels: the return of the African migrant in the diaspora, including first-generation Africans or children born in the diaspora and the return of characters of African descent—African Americans and Caribbeans—to their ancestral homeland. My analysis of the return of Africans historically connected to the continent in *So the Path Dies Not Die* (2008) provides an additional layer to understanding the complications of return in the context of history, culture, and identity.

Madhu Krishnan's postulates on return migration further elucidate my conception of the subject and its exploration. In "Reading Space, Subjectivity, and Form in the 21st Century Narrative of Return," she writes of return migration as having "suffered from its conflations of varying types of migratory activities and a generally reductive perspective on its sociological purview." She references Brah's *Cartographies of Diaspora* and Lynellyn D. Long and Ellen Oxfeld's "Introduction: An Ethnography of Return" in *Coming Home? Refugees, Migrants, and Those Who Stayed Behind* to elaborate on his theory of "enabling alienation" as a productive way of viewing return migration.

In exploring the topic of migration, my book makes another significant contribution to African diaspora literary studies: its focus on a number of themes including racial identity, alterity, precarity, acculturation, and integration that unveil the complexities of migration. Three interrelated themes are pertinent to my argument and deserve some critical attention. They are "home," "success," and "return." I discuss these themes with reference to ongoing conversations on Afropolitanism, spatiality, and identity. I begin with the concept of home and its connections to the meaning of success. In many African societies, success is predicated on leaving home. As long as the individual is able to leave the shores of the continent, he or she is deemed successful or on the path to success. That perception is clearly faulty and untrue, not only because it falsely posits staying at home as failure but also because it does not take into consideration that the Atlantic Ocean is one of several borders the migrant will have to cross—and the most dangerous. In fact, it is becoming increasingly clear that the good majority of those who

INTRODUCTION ❧ 13

stayed are better off socially and economically than those who left. Marame Gueye's notion of *toog jolof* would gain some currency here. Other African writers that have criticized the notion of home as failure include Ama Ata Aidoo and Fatou Dime.

Four recent essays in Simon Gikandi's *Negotiating Afropolitanism: Essays on Borders and Spaces in African Literature and Folklore* have been influential in the shaping of my argument of return. These are Theano S. Terkenli's "Home as a Region," Marame Gueye's "Fatou Diome's *Le Ventre de l'Atlantique: Reconfiguring Local Discourses of Emigration*," Naline Iyer's "No Place to Call Home: Citizenship and Belonging in M. G. Vassanji's *The In-Between World of Vikram Lall*," and Maria Jesus Caharlos Traseria's "Between Diasporic Identity and Agency: Versions of the Pastoral in Gumah's *Pilgrim's Way* and Mohjoub's *Navigation of a Rainmaker*."

Terkenli defines home as "regions culturally constructed and geographically and historically contingent." He adds that they "exist to serve fundamental individual and group needs, and, as human constructs and cultural products, they also sustain those needs." The author further notes two significant features of home: first, it fulfills the need for refuge, for a frame of reference, and for a context of self-identification and, second, it connotes not only a physical or spatial condition but also a social and habitual condition in a context with which people personalize and identify through some measure of control. In the axis of self-identification and control lie the roots of belonging and inclusion. In the juxtaposition of the phrase "to head home" with the special location "home," the emotive, physical, and spiritual manifestations and significance of home are here. To be home, at home, or at a place called home is to be emotionally and spiritually connected to a physical or imaginary place with deep ties to its history and culture. The social and historical conditions that it offers and possibilities for self-identification it promotes constitute the spiritual dimension of home, rooted in time and place. It is only in so doing that people can feel at home, a feeling that the in-between wants to deconstruct and eventually contradict. As Terkenli writes, "People feel at home with themselves as a rule, because they are familiar with both their past actions and their ongoing attitudes, feelings, preoccupations, tendencies, and intentions, which are anchored in the self and spatially expressed through personal geographies."

Another important idea expressed by Terkenli is that of the social component of home. He writes that this component "becomes salient in the development of the idea of home by establishing a circle of social relations that validate an individual as a human being." Deeply instrumental in its literal and figurative manifestations, the social component of home affirms the depictions of the migrant as crucial to the transformation and transcendence of the binaries of the in-between, in the absence of which the migrant

14 ❧ INTRODUCTION

is devolved, dehumanized, and ostracized. In this situation, individuals then gravitate to their collective home that is "delineated by ethnic, naturalistic, civic, or ideological parameters." It is the future of the need for affirming the dignity of the migrant through the precarity of the lives they lead that engenders the idolized transfer to states of nostalgia and naturalism and the desire to return. Nativism, Western homogeneity, and cultural purity deny migrants the ability to personalize their environment in ways that can promote self-identification and control. I argue therefore that home necessitates a relationship between self and the environment that allows for a projection of inner psychological states onto the physical. In this case, the landscape is personalized and becomes an extension of inner states of being, hence, self-identification and control, intentions, motives, feelings, and preoccupations. The level of success or failure is defined by the extent of achievement of these determinants because they allow for defiant levels of attachment to place and the sense of belonging that comes with it. The physical landscape is a symbolic human emotion and geographical place. Home is spiritually constructed and emotionally conceptualized but physically and spatially manifested in a landscape that reflects unique culture and historical variables. While the physical determinants of home are being defined and reconfigured or reformulated, the spiritual and emotive have largely remained constant and are noted in history and culture. This accounts for rootedness, and as Terkenli argues, has "acquired temporal, cultural, and psychological connotations," emphasized through "a state of mind or being." Hence, I agree with the notion that "the expansion of home reinforces the need for human beings to attach themselves to a context that is questionably theirs, so that they are secure in the changing associations with place, society, and time."

Marame Gueye's salient article "Fatou Dionne's *Le Ventre de l'Atlantique*" not only interrogates integration and success but goes further to question the rationale for the whole enterprise of migration and advocates that the process not be initiated in the first place. Deploying idioms from the Wolof language in the context of the novel, she questions the quest, undercuts its grandiose expectations and hints at the need for return. Gueye proposes staying in Senegal as the alternative to the quest and return. She writes that while migration has come to "convey positive outcomes in the imagination of the migrant, they also, and ironically, have negative connotations attached to them, hinting at the challenges that many Senegalese immigrants face in France and in Europe in general." She adds that "while the expected upward mobility supposed by *dem ci kaaw bi* is a reality for some, it is not the experience of the majority of immigrants."

Gueye points out the complications of return, but my argument in this study is that this does not preclude the return itself. While nostalgia, as I argue, celebrates the return journey, it does so with a sense of ambivalence,

INTRODUCTION ❧ 15

for it also hints that return might be foundational to tragedy. I argue that notwithstanding this ambiguity, a return is more beneficial to the migrant than continuing to languish in the "causes of illegality, disillusionment, and loneliness," as Gueye puts it.

In her article "No Place to Call Home: Citizenship and Belonging in M. G. Vassanji's *The In-Between World of Vikram Lall*," Nalini Iyer addresses the multiple identities across three generations of Indians in Kenya. Pointing out Vassanji's philosophical connections to Afropolitanism and drawing from the theorizations of Mbembe, Iyer explores areas of departure from Mbembe. In documenting the "predicament of the Indian diaspora in East Africa—a people who inhabit multiple geographical spaces and for whom citizenship and belonging are constantly negotiated and reformed," Iyer puts her finger on what constitutes the in-between spaces migrants occupy and the sense of fluidity, rootlessness, and anxieties that come with it. Therefore, critical to my argument of the relationship to the environment, she points out the differences in the lived experience of three generations of Indians in Kenya and hence different perceptions of home and other geographical spaces. How African migrants negotiate this in-between space is both a consequence of their experience abroad and their willingness to transcend the barriers to reintegration upon return. My argument of return advances this perspective as I emphasize that flight and return are both critical to reform and the construction of the new hybridity, as well as the liminality that allows returned migrants to straddle dual identities.

Afropolitanism also comes up in sections of this book in discussions on return. Studies on the African diaspora have lauded constructs such as Afropolitanism, conformity, and hybridity as critical to the success of the African migrant. To come to terms with the full extent and burden of my argument, I contend with the notion of Afropolitanism and its implication for return. The term "Afropolitanism" and its current use in cultural discourse are associated with Taiye Selasi in the widely acknowledged article, "Bye-bye Babar (or What Is Afropolitanism?)." In that article, she defines Afropolitanism as "the newest generation of African migrants. Selasi's description encapsulates discourses of language, ethics, culture, fashion/ lifestyles, and social aspirations that transcend regions, borders, ethnicities, nationalities, and linguistics. *Ghana Must Go*, Selasi's novel, provides an opportunity to engage Afropolitanism in its depiction of border crossings and the possibilities of cultural integration for diasporan Africans.

In his foreword to *Negotiating Afropolitanism* titled "On Afropolitanism," Simon Gikandi writes: "Initially converted as a neologism to describe the social imaginary of a generation of Africans born outside the continent but connected to it through familial and cultural genealogies, the term Afropolitanism can now be read as the description of a new phenomenology

16 &♥ INTRODUCTION

of Africanness—a way of being African in the world." He further notes that Afropolitanism is prompted by the desire to think of African identities both as rooted in specific local geographies and transcendental of them. To be Afropolitan is to be connected to knowable African communities, nations, and traditions, but it is also a life divided across cultures, languages, and states. It is to enhance and celebrate a state of cultural hybridity—to be of Africa and other worlds at the same time. I agree with this conception of identity as it offers diasporan Africans, for instance, Kweku' Sai's family in *Ghana Must Go*, the possibility of being both American and Ghanaian. Sadie's acceptance of Ghanaian culture as well as Ghana's recognition of her contributions to that culture creates the hybrid that Gikandi describes above.

Another theoretical construct useful in shaping the arguments in this book is liminality. I use liminality to describe the status of migrants as one of in-betweenness. I am drawn to the work of the psychologist, Guiseppina Marsico, who described the in-between as "natural fluidity." In her article "The 'Non-Cuttable' Space in Between: Context, Boundaries and Their Natural Fluidity," she notes: "the space in between is neither the cuttable and divisive presence into discrete things, nor a mere 'holding' that could be cut off from our conceptualization. Rather, it's a ground (for a figure) in which flow and counterflow in [which] a fluid interplay amidst a distinct bonded context takes place."

In the main body of the book, I take Musila's argument one step further by exploring the construct of liminality around the frame that constitutes the dilemma between integration and return, as the in-between space that migrants find themselves in the diaspora. I must acknowledge that Marsico recognizes the importance of this space, and she raises a host of questions about it: "What is the nature of the relationships between the contexts in which a person lives? And what are the dynamics of communication, migration, and switching from one context to another? How does this switch take place? What facilitates or inhibits it? And what is the nature of the boundaries of these contexts? What lies between one context and another? What is the middle, between the different contexts? What is the Space-In-Between made of?" However, despite her recognition of the productive capacities inherent in this space, I argue that it is in the ability of migrants to navigate the complexities of the in-between that their success primarily lies.

At the end of the book, I explore another view of liminality, one that I frame as "constructive liminality" and the construct of the "new hybridity." I use Adichie's *Americanah* (2013) and Hollist's *So the Path Does Not Die* (2008) to analyze this perspective. While the current study does not explore this frame in detail, it emphasizes it as a potential trajectory for new literary and creative endeavors of African writers. It is forward looking and, hence, futuristic in its focus on the protagonists' contemplation of liminality

INTRODUCTION &♦ 17

in straddling both worlds: the homeland and the adopted country. Finaba and Ifemelu's contemplative gesture of living in both spaces in *Americanah* indicates new directions for engaging ideas relating to identity, belonging, home, exile, nationalism, transnationalism, and integration for both migrants and their descendants. I refer to this idea as "constructive liminality" and evidence of the "new hybridity" in diaspora/African literature.

Using the construct of home, identity, and return in this study to theorize spatial geographies is another significant contribution of this work to African migration studies. I use these themes to explore the connections between space and identity in the context of belonging, inclusion/exclusion, violence, trauma, and how they collectively shaped the postcolonial body in different geo-cultural spaces. Spatial geographies help us understand how novels like *Americanah* (2013) and *So the Path Does Not Die* (2008), which depict our positions as insiders or outsiders, at the center or the margin, or at the core or periphery, are historically produced and politically constructed. And based on these productions and constructions and the positions we occupy, these novels remind us that our identities are constantly reformulated, defined, and configured. Geography helps define the state of the in-between and its features, possibilities, and limitations. It allows for the creation of what I call an "aesthetics of transformation" by which notions of identity and belonging are contextualized and, through temporality and location, transformed. I theorize that temporality and location engender geospatial trajectories of transformation. I examine nine novels in this study to posit that spatial geographies shed light on the configurations and meanings of space and highlight the connections between dislocation and identity. I use *We Need New Names* (2013), *Behold the Dreamers* (2016), *Harare North* (2009), and *Blue White Red* (1998) to argue that the production of spaces is linked to the construction of human subjectivity. Thus, the identity of characters or the postcolonial subjects emerges from the places or spaces they occupy and from their relationship to them.

I also attest to the fact that spaces are politicized and that in theorizations of the politics of space, we must affirm the significance of the personal in defining or claiming/reclaiming identities within spaces. In a sense, as Kirsch and Ritchie put it, "How do we affirm the importance of location and yet understand the limitations of our ability to locate ourselves and others?" As Joan Borsa notes, the task of the social critic (and I will add postcolonial writer and critic) is "to be able to name our location, to politicize our spaces and to question where our particular experiences and practices fit within the articulations and representations that surround us."

I use spatial geographies to analyze the postcolonial novel and to thematize multiple spaces—public, private, legal, political, cultural, geographical, psychological, philosophical, literal, and figurative—to examine their

18 &► INTRODUCTION

connections to power, oppression, and resistance, as well as their institutionalization in other political spaces where violence can be systemic, epistemic, and systematized through discrimination. The novels selected for study in this monograph speak to the pain of isolation that illegal African migrants face in Western societies and the psychological depression that comes with failure to accomplish the dream. These novels question the validity of the whole experience while unveiling a significant aspect of the human condition: the deep-seated fear of the Other, especially migrants of color, and the racial prejudice associated with difference. My book adopts a unique approach in exploring the three phases of the migration process. It uses the body of the migrant to foreground race and ethnicity as the defining feature of the migrant experience. It emphasizes that the diasporic experience of the African migrant demonstrates what it means to be Black bodies in white spaces: the realities of Black life and existence in Western societies, among other things, the essentialization and dehumanization of black bodies. This realization of exclusion has produced a new essential gesture: to return home. It is against this background that I draw from spatial, border, and migration theories to make the case for return by examining the experiences of African migrants in nine novels: *Open City* (2011), *The Other Crucifix* (2010), *Ghana Must Go* (2013), *We Need New Names* (2013), *Harare North* (2009), *Blue White Red* (1998), *Behold the Dreamers* (2016), *Americanah* (2013), and *So the Path Does Not Die* (2008).

I divide the book into three parts to reflect three stages in the migration process: flight, arrival, and return. Each novel selected for critical study illustrates a specific aspect of a particular phase of the migration process. There is the main argument of return and the exploration of the migrant experience at three stages of the migration process that warrants return to the homeland, even though it is a decision fraught with both challenges and possibilities. The main argument in Part I is the pain and suffering that comes with flight or departure from the homeland. The three novels selected for study articulate how each contributes to this overall argument. The novels are *We Need New Names*, *Blue White Red*, and *Behold the Dreamers*. The main argument in Part II is the precarity that defines migrants' experience and the resulting disillusionment and psychological depression that come with the failure to accomplish the dream. The novels selected demonstrate their specific contributions to this overall perspective. I use *Harare North, Open City*, and *The Other Crucifix* to highlight how each contributes to the overall argument of reversal of expectations, depression, and sometimes death in the migratory country. In Part III, I explore the novels' reflection on the cost to migration and their advocacy of return to the homeland despite the complications. I use *Ghana Must Go, Americanah*, and *So the Path Does Not Die* to discuss the main argument and the novels' individual contributions to it.

In sum, chapter 1 elaborates on the reasons for departure in *We Need New Names*, chapter 2 explores the promise and reversal of expectations in both *Open City* and *The Other Crucifix*. Chapter 3 examines disillusionment in *Blue White Red* and insanity and death in *Harare North*, and chapter 4 deals with exclusion and psychological depression in *Behold the Dreamers*. Chapter 5 instantiates the process of reintegration after return and the struggle to reintegrate in *Ghana Must Go*. Chapter 6 elaborates on the experience of return by demonstrating the possibilities that come with the new hybridity in *Americanah*, and chapter 7 concludes the experience of return through exploring liminality as a construct by which the returned migrant strives to straddle both worlds in *So the Path Does Not Die*. I conclude with a brief chapter on historical and literary evidence that supports my argument of return.

Part I

Flight

The first phase of the migration process, "flight," is explored through examination of three novels: *We Need New Names, Open City,* and *The Other Crucifix.* Each of them indicates a different component of flight.

This section of the book is divided into two chapters. Chapter 1 looks at NoViolet Bulawayo's *We Need New Names* and the reasons migrants leave their homeland. It examines the sociopolitical and economic conditions in Zimbabwe that necessitate the migration of the principal narrator, Darling, to the United States and the culture shock she experiences upon arrival in Detroit, Michigan.

Chapter 2 picks up the trope of flight to expound on the reversal of expectations by foregrounding the psychological depression that comes with unrealized dreams. I use Teju Cole's *Open City* and Benjamin Kwakye's *The Other Crucifix* to explore the myth of open city as evident in the migrant's experiences in New York City and Brussels. The chapter interrogates the notion of open cities with endless possibilities by pointing out the isolation, exclusion, and frustrations that come with migrancy, even for those like Jojo Badu who, arguably, accomplished their dreams.

Both chapters demonstrate that while flight may be critical to the migrant's success, the realities in the migratory country might prove otherwise. The dream might not be accomplished or it would be achieved at some cost to the migrant. The similarities in migrant experiences in both the United States and the United Kingdom help reinforce the indeterminacy of flight. What emerges in the exploration of migrant experience in these novels is the inaccessibility of the structures necessary for the accomplishment of the African migrant dream, and this underscores the fragility of the dream given the racial prejudice and economic exclusion they face.

Chapter One

Reasons for Departure

Look at them leaving in droves, the children of the land, just look at them leaving in droves. Those with nothing are crossing borders. Those with strength are crossing borders. Those with ambitions are crossing borders. Those with hope are crossing borders. Moving, running, emigrating, going, deserting, walking, quitting, flying, fleeing—to all over, to countries near and far, to countries unheard of, to countries whose names they cannot pronounce. They are leaving in droves.[1]

America is too far . . . I don't want to go anywhere I have to go by air. What if you get there and find it's a kaka place and get stuck and can't come back? . . . you have to be able to return from wherever you go.[2]

NoViolet Bulawayo's *We Need New Names* provides insight into the motivations for flight and the precarity surrounding life in the country of origin. The novel is situated at the intersection of motivations for departure and the uncertainty of the conditions to be encountered in the migratory country. While the novel spells out the reasons for departure, it subtly hints at the possibility of dreams unaccomplished. The above lament is double-edged: it articulates both the pain at the sight of people leaving the country and the terrible reality of getting stuck in a foreign land. The lament presents the migrant with a choice that is seemingly a conundrum: the suffering at home or the privations in a foreign land.

The lament specifically identifies the migrants as "children of the land" and in this way gestures to the brain drain in the country of origin. It specifies a host of reasons for departure—poverty, ambition, hope, and persecution. To these, the author ties in the manner of departure—running, moving, fleeing, flying, fleeing, and walking. The motivation defines the circumstance of the migrants and in turn influences the choice of escape routes open to them. However, the second excerpt ushers in a note of caution: What if the

---

1   Bulawayo, *We Need New Names*, 147.
2   Bulawayo, *We Need New Names*, 16.

24 ❧ CHAPTER ONE

dream is not realized and the migrant finds himself or herself stuck in a place of no return? Distance and the possibility of return are advanced as crucial factors to be considered in the decision to depart from one's homeland. The excerpt suggests that a journey that precludes the possibility of return is not worth undertaking, regardless of its attractions and promises. Thus, while flight is understandable, and even unavoidable in certain circumstances, return is crucial to motivation for departure for it offers the migrant an alternative to precarity in the migrated country.

We Need New Names focuses on the reasons for the departure of Zimbabweans from their homeland. In spite of the warning encapsulated in the lament cited at the opening of this chapter, evidence abounds that Zimbabweans, indeed Africans as a whole, are fleeing their countries of origin for Western societies. Bosede Funke Afolayan attributes this influx of African migrants to the political and economic conditions prevailing in their homelands: "The developing countries in Africa are the direct opposite of the West. Black Africa suffers from poverty and lack of development. Africans are ruled by insensitive leaders who are kleptomaniacs. Blessed with many natural resources, the African nations could have been developed but for the kind of leaders they have and the conspiracies of the West that have turned Africa into a consumer nation."[3] In this situation, African migrants seek to escape the harsh realities of life at home by embarking on the journey to the West. As Afolayan further notes, "The hopes are usually very high in view of the American creed, the American dream" and describes this as "a rags-to-riches philosophy that motivates the inhabitants that a beggar can become rich through hard work."[4] And so having been exposed to the promise of opportunities by the media and popular literature, "many Africans leave their countries armed with this belief"[5] of material prosperity, freedom, and integration in the West. This desire to escape the perils of life in the home country for the promise of material success in the West is reflected in the country game (to which I return later in this chapter) played by Darling, the protagonist, and her friends in the opening sections of the novel. As Polo Belina Moji writes, the description of the migratory countries to which they aspire "include the power of names—notably African and international country names—the trope of migration and the association of political disillusionment with material lack."[6]

Maria Rocio Cobo Pinero references the country game played by the children as indicative of the motivation for departure and the preference for

---

3   Afolayan, "Politics of Migration," 39.

4   Afolayan, "Politics of Migration," 39.

5   Afolayan, "Politics of Migration," 40.

6   Moji, "New Names, Translational Subjectivities," 186.

Western societies as migratory destinations of African migrants. She views the imaginary maps drawn on the ground by the children as "a game that sarcastically represents the unfair economic and power distinctions that arise depending on the piece of land where one is born."[7] Further, she agrees with Pier Frasinelli that the "playful geopolitical dynamics establish that first the kids have to fight over the names, because each of them wants to be certain countries like everybody wants to be the US, and Britain and Canada and Australia and France and Sweden and Russia and Greece. These are the country-countries."[8] Furthermore, they illustrate the contrast between the privations in developing countries and the promise of prosperity in the West. What the migrants are not prepared for are the challenges in the migratory countries. As Afolayan notes, "No one warns them of racism, loneliness, and loss of identity that come with the movement. Unfortunately, the realities in the United States have shown . . . that life in the United States for a stranger is harsh especially when the stranger is an illegal one. He finds this out too late and becomes disillusioned, unable to return to his homeland."[9] The shattering of the migrant's dreams, as Darling comes to experience in Detroit, Michigan, creates a situation of precarity. The precarious life of migrants, especially illegal ones in the West, is a recurring theme in the works selected for study. Cobo Pinero summarizes this situation in three of these novels in this way: "Adichie's *Americanah* (2013) and Mbue's *Behold the Dreamers* (2016) also explore the inaccessibility of the American Dream for African migrants. . . . Selasi's *Ghana Must Go* (2014) addresses the tensions of how a family of Ghanaian and Nigerian descent copes with the consequences of achieving the dream; they realize that it was not created with black people in mind, and that it is gender biased."[10] Flight is not necessarily the answer to the problems in the homeland.

The novel depicts the first-person narrative method by which events are filtered through the consciousness of children and young adults. The innocence of the narrators as they relay their impressions of crucial incidents to the reader is striking in both its simplicity and its innocence, as well as its poignancy and effectiveness. Its ability to shock the reader into a realization of the significance of incidents and events critical to the lives of members of the community is telling. The choice of children as principal narrators is therefore instructive; for in all its transparency, children are more prone to unvarnished truth-telling than adults are. Their propensity to report events as they happen without embellishments accounts for their choice as

---

7   Cobo Pinero, "NoViolet Bulawayo's *We Need New Names*," 477.

8   Cobo Pinero, "NoViolet Bulawayo's *We Need New Names*," 477–78.

9   Afolayan, "Politics of Migration," 40.

10   Cobo Pinero, "NoViolet Bulawayo's *We Need New Names*," 479.

26 ❧ CHAPTER ONE

narrators. They register the privations of life in Zimbabwe with a degree of clarity and transparency that would be dubious in adult narrators. In fact, the power of the narrative content is anchored in the simplicity of tone and frighteningly crystal innocence of the children.

Bulawayo uses the names of the children and the places they live to shed light on the poverty and oppression in Zimbabwe. This act of naming provides a context for engaging the political history of the nation. The names of the narrators are Chipo, Darling, Bastard, and Forgiveness. There are other characters in the narrative, such as Mother Love and Mother of Bones, whose names also carry symbolic cultural, historical, and political significance in the novel. The act of naming is crucial to understanding Bulawayo's message of poverty and the motivation for departure. As Moji contends: "Bulawayo's naming practices eloquently connote the character of each space. Budapest, although a neighboring suburb, is as far removed from the reality of Paradise as the eponymous European city. This contrasts with the ironic naming of a shantytown as Paradise, where life there is hellish. Naming is also used to anchor the story in a Zimbabwean location."[11] Bosede Afolayan also deals with this issue of naming in the novel. She points out the symbolic connections between the names of places and the characters' attempts to escape the horrors inherent in them, for instance, through the games the children play. Hence, "Paradise children symbolize the horrific life the whole community is subjected to. They're like street urchins who go about without adult supervision and control. The children's games—'Find bin Laden,' 'Andy-over,' 'Country-over'—are replays and mimicry of adult experiences."[12] Naming is focalized through multiple strands of names of characters, names of places, and names of games that the children play.

NoViolet Bulawayo connects these strands in the chapter "We Need New Names," where the children mimic an abortion procedure on the pregnant Chipo. While focusing on the role-play, the narrative also gestures to the history of the nation and the precarity surrounding its birth. In the first instance, the pregnancy of Chipo is the result of a rape, an assault perpetuated by her grandfather. The rape of Chipo is the rape of the nation by the colonialist and the exploitation of its resources by violent assault. Chipo's body represents the assault on the body politic of the Zimbabwean nation by Western powers and provides a template to read the destruction of a nation at a premature stage of development. Of crucial significance is Chipo's ignorance of her rape, partly because the assault was perpetuated by someone she trusted. Chipo's vulnerability is also that of precolonial African societies, exploited by Western powers masquerading as trusted partners in development.

---

11   Moji, "New Names, Translational Subjectivities," 184.
12   Afolayan, "Politics of Migration," 12.

The birth of Chipo's baby mirrors both the historical birth of colonial Zimbabwe and the possibility of a new nation. The pregnancy gestures backward to both the colonial assault and the 115 years of British rule in Zimbabwe, then Southern Rhodesia. History and the struggle for independence have made explicit that the colonized nation was exploited and its people dehumanized. On the flip side, the pregnancy offers the possibility of a new birth: that of an independent nation. However, the circumstances surrounding the pregnancy cannot be divorced from its conception, nor the prevailing conditions for delivery overlooked. If Chipo's birth is to signify the beginnings of a new postcolonial Zimbabwe, then history and memory would necessitate a revisiting of the past anchored on forgiveness (as the name of one of the characters indicates). How history is remembered and the extent to which forgiveness is exercised would determine the contours around which the new nation is shaped. For the birth to be successful, it would require the work of skilled medical practitioners in the delivery process. A new modus operandi executed by a new set of professionals is required for the successful delivery of a new nation. Bulawayo also suggests that the practitioners would need a new set of names for them to be successful in their practice. The narrative points to obstacles in the delivery of the new nation and hints at a nation on the precipice of disaster. In fact, it is in the choice of new names that the narrative hints at the danger in this process. In the role play, we note that the characters assisting in the delivery, who symbolize the medical practitioners and politicians in the larger society, are named Dr. Cutter and Dr. Bullet. The choice of labels suggests two possibilities: a Caesarean section delivery, as indicated by cutting, or a stillbirth, as suggested by Bullet. The potential outcome is an unveiling of the precariousness of life in postindependent Zimbabwe for it gestures to the fact that the new nation was either born prematurely—and therefore not likely to survive in the hands of unqualified medical and political practitioners—or a stillbirth, dead on delivery. In both instances, the life of the mother cannot be assured.

Importantly, while the narrative suggests the need for a new birth, or at least a rebirth, the author points out that the practitioners navigating the birthing are more important. If the birth of the new nation is in the hands of impostors, fraudsters, and corrupt practitioners like Cutter and Bullet, then the future of postindependent Zimbabwe is questionable, if not doomed. Chipo's pregnancy provides a canvas on which to explore the trauma of the nation and a context to engage the broader themes of exploitation and oppression in the novel. Chipo's silence is instructive—it registers both the silence of trauma and the silencing of the victim or survivor. Her inability to articulate such an intimate and personal experience confirms the extent of her trauma and the psychological toll the assault took on her psyche. Her

28 &❧ CHAPTER ONE

silence is also the silence of the nation—a deeply traumatized nation going through the brutal legacies of colonialism and the reversal of expectations at independence. Chipo's trauma and her inability to articulate her suffering mirror the historical trauma that characterize colonialism and the pathology of postindependence disillusionment.

The hegemony and power differential surrounding culture and politics are also significant here. Chipo's grandfather is not only in a position of power; he is also in a position to commit a sexual assault with impunity because of the culture of male domination and domestic violence. Chipo's narrative of the assault could even be questioned, and in some ways, this confirms her rationale for silence. The symbolic recollection of power and hegemony as they played out in the colonial exploitation of the land and the people is replayed in the grandfather's abuse of Chipo. It is in this context of power differential that the silencing of Chipo is fully realized. Silencing becomes a coping mechanism for traumatized survivors; in cases of atrocities such as rape, speech potentially attracts reprisals, and the fear of retribution forces survivors to acquiesce and suffer in silence. The situation is even more acute for survivors of rape, as rape carries a stigma in most African societies. In addition, the stereotype that the woman must have somehow provoked the assault further keeps survivors from speaking. They stay silent and eventually give birth to a bastard child, which, importantly, inspires the name of one of the young adult narrators in the novel, Bastard. The implication is that Zimbabwe is the product of a colonial rape, and the result is a bastard nation. Regardless, there is an opportunity to transform society into a beloved nation, as lovely as a darling ("Darling" being the name of another of the child narrators). Such a transformation would require a redefinition of roles and relationships, an engagement with history and memory, and a willingness to exercise grace and forgiveness. It would require that the delivery process be placed in the hands of skilled professionals who are committed to the task and not by impostors or fraudsters. The process of transformation would further require that the social and economic inequities between Paradise and Budapest be readjusted and the religious exploitation of the masses addressed.

As mentioned earlier, *We Need New Names* answers the fundamental question: Why are migrants fleeing from their home countries? The novel provides an insight into the conditions of living that necessitate departure. The names of characters and places reveal identity, define actions, and illustrate themes. The ironic depiction of Paradise is critical to understanding the poverty of the Black population. Paradise sharpens the economic disparities between Blacks and whites and provides a trajectory of dispossession and displacement occasioned by the confiscation of the land by white settlers and the evacuations by bulldozers. What Paradise and Budapest offer are two sharply contrasting modes of existence for the citizens of Zimbabwe: one predicated on hunger, starvation, and destitution—the other on abundance, wealth, and opulence. The two settlements are barely separated by Mzilikazi Road, but the conditions of living could not be more different. The journey from impoverished Paradise to abundance in Budapest represents the first act of crossing borders by the Black citizens of Zimbabwe. Motivated by hunger, the children's action mimics and reflects the first act of migration into the land of opportunities inhabited by white people, only that this time, it is in their very home country. In a subtle case of reversal of expectations, the narrative demonstrates that what the children accomplished turned out to be far below what was expected. In fact, the consumption of the guavas and mangoes on empty stomachs turned out to be ill-advised, as it resulted in constipation and stomach pain—the first indication that crossing borders in search of greener pastures might not yield the much-expected fruits. In fact, there is a huge possibility of harm befalling the crossers in the process. The lamentable aspect of the situation is that the crossers are not asking for much—merely food as simple as guava and mangoes. However, the sad reality is that such necessity could come at a high price. The Black population experiences the brunt of the hardship and is confronted with the force of destitution that the white population can only imagine. The realities of life in Paradise are so far removed from the experiences of whites in Africa that white settlers can only demonstrate their connection to it by attachment to symbols as a necklace of the continent secured around their necks. White experience of Africa is radically different from that of Black people. In fact, a white settler was so taken aback by Black children begging for food at her doorstep that she proceeded to document the experience by taking photos of the destitute children. This act not only confirms her living in an alternative reality to that of the children, but the attempt at documentation of Black poverty also indicates the desire to permanently preserve white power and privilege.

Compounding the economic situation is the political state of the nation. In many ways, the two are connected; one illuminates the other. The struggle of the grandmother to count the new coins is an indication of the change in the economy from agricultural to capitalist brought about by political reform. The local currency loses its purchasing power, inflation is on the rise, and the preference for the American dollar is increasing. The dominant impression is the destruction of the traditional economy by an exploitative capitalist system. Further, the capitalist overthrow of the traditional economic system is tied to the loss of the land. The confiscation of the land by the white settlers is more evidence of the material dispossession of the Black population. The consequences are harsh—dispossession and trauma—and this is reflected in the lives of ordinary characters such as the grandfather.

30 &❧ CHAPTER ONE

The plot of the novel asserts that political reform is not the panacea to the economic problem. We are presented with the disadvantages of a political system that is shaped by corrupt politicians, leaders without vision, and incompetent government officials. In a biting satirical depiction of political leadership (a parody of the Mugabe government), Stina tells us that "you have to be an old, old man to become president" and that "the president of Zambia and Malawi and South Africa and other presidents . . . were all old; you have to be like a grandfather first."[13] The lack of visionary leaders has been a perennial problem in the African continent, and their missteps are one of the reasons for the departure of millions of Africans across the continent. African leaders have not only demonstrated incompetence in holding public offices but have also stubbornly refused to give up power, in some cases, after decades of brutal dictatorships. Godknows sees no possibility of improvement in the political situation in the country.

The oppression of the people is further illustrated in the evacuations carried out by the government. The terror of the bulldozers translates into nightmares and subsequent trauma for Darling. The terror is palpable in her description of a moment of evacuation. She describes the ferocity with which the bulldozers tear down the houses as "boiling," and at the completion of the demolition, she describes a scene of "broken walls and bricks," indicating the extent of the destruction.[14] The violence of the demolition and the indifference with which the process was conducted illustrates the lack of concern for the welfare of the people. In the face of such devastation, the government partners with Chinese investors to build shopping malls—not affordable housing, schools, or hospitals—that the local population cannot access or afford. The Chinese investors turn out to be exploiters of the nation's resources and openly involved in trafficking local women for sex for their Chinese workers.

The arrival of the NGOs completes the picture of exploitation. The NGO workers, like the white lady taking photos of Chipo and her hungry compatriots, are more interested in documenting the poverty of the people than in actually alleviating it. The scene is portrayed as an intentional moment of creating a spectacle of their poverty, rather than in helping needy people. The attention to the photos is a clear gesture of the publicity stunt that international agencies engage in under the guise of humanitarian work. It is more performative in its gesture to assistance than concrete in its alleviation of poverty. Darling notes, "After we sit, the man starts taking pictures with his big camera. They just like taking pictures, those NGO people, like maybe we are their real friends and relatives. . . . They don't care that we are

---

13   Bulawayo, *We Need New Names*, 62.
14   Bulawayo, *We Need New Names*, 66–67.

REASONS FOR DEPARTURE   31

embarrassed by our dirt and torn clothing, that we would prefer they didn't do it. . . . We don't complain because we know that after the picture-taking comes the giving of gifts."[15] The power differential is clear, and it is evident the NGOs are framing the incident using the lens they desire. In the process, they objectify and dehumanize the children. The workers make a spectacle of their poverty over trifles, as Darling tells us, "each one of us gets a toy gun, some sweets, and something to wear."[16] Africa's success in poverty alleviation will not come from foreign assistance, for what they offer at best is cosmetic change. It is evident that poverty plays into the façade of humanitarian assistance, and so NGOs are better off showing the poverty of the people than in alleviating it. Assistance from the NGOs in this context is publicity stunts designed to promote their interests.

It is in such a context of privations that the motivations for departure are understood. As the children contemplate migration, they engage in the country game designed to show their preference for migratory countries. The choices are reflective of the perception of migration in most African societies:

> But first we have to fight over the names because everybody wants to be certain countries, like everybody wants to be U.S.A. and Britain and Canada and Australia and Switzerland and France and Italy and Sweden and Germany and Russia and Greece and them. These are the country-countries. If you lose the fight, then you have to settle for countries like Dubai and South Africa and Botswana and Tanzania and them. They are no country-countries, but at least life is better there. Nobody wants to be the rags of countries like Congo, like Somalia, like Iraq, like Sudan, like Haiti, like Sri Lanka, and not even this one we live in—who wants to be a terrible place of hunger and things falling apart?[17]

The children's preferences create a hierarchy of countries, a three-tier system, the first of which no African country belongs to, as these are countries in North America, Australia, and Western Europe. The majority of African countries belong to the third tier, and these are countries plagued by famine and civil wars. Here lie the roots of African migration: the desire of migrants from Africa and the Middle East to seek a better life in the West (and in a few relatively stable African countries in East Africa) as they flee from persecution, economic hardships, political oppression, and social unrest. As Darling tells us, "I don't go to school anymore because all the teachers left to teach over in South Africa and Botswana and Namibia and them, where there's

---

15   Bulawayo, *We Need New Names*, 54.

16   Bulawayo, *We Need New Names*, 57.

17   Bulawayo, *We Need New Names*, 51.

32 ❧ CHAPTER ONE

better money."[18] Regional migration is depicted in the biblical symbol of the Israelites' crossing the Jordan as they fled from persecution and bondage in Egypt. Darling expresses her desire to go to a place "like in the Bible, when those people left that terrible place and that old man with a long beard like Father Christmas hit the road with a stick and then there was a river behind them."[19] The biblical image undercuts the significance of the children's aspiration for, ironically, they are aiming to go to Paradise, which the narrative content of the novel already showed to constitute incongruities between the biblical illustration and the grim reality of its manifestation in Zimbabwe. The conflation of Moses with Father Christmas heightens the fantasy with which the crossing is associated. The migrants' perception of the other side of the journey is riddled with fantasy and myths such as Father Christmas.

Earlier in the narrative, the author hints at this misconception of the opportunities on the other side in her depiction of the returned migrant: Darling's father. He came back empty-handed, broken, and dying of AIDS: "Father comes home after many years of forgetting us, of not sending us money, of not loving us, not anything us, and packs in the shack, unable to move, unable to talk properly, unable to anything, vomiting and vomiting, Jesus, just vomiting and defecating on himself, and it smelling like something dead in there, dead and rotting, his body a black, terrible stick."[20] The father's ailment shows the cost of migration and the elusive nature of the dream. The opening excerpt of the novel illustrates that every migrant is on the road, but the truth about mobility is that being on the road is not an assurance of reaching one's destination. As Teju Cole demonstrates in *Open City*, the truth about migration is that not every migrant gets to accomplish the dream, and even for those who succeed, success can come at a high price. The costs of migration are many and varied. In Darling's case, it is the trauma she experiences in her father's absence and of witnessing his death upon his return. It might be important to point out here that internal migration, or the disastrous consequences associated with it, is a mirror of international migration. There is a sense in which the failure of Darling's father to accomplish his dream in the journey to South Africa prefigures the failed migration of Aunt Faustina, Uncle Kojo, and Tshaka Zulu later in the novel. Darling's father epitomizes the migrant who goes in search of greener pastures but returns home empty-handed, physically and psychologically broken, and eventually dies from his physical ailments and psychological trauma. As Afolayan notes, his case "is symbolic of African migrants who are worse off by migrating."[21]

---

18   Bulawayo, *We Need New Names*, 32–33.

19   Bulawayo, *We Need New Names*, 19.

20   Bulawayo, *We Need New Names*, 91.

21   Afolayan, "Politics of Migration," 47.

NoViolet Bulawayo also depicts the insecurities of the political system in the vigilante justice conducted by local militia as a contributory factor to migration. Spurred on by the need to reclaim the land from the white farmers, the indigenes organized themselves into local militias that conduct regular raids of farms owned by white farmers. The senseless violence displayed on these occasions and the damage to lives and properties undermine state security and protection of citizens. As the violence escalates, so too does the insanity of the killings. White farmers were the primary targets, but those Blacks who were seen as sympathetic to the plight of the white farmers and deemed traitors were also violently attacked. As Brian Chikwava shows in *Harare North*, escape from political violence and persecution is among the reasons many Zimbabweans migrate to London. In presenting the destruction of the white neighborhood in Budapest through the eyes of the innocent narrators, the author accomplishes two major points: a depiction of gross inequities between white settlements and the Black urban districts and the senseless violence and destruction that accompany the militias' claim to the land. Both situations, characterized by violence, are reflective of the human rights violations that define the Mugabe regime in Zimbabwe.

The scourge of the AIDS epidemic is another reason why Zimbabweans depart for Western societies. The spread of AIDS, without cure or treatment, worsens an already precarious situation and accelerates mass migration into foreign countries. The reality of the disease is portrayed in the final days of Darling's father, after his return from South Africa. The physical and mental toll the disease took on his body was astonishing. The funeral of Bornfree also registers the toll AIDS is taking on the population. It is reflected in the "mounds and mounds of red earth everywhere [in the cemetery], like people are being harvested, like death is maybe waiting behind a rock with a big bag of free food and people are rushing, tripping over each other to get to the front before the handouts run out. That is how it is, the way the dead keep coming and coming."[22]

In desperation, the people turn to religion for solace. The novel is rife with heavy sarcasm and biting invectives toward religion. Far from providing hope, religion is another instrument of exploitation. Bulawayo's novel would perhaps best be remembered for its satire of religion, and the figure of Prophet Revelations Bitchington Mborro concretizes this assertion. In the opening section of the novel, Bulawayo depicts Mborro sexually assaulting a member of the congregation at church under the guise of spiritual exorcism. The whole incident is a caricature of the ritual of exorcism, and its meaninglessness is reflected in the empty phrases Mborro recites as spiritual exhortation. The charade is ridiculous, but the message is pointed—the physical

---

22   Bulawayo, *We Need New Names*, 134.

34 ❧ CHAPTER ONE

and spiritual exploitation of an already impoverished and destitute people by those purporting to care for them.

It is in the conflation of spiritual and sexual exploitation that the damage is clearly felt. The narrative reveals that in the process of casting out demons from the woman, Prophet Mborro "places his hands on her stomach, on her thighs, then he puts his hands on her thing and starts rubbing and praying hard for it, like there's something wrong with it."[23] A case of sexual assault is depicted, and the body of the woman is the canvas for spiritual and sexual exploitation. The assault is so graphic that it breaks the silence of Chipo and triggers memories of her own assault at the hands of her grandfather. Chipo recalls, "He did that, my grandfather, I was coming from playing Find bin Laden and my grandmother was not there and my grandfather was there and he got on me and pinned me down like that and he clamped a heavy hand over my mouth and was heavy like a mountain."[24] Chipo's grandfather is a pedophile, and the fact that he gets away with sexual assault of a minor highlights the precarious position of the woman or girl child and hints at the level of patriarchy and cultural impunity in society. Mborro's assault allows for the conflation of the two incidents, and on both occasions, the physically assaulted body of the woman provides a template to read the brokenness of the society. The broken body of the woman mirrors the broken body politic, and the rape of the female body is the spiritual and economic abuse of the nation. The attempts of Chipo's friends to abort the pregnancy point to the need to reimagine a new nation predicated on a new birth. The author suggests that the reconstruction of the nation must go beyond name changes in order for new visionaries to bring about meaningful change. In the meantime, Zimbabweans continue to leave the country in droves. As the narrative voice notes, "When things fall apart, the children of the land scurry and scatter like birds escaping a burning fire."[25]

Flight also overlaps with disillusionment in the migrants' experiences in their new environments. Darling's experiences in Detroit indicate a radical departure from her expectations. The reversal becomes a rude awakening to the realities of life for the migrant overseas. She informs us of the culture shock, the hostile weather, the otherness of the migrant, and the social alienation that comes with it, as well as the racism and trauma that underpin the struggle to belong. This struggle in turn triggers nostalgia for the homeland. Memories of home that the migrant initially overlooked are now amplified and become a source of motivation for return. The migrant straddles two worlds: the memory of the homeland that excites nostalgia and precipitates

---

23   Bulawayo, *We Need New Names*, 42.
24   Bulawayo, *We Need New Names*, 42–43.
25   Bulawayo, *We Need New Names*, 147.

REASONS FOR DEPARTURE &❧ 35

return, and the exclusion in the new environment that contests integration. The resulting limbo characterizes the dilemma of return as the migrant, while contending with the difficulty of integration into the migrated country, is uncertain about reintegration upon return to his or her home country. In Detroit, Darling gives us firsthand information on the realities of life in Michigan for the African migrant. The relationship between Aunt Fostalina and Uncle Kojo registers this reality. Crucial to the struggle to survive in this environment is the question of identity. The migrants struggle to walk the line between a retention of African traditions and an embrace of American culture. Aunt Fostalina and Uncle Kojo represent two contrasting approaches to this dilemma. For Fostalina, cultural assimilation is critical to survival and the accomplishment of the dream. Kojo, on the other hand, still believes in his traditional African values and questions Fostalina's rationale for transforming into an American woman. Unable to reconcile the two different ideologies, the couple gradually drifts apart from each other. Kojo gradually sinks into alcoholism and depression, and Fostalina seeks attention in infidelity. Kojo's depression is accentuated by nostalgia for Ghana and his recognition that assimilation into American culture is a pipe dream. Even Darling begins to reckon with nostalgia as she tells us, "There are times, though, that no matter how much food I eat, I find the food does nothing for me, like *I am hungry for my country and nothing is going to fix that* [emphasis added]."[26] Darling's insatiable hunger is the hunger of migrants—the void in their hearts that cannot be filled with anything the West has to offer. This void has a twofold effect on migrants: it deepens their longings for their homeland and heightens their reservations for the migratory country.

It is in this section that Bulawayo spells out the cost of migration. The trauma of displacement is palpable not only in the pioneer generation of migrants, represented by Aunt Fostalina and Uncle Kojo, but also in the second generation, that is, Prince, their son. Transgenerational trauma is seen in the struggles of the children of migrants in the migratory country. Prince recalls his exclusion in school because of his Ghanaian accent. He is angry at his alienation and describes America as "mother fucker" and his Ghanaian ancestry as "African shit."[27] His trauma is demonstrated in the time he spends with wooden animals as a coping mechanism for his anxieties. While claiming Americanness by virtue of their birth, second-generation Africans in the diaspora are also made aware by white society of their African ancestry, which is negatively presented in the media, books, and other platforms. The cultural dilemma also extends to the parents of second-generation Africans in the diaspora. They are faced with a double dilemma: they don't know

---

26 Bulawayo, *We Need New Names*, 155.
27 Bulawayo, *We Need New Names*, 149.

36   CHAPTER ONE

the children born in their absence back home nor do they know their own children born abroad. The narrative reveals part of this complication in the naming of children born in the diaspora: "We gave them names that would make them belong in America, names that did not mean anything to us. Aaron, Josh, Dana, Corey, Jack, Kathleen."[28] Because they do not have immigration papers that would allow them to travel out of the country, illegal migrants will never attend the funeral ceremonies of their parents, and when they explain their customs and traditions to their children, they are unwilling to embrace their parents' culture. In the end, when the parents grow old, they are put into nursing homes by their children, and when they die, they are not mourned or buried according to the traditional rites of passage in their culture. As the pioneer generation contemplates these issues, they begin to ponder whether return to the homeland would not be a better alternative.

While Darling doesn't have to contend with this duality, she is confronted with a different reality—the racism shown to the African Black by the white society as distinct from the American Black of African descent like Prince. At the wedding in South Bend, Indiana, Darling gives us her assessment of her life as Other in the United States: "In the end I just felt wrong in my skin, in my body, in my clothes, in my language, in my head, everything."[29] Darling points out the jungle of South Bend as a reversed trope of barbarism and lack of civilization in America. She recalls the epidemic of bullying in American schools and the horrors of suicide as in the case of her schoolmate, Tom. She reveals the pathology in the marital relationships of Africans who are forced into marriage with obese white women in order to secure immigration papers and regularize their residency status. And she exposes the social prejudice in the perpetuation of stereotypes about Africa in the media—the continued focus on the atrocities of civil wars, famine, political unrest as unique to the African experience. At the wedding in Indiana, Darling has to put up with the intransigence of the white lady who keeps asking about the rapes and killings in the Congo. She tells Darling about the tears she sheds from watching CNN's portrayal of the plight of a little cute girl in the midst of the killings in the Congo. The woman goes on to inform Darling that her niece would be going to Rwanda as a Peace Corps volunteer and recalls a generous donation of "clothes and pens and medicines and crayons and candy for those poor African children" she met in South Africa while teaching at an orphanage.[30] The image of Africa as a poor dark continent in need of redemption by a white savior is misleading and patronizing.

---

28   Bulawayo, *We Need New Names*, 249.

29   Bulawayo, *We Need New Names*, 167.

30   Bulawayo, *We Need New Names*, 178.

REASONS FOR DEPARTURE ❧ 37

It furthers the dichotomized narrative of white superiority and Indigenous barbarity and perpetuates Western insistence on telling a one-sided story of Africa as underdeveloped and uncivilized.

This narrative of inferiority is further demonstrated in Darling's recollections of the story of Tshaka Zulu, the migrant from Africa dying slowly in a nursing home for the mentally ill. Embedded in her story is the plight of the migrant who suffers the loss of body and mind in pursuit of the dream. Tshaka Zulu's experience parallels the unnamed narrator in Brian Chikwava's *Harare North*, who also suffers a mental breakdown at the end of the novel. In *We Need New Names*, Tshaka not only loses his mind but also his life in a gruesome encounter with the police at the end of the novel. His body could not be taken home for burial, and so he was incinerated and his ashes kept in Faustina's home. The pictures on the wall in his room at the nursing home denote his acute loss of memory but also his desire to reclaim the past. His life is a testimony to the fact that migration comes at a cost, and migrants pay this price with their minds and their bodies. At times, the price is paid with their lives.

Tshaka Zulu's story in the West has received much critical commentary. Polo Moji reads Zulu's predicament as illustrative of "migration as a ruptured genealogy."[31] She points out that despite his mental illness, Tshaka "engages in elaborate rituals of remembrance" with photos and clippings of African political stalwarts as Nelson Mandela and Kwame Nkrumah.[32] Through these "naming rituals" that recall the history of resistance of his people to colonial hegemony, he "remained inserted in the social matrix of his country of origin,"[33] He develops a split personality and is depressed. For Bosede Afolayan, the death of Tshaka Zulu at the hands of the police is a reminder of the precarious lives Black people, including African Americans, are forced to live in America, as well as the threats of violence and horrible deaths that sometimes occur during encounters with the police. She writes of his tragic end: "Tshaka Zulu runs outside the facility carrying his spear and is shot dead by the police. His plight is reminiscent of those of black young men like the late Trayvon Martin shot dead in America who cannot be understood and are murdered in cold blood out of ignorance."[34]

In a pivotal chapter in the novel, "How They Lived," Bulawayo presents the challenges to the dream through the pathologies in the lives of African migrants in the diaspora. First, she spells out the representation of the African in the American imagination that is shaped and conditioned by the

---

31   Moji, "New Names, Translational Subjectivities," 188.
32   Moji, "New Names, Translational Subjectivities," 188.
33   Moji, "New Names, Translational Subjectivities," 188.
34   Moji, "New Names, Translational Subjectivities," 50.

38 ❧ CHAPTER ONE

media—a story of famished children, wars and violence, poverty and disease, political turmoil and death. Herein lies Western ignorance, propaganda, and the deliberate, continued attempt to make Africa not only Other but also unique for its wars, famine, and disease. The impression is that Western societies are free of these conditions. It is in this attempt to make violence and poverty peculiar to Africa that the roots of racism and other forms of social marginalization lie. The image of Africa as the heart of darkness is a white construct aimed at elevating whiteness and promoting racial superiority. For this strategy to be effective, it needs an Other that would serve as the antithesis of the West. That Other is found in Africa and in Western determination to keep that stereotype alive. There is the need for a balance of stories if only to ascertain that Africa is not a country but a continent with fifty-four countries.

A critical component of the othering of African migrants is language, or more precisely, the accent with which they speak English. In his discussion of the role of language in the exclusion of African migrants in *Americanah*, Jack Taylor states, "Language also functions as a marker of assimilation and explores the political concerns of *Americanah* and by extension the politics of migration faced by Afropolitlikeely experience the host countries' demand for further assimilation."[35] Ifemelu's experience with accent in *Americanah* is similar to Jojo Badu's in *The Other Crucifix* and Darling's in *We Need New Names*. The struggle of the African migrant to eliminate all traces of their accent by imitating an American one is best realized in Aunt Faustina's efforts to learn to speak like an American. Taylor writes: "This theme is shared in *We Need New Names* when Darling's aunt sheds her accent after a customer service representative has trouble understanding her, and Darling herself eventually turns to popular American television shows to learn an American accent."[36] As Taylor contends, "language—and the capacity to speak English 'properly'—becomes racialized and based on one's national identity; language is a marker of difference signifying one's outsider status, and changes in one's language are indicative of changes to oneself, highlighting the pains immigrants face to belong to their host countries."[37] Taylor perceives this process of othering and migrants' attempts at appropriating the American accent as mimicry predicated on "the doubling and fracturing of identity between one's original culture and the new culture being occupied."[38]

---

35   Taylor, "Language, Race, and Identity," 74.
36   Taylor, "Language, Race, and Identity," 74.
37   Taylor, "Language, Race, and Identity," 74.
38   Taylor, "Language, Race, and Identity," 76.

REASONS FOR DEPARTURE ❧ 39

Another component of flight is the exclusion of the migrant in the migratory country. Bosede Afolayan also notes the exclusion of African migrants on the basis of their accent. She notes, "For an immigrant, accent is a big issue. . . . The African brings his accent to bear on his interactions with people. Darling's accent also becomes a point of ridicule in the school. She is mercilessly ridiculed and is only saved by the coming of another student who could not tolerate being the object of humor and taunts and hangs himself."[39] She concludes that "while the boy's action is a rude shock to darling, it goes to assert the psychological trauma a foreigner experiences in the hands of natives and the horrific result of such taunts."[40] Afoloyan further suggests that in a bid to escape the taunts and humiliation that come with their otherness, African women migrants seek to perform whiteness in order to fit into American cultural norms and practices. One way in which this is accomplished is by striving to adopt the standards of femininity, especially those relating to beauty and weight as prescribed by American society. She explains: "Darling is also bewildered at Aunt Fostalina's excessive urge to lose weight even when she is all bones. Her refusal to eat is another shock. . . . The sharp contrast between Zimbabwean women in Zimbabwe and Zimbabwean women in diaspora is not lost on the teenager. Some are like Fostalina craving to be like white women."[41] In starving herself to assume the slim figure of the white woman, Faustina is performing whiteness to escape the stereotype of the robust African woman considered a deviation from the standard of femininity in American society.

This characterization of Africa and Africans has promoted a feeling of inferiority that makes migrants from the continent an ethnicized Other and vulnerable to exploitation. Once they come to accept their otherness, used here in the sense of dehumanization, they can be easily manipulated and exploited. The effectiveness of this strategy of domination is seen in the contrast between the two societies: against the background of African destitution is America's abundance. Darling marvels at this abundance when she tells us that America is a place where "we saw more food than we had seen in all our lives"[42] and uses this inequity to question the benevolence of God. She questions God's compassion for other peoples and suggests that he must be biased in favor of white people; for how can he allow such disparities in people, all of whom he created in his image and likeness? To Darling, God is either a white God, or he has been rejected by African people. The satire is compounded by the sardonic humor of Africans gorging themselves to

---

39   Afolayan, "Politics of Migration," 48.

40   Afolayan, "Politics of Migration," 48.

41   Bulawayo, *We Need New Names*, 49.

42   Bulawayo, *We Need New Names*, 240.

40 &❧ CHAPTER ONE

death in their newfound abundance of food. She notes, "We ate like pigs, like wolves, like dignitaries; we ate like vultures, like stray dogs, like monsters; we ate like kings, we ate for all our past hunger, for our parents and brothers and sisters who were still back there."[43]

In *We Need New Names* and later in *The Other Crucifix*, language and communication recur as two significant barriers that African migrants have to cross in order to belong. The language situation calls for the speaking of American standard English and not the language variety in use in the migrant's country of origin. Given its ability to exclude, language creates a barrier between users and nonusers and sharpens the isolation and exclusion that come with its use. Communication is a struggle, and the migrant feels the isolation that comes with language in social context. Migrants are daily reminded of their foreign accent, and this sharpens their sense of alienation and position as outsiders.

Confronted with these difficulties, Darling ruminates on both the obstacles and the extent to which migrants can go to flee their homeland in search of the dream. From the benefit of hindsight, she begins to assess the cost to migration: "How hard it was to get to America—harder than crawling the anus of a needle. For the visas and passports, we begged, despaired, lied, groveled, promised, charmed, bribed—anything to get us out of the country. . . . Girls flat on their backs, Banyile between their legs, America on their minds."[44] On getting to America, they realize that the reality is far different from what was anticipated. In her stay in Detroit, Darling begins to question the feasibility of the dream: "In the footsteps of those looted black sons and daughters, we were going, yes, we were going. And when we got to America we took our dreams, looked at them tenderly as if they were newly born children, and put them away; we would not be pursuing them. *We would never be the things we had wanted to be: doctors, lawyers, teachers, engineers* [emphasis added]. No school for us, even though our visas were school visas."[45] The excerpt registers the grim reality of migration for a very high percentage of African migrants. That others do accomplish the dream and become professionals is largely true. But they account for a very small percentage of migrants, and they are mostly legal migrants. The texts selected for study reveal that a good percentage of illegal migrants must work menial jobs and under dangerous conditions. Others, who overstayed their visits and school visas, end up doing shady jobs and in equally inhumane conditions. Darling summarizes the life of the illegal migrant in terms of anxiety and desperation. It is a life of silence, of living in the shadows, and under constant threat

---

43   Bulawayo, *We Need New Names*, 241.
44   Bulawayo, *We Need New Names*, 242.
45   Bulawayo, *We Need New Names*, 243.

of arrest and deportation, if not incarceration. As Marcel Bonaventure tells us in *Blue White Red*, it is a life of performance and deception, while living with multiple identities.

With the elusiveness of the dream come disappointment and regret. This is the beginning of nostalgia. Darling reveals the pangs of disillusionment at the migrants' recognition that perhaps the struggles to get to America weren't worth it and that maybe life would have been better managed back home. It may not have been the preferred life of the migrant, but it was certainly not the life of fear they are compelled to live in the West. They cling to the hope that things might improve while the hands of the clock mercilessly tick on. Memory of the homeland provides some degree of comfort, and some migrants, as Darling notes, would then "show us faded photographs of mothers whose faces bore the same creases of worry as our own very mothers, siblings, bleak-eyed with dreams unfulfilled like those of our own, fathers forlorn and defeated like ours."[46] To keep the dream alive, migrants resort to doing all sorts of jobs: "And the job we worked . . . low-paying jobs. Backbreaking jobs. Jobs that gnawed at the bones of our dignity, devoured the meat, tongued the marrow. We took scalding irons and ironed our pride flat. We cleaned toilets. We picked tobacco and fruits under the boiling sun until we hung our tongues and panted like lost hounds. We butchered animals, slit throats, drained blood."[47] The jobs are not only dehumanizing; they are also dangerous. For instance, we learn that "Adamou got murdered by that beast of a machine that also ate three fingers of Sudan's left hand. We cut ourselves working on meat; we got skin diseases. We inhaled bad smells until our lungs thundered. Ecuador fell from forty stories working on a roof and shattered his spine."[48] Migrants work in these life-threatening conditions all because they have to send "monies back home [to relatives] by Western Union and MoneyGram" in order to buy "food and clothing for the families left behind" and to pay "school fees for the little ones."[49] This is the same story of migrant life in *Blue White Red* and *Harare North*.

As migrants reflect on their circumstances, they think about what could have been done to arrest the flight from their homelands. A critical consensus instructive to other migrants' intent on pursuing the dream was expressed: "They came in droves, abandoning the tatters that were our country. *We did not think about mending the tatters, all we thought was: Leave, abandon, flee, run—anything. Escape*"[50] (emphasis added). Darling's experience working

---

46   Bulawayo, *We Need New Names*, 245.
47   Bulawayo, *We Need New Names*, 246.
48   Bulawayo, *We Need New Names*, 246.
49   Bulawayo, *We Need New Names*, 246.
50   Bulawayo, *We Need New Names*, 247.

42   &   CHAPTER ONE

at the bottle-return department at Walmart and cleaning Eliot's house provides a basis for rethinking departure and suggests that mending the tatters could have been a more profitable approach in their flight. Perhaps departure could have been arrested by a propagation of the ideology of mending one's own tatters rather than fleeing to the other side in search of already mended tatters. It would have been simply a decision to water one's own grass instead of fleeing to the grass that is supposedly greener on the other side.

Darling's experience in Detroit is also critical to the argument of nostalgia and return. Nostalgia is not necessarily a romanticization of the past or an unwillingness to acknowledge inherent problems in that past; rather it is a recognition and an embrace of aspects of the past that are critical to identity and whose importance in shaping lives cannot be overlooked or minimized. Nostalgia is taking pride in the forces that have contributed to defining the inherent being of the self, as well as the sense of human dignity that comes with that recognition. It is not a denial of the difficulties of the past, a past that for some migrants was anchored in memories of brutal atrocities of civil wars and various forms of persecution. It is rather a process of way finding that offers an alternative to the dehumanization of the present by a recalibration of those experiences in the context of self-esteem and human worth. Nostalgia is not the absence of the atrocities, but rather it is finding a way in spite of them. In this view, nostalgia gestures to what was once taken for granted and to see it in a new and more productive light. It emphasizes that the past is a psychological phenomenon that is never far away from us nor eliminated from our present lives. On the contrary, we carry the past with us regardless of changes in location. The past is always in the present, and it is a contributory factor in determining the meaning of the present. Nostalgia is a spatial and temporal tool in determining the meaning of the present. Here is Darling's reflection on her past:

> With time I stopped writing altogether. . . . But it didn't mean I'd forgotten about them; I missed [my childhood friends], missed them very much, and there were those times I'd be doing something and get this terrible feeling of guilt for not keeping in touch. I do missed Budapest, missed Fambeki, missed Paradise, missed Mother and Mother of Bones and MotherLove, all those people, even Prophet Revelations Bitching Mborro, with his craziness, I missed them all. And when I got the guavas the gang sent with Messenger, these years later, it felt good knowing they remembered me as well.[51]

The crucial significance of location in shaping identity and lasting connections to place despite physical displacement cannot be overlooked. Darling

---

51   Bulawayo, *We Need New Names*, 190.

emphasizes that the influence of the environment on human life is stronger than she had ever imagined and that the mental and emotional connections to a place are never broken. The narrative asserts that it is in the realization of the spiritual and emotional connections to place that nostalgia is registered. While it stresses its influence, the narrative also sheds light on its duality, a sense of double self that is not fully anchored in either place. After one of her telephone conversations with Stina, Darling describes her nostalgia: "It's hard to explain, this feeling; it's like there's two of me. One part is yearning for my friends; the other doesn't know how to connect with them anymore, as if they are people I've never met. I feel a little guilty but I brush the feeling away."[52] This double consciousness of self sharpens Darling's isolation and recognition of the difficulty of belonging to her new environment. Darling's difficulty is the predicament of most African migrants: the void occasioned by both the displacement and the dual consciousness, and the resulting struggle to reconcile the two selves. This struggle is an ongoing process, and the void in the migrant's soul may never be reconciled.

In contemplation of the effect of this struggle, Darling again gestures to return. At this point in the narrative, memory of home unveils the cost to migration and the complications of returning to that place. Darling tells of this dilemma:

> Stina also said leaving your country is like dying, and when you come back you are like a lost ghost returning to earth, roaming around with a missing gaze in your eyes. I don't want to be that when I go back to my country, but then I don't really know because will Paradise be there when I return? Will Bastard and GodKnows and Sbho and Stina and Chipo and all my friends be there when I return? Will the guava tree be there when I return? Will Paradise, will everything, be the same when I return?[53]

Darling's thoughts echo both the complications of living in an environment to which one may never belong and the complexities of returning to a place that was once familiar but that may have undergone significant changes in the absence of the migrant to the point of nonrecognition of the old or its extinction. Return exists at the crossroads of despair and uncertainty, hope and fear. It is characterized by the expectations of reclaiming the past but also by the fear that might prevent the accomplishment of that expectation. What the migrants would be returning to and how they would handle whatever they find on their return are crucial considerations for a successful process of return.

---

52   Bulawayo, *We Need New Names*, 212.

53   Bulawayo, *We Need New Names*, 162,

44 ❧ CHAPTER ONE

We Need New Names is also instructive for its contemplation of return and the complications inherent in such a move. The uncertainty of return is further deepened by the changing attitude of society in its perception of the returned migrant. In her conversation with Chipo regarding the pain she suffers from seeing the destruction of Zimbabwe over the BBC, Chipo tells Darling: "But you are not the one suffering. You think watching BBC means you know what is going on? No, you don't, my friend, it's the wound that knows the texture of the pain; it's us who stayed here feeling the real suffering, so it's us who have a right to even say anything about that or anything and anybody."[54] Return is not going to be a red-carpet welcome for most migrants. On the contrary, the narrative suggests that migrants will have to navigate a host of complications stemming from the changes in the homeland, the perception of the returned migrant, and society's attitudes toward them. In one instance, Chipo even accuses Darling of abandoning the homeland at its time of greatest need. She accuses her of abandoning a house on fire instead of finding water to put out the fire. Darling cannot return with a clear conscience to a country she abandoned and where others have persisted in their efforts to restore hope to the country. Migrants' predicament is clear: they are outsiders both at home and abroad. They struggle with a sense of double consciousness and cannot fully integrate into either environment. Tired of the racism and exclusion in the West and plagued by nostalgia, they long to return but are also uncertain of how they would be received.

---

54   Bulawayo, *We Need New Names*, 287.

Chapter Two

Unfulfilled Dreams

Open City and *The Other Crucifix* explore another component of flight—the frustrations that come with unrealized dreams. This chapter examines the American Dream as one of the motivating factors for flight and its inaccessibility by the migrant upon arrival in America. What emerges in these two novels is that, regardless of the promise of freedom and liberty, the realities are different. Julius in *Open City* and Jojo in *The Other Crucifix* struggle to overcome social exclusion and the economic barriers to improvement. The references to similar migrant experiences in the scenes in Brussels in *Open City* again speak to a broader conception of fragility and brokenness in migrant life abroad. While Jojo arguably achieves his dream, the novel's end suggests that the upward climb to social integration has only just started.

Teju Cole's *Open City* can be read as a prologue to *The Other Crucifix* in terms of the promise of migration and the subsequent reversal of the migrant's expectations. Its protagonist, Julius, is from Nigeria, on a psychiatric fellowship conducting a clinical study of affective disorders in the elderly. Based in New York City, a place that can be characterized as an "open city" with endless possibilities and where dreams are accomplished, Julius goes through a process of psychological turmoil as he comes face to face with the realities of life in the West. Like Jojo Badu, Julius's sense of migration is based on the ideologies associated with the promise of "life, liberty, and the pursuit of happiness," which they would have read about back home in Ghana and Nigeria and are now striving to achieve in the United States.

The character and role of Julius illustrate this contrast between expectations and reality. Cast in the figure of the postcolonial flâneur, he is "a simultaneous chronicler of history, a keen observer of the present, and an augur of the future."[1] Using the narrative structure of the outsider who examines the dominant narrative of openness with which New York City has been described, Julius offers a contrapuntal reading of the contours of the city, which Alexander Hartwiger sees as a way of "understanding how

---

1   Hartwiger, "The Postcolonial Flâneur," 92.

46 ❧ CHAPTER TWO

marginalized histories are often embedded within dominant narratives."[2] Hartwiger further suggests that Julius's position as flâneur allows the narrative content to "read history back into the city through Julius' wanderings, in which he observes and uncovers the lost histories that contributed to make New York City what it is today."[3] In this way, the novel offers a reading that depicts the conflict between promise and reality by exploring the tensions between official narratives of history and buried and unofficial ones. As Julius struggles to reconcile various narratives of histories and the identities of the different groups of people whose lives were influenced and shaped by those histories, he comes to realize that the promises of migration are not as clear-cut or readily accessible as previously imagined. Hartwiger concludes that "for many people in the world, New York has developed a complicated identity as simultaneously a location of economic and cultural freedom and as a site of disenfranchisement and discrimination."[4] This dialectical construction and its resulting tensions have to be navigated for the migrant's dream to be accomplished.

Madhu Krishnan points out the relationship between space and movement in the novel as indicative of the continuation of violence and stresses through textual deconstruction of neoliberal visions of cosmopolitanism in the novel that, far from being liberatory, "postcolonial spatiality is continuation of the abstract formations of colonial space."[5] The resulting clash between expectations and reality are laid here in the constructs of space and movement anchored in several aspects of the liberal and fine arts, including literature, music, and painting. The symbol of the open road is critical to this conception of the dream and the new environment. Julius develops the habit of going on a walk through the streets of Manhattan and Brooklyn. As he walks through the city, the novel assumes a cartographic quality in that its plot construction is integral to the geographical mappings of the city. Taken on a conducted tour of the city, the reader observes the various aspects of its life and rhythm and its architecture, history, and allure. Like the protagonist who must try to successfully integrate into society, the reader is being introduced to a new geographical space with its own social, economic, and cultural challenges and must make sense of it. Julius's observations of the city are his attempt to give meaning to the different historical and cultural artifacts and situations he encounters. He ruminates on the nature of this new geographical space and what it would take to occupy it meaningfully

---

2   Hartwiger, "The Postcolonial Flâneur," 4.

3   Hartwiger, "The Postcolonial Flâneur," 3.

4   Hartwiger, "The Postcolonial Flâneur," 3–4.

5   Krishnan, "Postcoloniality, Spatiality, and Cosmopolitanism," 674.

and productively. The scope of the city suggests the extent of the challenges to integration that it poses to the outsider.

Hartwiger characterizes this structure of the novel as illustrative of the urban palimpsest in which the protagonist's walk in the city provides a basis for excavating and reclaiming occluded and buried narratives of marginalization and foregrounding them as contributing to the collective histories and identities of the city. In this process, the novel invites and offers migrants a place in the sociocultural landscape that constitutes the city.[6] As she argues, "Julius' walks in the city become palimpsestic exercises that expose histories that have been erased and written over. . . . The coupling of the aerial view, which offers an uncritical, unified portrait of New York and the surrounding historical look at the city from the street level, which uncovers and offers a counter narrative to New York's 'official' history, provides a multidimensional space time configuration from which to situate New York in larger historical narratives."[7] What Hartwiger's characterization points to is that the culture of the city is a product of migration, and the recognition of its "double histories" is critical to the migrant's understanding of the realities of migration and what it will take to succeed in this place.

The walk further illustrates a critical phenomenon of life—the open road as a metaphor of man's journey through life. Life is a road on which people journey toward their destination. The road constitutes a promise—to take the traveler to his destination. However, the fulfillment of this promise depends on a lot of factors. While it promises opportunities and the accomplishment of desire, the road cannot guarantee the fulfillment of its promises. In fact, it can denote aimless wanderings, loss of direction, displacement, and isolation. The metaphor of the road and the walk on it are critical to understanding both the promises and limitations to migration. If New York City is an open city, the implication is that traveling on this road promises endless opportunities for the realization of dreams. However, the city itself, or rather success in the city, depends on a host of factors, some simply because of the vastness of the space and its complex design. In that sense, it offers no guarantee of accomplishing the dream. In fact, evidence abounds to the contrary, and a high percentage of migrants, as the narrative shows, have witnessed the death of their dreams in this supposedly open city. For migrants to succeed in this space, it is critical then for them to go on a walk in order to be acquainted not only with its design, spaces, and infrastructure but also with the components of those structures and the mechanisms by which they operate.

---

6   Hartwiger, "The Postcolonial Flâneur," 8.

7   Hartwiger, "The Postcolonial Flâneur," 8–9.

48 • CHAPTER TWO

Another aspect of movement crucial to understanding migration is the marathon that Julius observes. The marathon serves as a contrast to the walk, not only in terms of pace and time but also, and more importantly, in the nature of the event and what it takes to complete it. The marathon requires a different level of training, commitment, energy, and determination than walking. It is physical and mental, attitudinal and psychological and, in the context of overcoming challenges, achievable only over a long period. The moral then is the reality of migration. It is an open race in an open city. Everybody is welcome to join the race. However, not everyone gets to complete it, and even those that do are required to demonstrate a very high level of human endurance. The marathon calls for an understanding of the terrain—its layout or topography, of the rules of the game, and of the energy and resilience it takes to complete it. This requires knowledge of one's own body to control and regulate pace, focus, consistency, hydration, and a host of other variables. In the same way that not every runner can be a successful marathon runner, so too not every migrant can be a successful one. The successful migrant is the marathon runner who completes the process with the knowledge and understanding of its various components.

It is also important to point out the dynamics of completion. With the marathon, runners complete the process at different times. The process takes a different kind of toll on different runners. One thing is clear, however: there is a cost to completion, and this symbolically parallels the cost to migration. Overcoming the many hurdles to migrant success is comparable to transcending the physical, mental, and psychological hurdles in a marathon. Completion of both races comes at a cost. Who or what we become at the end of the race is critical to assessing the cost and its significance for the journey.

The marathon is also significant for its depiction of humanity. Like the marathon runner, Professor Saito has completed the race but at a huge cost. When we meet him, he is a retired professor struggling with memory loss. In conversations with Julius, we recognize sparks of his intelligence as a literary scholar, but we are also taken aback at his present condition. His reflections on literature, classical music, symphony, and painting illustrate the vanity of life; youth, beauty, intelligence will all fade away with time. Professor Saito symbolizes the successful migrant whose accomplishments are neither recognized nor celebrated. Like the marathon runner Julius encounters who completes the race but with "no friends or family present to celebrate his achievement,"[8] Professor Saito lives and dies in isolation with few to recognize his contributions to society. Juluis's pity for the runner is also for Saito. The novel demonstrates that human desire and accomplishments are trivial,

---

8   Cole, *Open City*, 15.

ephemeral, absent of fulfillment. Professor Saito's condition invites the reader to question whether the demands of life match the truth of what it actually is. Cole delves into arts as a way of demonstrating the complications of life and living, and the liberal and fine arts offer us a canvas to reexamine desires, motives, and accomplishments. Almost ecclesiastic in conception, art interrogates life's meaning and man's quest for greatness.

It would be wrong to infer from this analysis that Cole is against the phenomenon of migration. Or conversely, Cole sees it as a natural phenomenon that illustrates the human condition. He describes the migration of birds in seasons in New York City and uses this as context to tease out the dynamics of human migration. Cole tells us about how Julius "had fallen into the habit of watching bird migrations from [his] apartment" and how "he used to look out the window like someone taking auspices, hoping to see the miracle of natural immigration" of humans.[9] In connecting human migration to "the apparition of migrating geese,"[10] Julius is echoing Cole's intention is to see the removal of the barriers and restrictions to immigration and to aspire to an aesthetics of nature that conceptualizes migration as a natural and necessary human phenomenon.

However, my reading of the episode suggests there are lessons to be learned from bird migration. Even though for birds migration is natural, the movement is predicated upon understanding the dynamics of seasons and cycles. They migrate at specific periods during particular seasons. Time is crucial to movement if the birds are to benefit from the changes in the weather and the environment to which they will move. Human movement, though unavoidable, can be better structured and implemented.

Open City is remarkable for its observations on migration and "the varying experiences of those who find themselves without the cultural and economic capital to move seamlessly across cultures and borders."[11] In contesting this limitation, Cole not only puts his protagonist in a position to excavate marginalized histories but also constructs a reading of the narrative that "challenges readers to distinguish between those who have the cultural and economic capital to be at home in the world and those who, in Homi Bhabha's terms, are unhomely."[12] In this way, Hartwiger contends that "migratory birds in particular, play a pivotal role in establishing a form of natural migration that when compared to human movement reveals the artificially constructed elements that stand in the way of unfettered movement. . . . The use of the term 'natural' here is telling because it emphasizes

---

9   Cole, *Open City*, 3–4.
10 Cole, *Open City*, 5.
11 Hartwiger, "The Postcolonial Flâneur," 1.
12 Hartwiger, "The Postcolonial Flâneur," 11.

50 ❧ CHAPTER TWO

movement and migration as something intrinsic to the world, not something that is unnatural, and therefore in need of monitoring and policing."[13] Cole draws from literature, art, music, and painting in conjunction with the movement of migratory birds to call attention to the power of art to transcend borders and uproot artificial barriers and aspire to "an idealized form of movement and oneness in the world."[14]

Further, Cole reminds us in chapter 5 that migration is a Western phenomenon and that it was critical to the establishment of Western nations. It is crucial to their history of fleeing persecution and taking refuge in a new home. This is the history of Western societies and the basis on which they were founded. The American Declaration of Independence states it brilliantly in life, liberty, and the pursuit of happiness. Migration is the history of the British, Dutch, Americans, Caribbeans, Africans, Europeans, and Middle Easterners. The history of nations and of societies is the history of human migration. Migration is a global phenomenon and has found expression in the construction of nations, as well as the cultural, historical, and social underpinnings of these nations. New York City is a conglomeration of the histories, cultures, and social values of countless peoples and races from all over the globe. It stands to reason that its greatness is a function of its character; a character defined and shaped by its migratory roots and the values of its migrant population. To see New York City as an American city is to miss the place of migrants and the role of migration in American history; to see New York City as an American city is to redefine what it means to be American. Theoretically and historically, it is an open city, founded, shaped, and nurtured by a myriad of cultures from across the globe and in many ways demonstrates both the benefits to migration and the role of migrants in defining the cultural contours of the United States.

A critical reading of the novel suggests that while the conception of openness accounts for the attractions of New York City, it is also the bane of its existence. Its openness is also illustrative of its willingness to accommodate a host of things, ideas, and concepts, some of which have negative consequences and are detrimental to society. It is paradoxically the beauty and the beast, a combination of opposites, and hence a place where dreams can both flourish and perish. Further, it is apparent that its openness can blind us to its unattractive side, and this tendency to see only one side of the reality could turn out to be an insurmountable barrier to success. Again, the openness of the road is no guarantee of reaching one's destination. Roads are fraught with danger and can be the scene of accidents and deaths. New York City is not immune to the hazards of the road.

---

13 Hartwiger, "The Postcolonial Flâneur," 11–12.
14 Hartwiger, "The Postcolonial Flâneur," 12.

The culture shock that comes with flight provides another indication of the migrant's frustration. Earlier in the novel, Cole gives us a sense of the seamy side of the city.[15] In the opening sections of the novel, he introduces the Take Back the Night protest in the city. The theme of the protest was the fight against gender discrimination, inequality, and inequity. This is the first indication that the gleam is not without blemish and that the journey on the open road might be characterized by several bumps. Alongside this construct is the symbol of the subway. Cole presents it as an assortment of humanity, a snapshot of the human condition. The symbol denotes a frightening image of an endless mass of people daily and constantly on the move, impersonal and distant. In this way, he forces the reader to critically engage the image of humanity depicted in this mass of people streaming endlessly in and out of the subway. The number of people points to the city's power to attract its inhabitants, but it also raises the question of how many of these individuals would succeed in this city. While the road may be broad and open to all, it does not guarantee that the dream will be accomplished. Many may be called, but at the end of the day, only a few would be chosen.

The cripple and the blind beggar add to the culture shock. We are forced to confront jarring destitution in the midst of abundance. But we are also reminded that this is a snapshot of the brokenness of humanity. New York City is a conglomeration of all aspects and shades of life. We read about the threats of global warming and the obtuse political discourse surrounding the debate. Cole also introduces America's original sin, the genocide against Native Americans, and the need to confront history in order to redefine the present. We are reminded of the history of mankind, a history of bloodletting, violence, trauma, and depression. Hartwiger suggests that *Open City* accomplishes two main objectives: on the one hand, it helps readers see the ambivalence of New York City, a metonymic representation of migration, as "at once a promise of prosperity and the symbol of uneven accessibility to it," and on the other, it illustrates that marginalized histories "of Native Americans whose homeland was seized and of Africans who suffered the Middle Passage . . . are omitted in the grand narrative of globalization."[16] As both narratives about migrant experience in New York City and Brussels demonstrate, the current Western conception of the migrant as criminal requiring stringent policies for residency suggests erasure of their own histories and a denial of access to the promise of freedom to contemporary migrants, even though they benefitted from such people.

Similarly, Delphine Fongang focuses on the migrant's exclusion and struggles for integration as constituting liminality. In her paper "Cosmopolitan

---

15   Cole, *Open City*, 23.

16   Hartwiger, "The Postcolonial Flâneur," 16.

52 ❧ CHAPTER TWO

Dilemma: Diasporic Subjectivity and Postcolonial Liminality in Teju Cole's *Open City*," she relates marginality in Bhabha's theorization of the "third space" to the "shifting subjectivities that define postcolonial migrants identities" and emphasizes that in the "wanderings of the transitional subject in the city, his status as outsider, developing a transitional identity, crisscrossing spaces and places in a city that remain strange and foreign to the aspirations of diasporic inclusiveness" is made concrete.[17] I agree with Fongang's conception, for there is a sense in which belonging or integration will continue to elude the migrant precisely because the "postcolonial diasporic subject navigates the metropolis from a position of marginality, constantly struggling to fit in by recreating and reinventing his identity in challenging spaces. Racial bias and cultural difference set the narrator apart from mainstream society."[18] Fongang concludes that Cole's novel "reveals how global racial hierarchies continue to negatively affect postcolonial migrant subjects in metropolises of the West."[19]

For Cole, marginality stems from history that is not unique to America but rather indicates a human history on a global dimension. It is the history of slavery and colonialism and the destruction of Indigenous societies. It is a reminder that human history is full of horrors, regardless of temporal and spatial differences. It is the reason why the Native American genocide is also the genocide of "The Last King of Scotland."[20] Human history interrogates the notion of a safe space because the meanings attached to spaces cannot be separated from their history. To characterize human spaces as endless possibilities is a utopia. The message is incisive but real: there is no other side to the human experience where the grass is greener. Circumstances might vary from one place to the other and at different times, but human life is essentially the same everywhere. In fact, historically, human life is one endless replication of atrocities.

Cole uses the destruction of the World Trade Center as a reminder that evil transcends geographical spaces to suggest a point of intersection of the human experience. He uses art, sculpture, and painting to demonstrate the limits to human accomplishments. The John Brewster paintings in the American Folk Art Museum indicate this idea of human brokenness, infamy, and disease, against which man struggles to succeed. The seamy side of life is depicted in the paintings, and the image of a child desperately holding on to a bird illustrates this struggle. In the scheme of life, we meet characters, once regarded as accomplished, struggling to hold on to life. We meet Professor

---

17   Fongang, "Cosmopolitan Dilemma," 141.
18   Fongang, "Cosmopolitan Dilemma," 141.
19   Fongang, "Cosmopolitan Dilemma," 138.
20   Cole, *Open City*, 29.

UNFULFILLED DREAMS   ❧   53

Saito and Dr. Martindale, shadows of Dr. Kweku Sai in *Ghana Must Go*, and their life stories question the reasons for departure. We also encounter shadowy characters like Nadege, the taxi driver, and Kenneth, who resides in the background, and one wonders at the struggles they are going through to simply survive in this city. The credibility or urgency of the situation that necessitated flight does not guarantee a humane reception in the West.

The stories of Saidu and Pierre, refugees from Liberia and Haiti, respectively, demonstrate another aspect of flight—the violation of the rights of migrants as they seek asylum and refugee status in Western societies. Pieter Vermeulen calls attention to the human rights issues in Cole's novel: the "panorama of cultural and historical differences that the novel develops is mainly made up of scenes of violence, abuse, and exploitation, almost always tinged by a racist comment."[21] Birgit Neumann and Yvonne Kappel also point out the novel's depiction of historical violence. They reference the structure of the novel and Julius's position as postcolonial flâneur as a framework for engaging its human rights concerns:

> Step by step, Julius' thoughts, together with the multiplicity of other voices, stories, and memories evoked in the text, uncover marginalized histories— largely histories of violence, ranging from Native American genocide, the transcultural slave trade, and European histories of colonial exploitation, to the attacks of 9/11 and the Iraq war. Contrary to what the many references in the novel to cosmopolitan values might suggest, these histories of suppression connect New York City to Brussels. The titular open city is a far cry from cosmopolitan harmony.[22]

Similarly, Igor Maver expounds on the novel's reconfiguration of violence, trauma, and war to depict the interiority of suffering and its effect on one's psyche and individual and collective memory.[23]

Scenes from the novel that depict instances of human rights abuse are numerous. On an invitation from Nadege, his girlfriend, to her church's bimonthly visit to detention facilities in Queens, New York, Julius had firsthand experience of the plight of undocumented migrants in the city. Inside the facility, he noticed that the inmates "appeared to consist of recent immigrants: Africans, Latinos, Eastern Europeans, Asians."[24] One of the inmates, Saidu, a former child soldier forcefully conscripted into the NPFL of warlord Charles Taylor during the Liberian civil war in the 1990s, narrates his experiences of the war and his journey through three countries across the Sahara

---

21   Vermeulen, "Flight of Memory," 44.
22   Neumann and Kappel, "Music and Latency," 35.
23   Maver, "Teju Cole's Nigeria," 4.
24   Cole, *Open City*, 63.

54 ❧ CHAPTER TWO

Desert—Mali, Mauritania, and Libya—into Europe and eventually America. The narrative speaks of the atrocities committed in civil wars and the trauma of witnessing such mayhem. Clearly, Saidu is fleeing from persecution and, under international law, qualifies for asylum in the United States. Given the historical ties between Liberia and America, in addition to his legitimate claim for asylum, one would have expected that Saidu would be granted protection in the States. His application was denied, and he was held in detention, where he could be incarcerated for several years or forcibly deported back to Lisbon, Portugal, his entry port into Europe, regardless of the fact that he is from Liberia.

Pierre tells a similar story of the atrocities he witnessed in his native Haiti. Like Saidu, Pierre is fleeing the atrocities stemming from autocracy and brutal dictatorship in his country. As he tells us, "I came here from Haiti, when things got bad there, when so many people were killed, blacks, whites. The killings were endless, there were bodies in the streets; my cousin, the son of my mothers' sister, and his entire family were slaughtered. We had to leave because the future was uncertain."[25] While Pierre is not in detention like Saidu, his status as a bootblack, or shoeshine boy, indicates the reversal of his expectations and the onset of disillusionment. He is grateful for the safety of his family, some of whom he could afford to bring into the country. But the fact still remains that getting to the States is only just the beginning for a host of migrants. Saidu would come to realize that the Sahara Desert was just one among many barriers he would have to cross; it was the beginning of the process of crossing many other artificial barriers such as immigration laws, employment policies, visa issues, racial discrimination, incarceration, and forcible deportation. Cole's message is poignant: the grass is not always greener on the other side. Saidu's and Pierre's stories raise questions about Western attitudes to migration and the migrant. Their narratives raise questions on the implementation of international law pertaining to refugees and asylum seekers. Their stories draw attention to the revisioning of history for, as Cole demonstrates, human migration has deep roots in Western history and the basis on which Western nations were founded.

Persecution, oppression, and displacement constitute part of the reasons for Julius's departure to the United States. His undergraduate days at the Nigerian Military School in Zaria, the exploitation of pupils under the guise of discipline, and the story of his mother's migration from Germany to the United States are constitutive of his encounter with and understanding of the constructs of the outsider, of otherness, and social exclusion. His background attests to encounters with poverty, emotional distance and separation from family, death, privation, and desire for a new beginning. Like

---

25 Cole, *Open City*, 72.

UNFULFILLED DREAMS &♦ 55

Jojo Badu and many other African migrants, education is the gateway to socioeconomic advancement. With money from his savings, Julius applies to schools in America and is granted admission and funding from Maxwell College. He notes, "My course had been charted. With borrowed money from my uncles, I bought a ticket to New York to begin life in the new Country, fully on my own terms."[26]

On vacation in Brussels, Julius gives us another picture of African migration in the diaspora. Through his encounter with Dr. Arnette Maillotte on the airplane, he gets a sense of the stereotypes associated with racial discrimination. Responding to Julius's disclosure of his Nigerian nationality, Maillotte brings up the arrogance of Nigerians, which she subtly suggests as the reason for their poor reception in the West. She prefers the subservience of Ghanaians to the supposed arrogance of Nigerians because it fits the stereotype of Black inferiority, even though she ironically references Brussels as color-blind in contrast to New York City that she describes as racist. Through the encounter, Cole reiterates an earlier theme in the novel—the notion of America as a haven in contrast to the recurrent wars and violence in Africa and other parts of the world. Maillotte's reflections on the Belgian-German atrocities of the Second World War, the destruction of lives and properties, and the kidnappings that followed the end of the war dovetail with Cole's suggestion that no nation is free of atrocities and that perhaps the idea of an open city with endless possibilities is also utopian. In fact, as earlier mentioned, war and destruction are indicative of the human condition, and it is therefore universal. As seen in the atrocities of the NPFL in Liberia, the gang violence in Haiti, the Native American genocide in the United States, and the wars conducted by the British and the Dutch, violence is human, nonspatial, nontemporal, and universal. In this construction, migration as a mechanism of escape from violence and human atrocities is unrealistic. Cole's depiction of crimes in Brussels, also considered an open city, is indicative of the universality of the human condition.

Several events and incidents in Brussels confirm the reversal of migrants' expectations. Originally conceptualized as an open city with values of freedom and equality, Brussels in the narrative ironically indicates the prevalence of xenophobia, Islamophobia, nativism and right-wing nationalism, otherness and Orientalization of foreigners, racial discrimination, and hate crimes. During a tram ride in the city, Julius recounts the "rally at the Atomium to protest racism and violence" and the racial hatred and violent backlash following the murder of a Flemish boy by two Arab youths with the PM appealing for calm while the bishop bemoans a callous society refusing to help

---

26 Cole, *Open City*, 85.

56 ❧ CHAPTER TWO

a dying boy.[27] Subsequently, foreigners are scapegoated, vilified, arrested, and extradited to their home countries. Several ugly incidents involving hate crimes are cited, including the beating of a Frenchman into a state of coma; the shooting of a Turkish girl, a nanny and a Flemish infant in her care; as well as the beating of a Black man at a petrol station that left him blind and paralyzed.[28]

Farouq, the immigrant from Morocco, in a conversation with Julius, uses Edward Said's theory of Orientalism to contextualize racial difference and the othering of Blacks and Arabs because of their race and ethnicity. In anger, Farouq refutes the political philosophy of non-violence grounded on Christian principles of forgiveness. He despises the notion or "expectation that the victimized Other . . . covers the distance, that has the noble ideas" and equally undermines the notion of what he labels "dignified refusal."[29] As Julius contends, "What Farouq got on the trams wasn't a quick suspicious glance. It was a simmering, barely contained fear. The classic anti-immigrant view, which saw them as enemies competing for scarce resources, was converging with a renewed fear of Islam."[30] These incidents in Brussels suggest that the framing of Arabs and Africans as racialized and ethnicized Other is a critical component of the migrant experience. His deductions on migrants' expectations and the resulting frustrations are worth citing:

> When we were young, he said, or I should say, when I was young, Europe was my dream. Not just a dream, it was the dream: it represented the freedom of thought. We wanted to come here, and exercise our minds in this free place. When I was doing my undergraduate degree in Rabat, I dreamed of Europe; we all did, my friends and I. Not America, about which we already had bad feelings, but Europe. *But I have been disappointed. Europe only looks free. The dream was an apparition.*[31] (Emphasis added)

Farouq's frustrations provide a point of intersection with some of the other novels selected for study that illustrate flight and arrival. In his analysis of the suffering of African migrants in the diaspora, the reader is reminded of overlaps in the experiences of Darling in *We Need New Names*, Jojo in *The Other Crucifix*, Massala-Massala in *Blue White Red*, and Jende in *Behold the Dreamers*. These characters who initially perceived the West as alternative to the oppression and lack of progress back home come to be disappointed in the racism that defines their lives and the barriers it erects in their paths to success. The message of frustration, culture shock, and exclusion that comes

---

27   Cole, *Open City*, 98.
28   Cole, *Open City*, 99.
29   Cole, *Open City*, 105.
30   Cole, *Open City*, 106.
31   Cole, *Open City*, 122.

with flight is reinforced. The frustration is handled differently by different characters. Some like Farouq became angry and vengeful; others, like Jojo Badu, are resigned to their situation; a few, like Jende, take the unlikely but important step to return home.

Farouq's encounter with Julius has received much critical commentary. I am indebted to Bernard Ayo Oniwe for his insightful reading of the significance of that encounter. Oniwe proposes a reading of the expression of cosmopolitan ideology in *Open City* that demonstrates a dichotomy between "a cosmopolitan aspiration to a worldliness not constrained by race, religion or nation" and the constraints of practicing that ideology through the "challenges to the cosmopolitan ideal, even though this is an ideal necessary to navigate a global world of difference."[32] Citing racial prejudice and the violence directed against the Other in society, in this case, Arabs in Brussels, Oniwe argues after the open lynching of a migrant of color in a public square in Brussels that it "is not really the pure racism that reared its ugly face in this particular case that is damaging to the cosmopolitan identity but the indifference to a violated stranger in a public space."[33] For Oniwe, this incident and many others in which Arabs from North Africa and blacks from Congo are attacked demonstrate the hypocrisy of the society because in order "to preserve and protect her historical antiquity from the wrecking violence of the Second World War, Brussels' leaders declared it an 'open city,' which literally spared it from bombings, but also metaphorically implies that all peoples, not only Flemish and Walloons, are welcome to make it a home."[34] The contrast and its implications for the postcolonial migrant subject could not be clearer.

Benjamin Kwayke's *The Other Crucifix* extends the conversation on flight by focusing on the culture shock that African migrants experience upon arriving in the migratory country. The novel tells the story of JoJo Badu, an international student from Ghana, who later becomes a resident migrant in the United States. It depicts the trajectory of his education, his relationship with various identity groups, and his decision to remain in the country at the completion of his studies. Jojo's story intersects with race, history, culture, and politics and provides a solid foundation for analysis of the frustrations that come with unrealized dreams.

Kwakye's novel presents reasons for the departure of Africans to the West, as well as conditions that necessitate residency at the completion of their studies. In its exposition of Jojo's cultural and economic background, his educational aspirations, and his encounters with different groups of people

---

32 Oniwe, "Cosmopolitan Conversation and Challenge," 46.

33 Oniwe, "Cosmopolitan Conversation and Challenge," 47.

34 Oniwe, "Cosmopolitan Conversation and Challenge," 47.

58 ❧ CHAPTER TWO

both in and outside the academy, *The Other Crucifix* seeks to address a host of questions relating to departure, residency, and return.

In the early sections of the novel, Kwakye draws our attention to Jojo's background. He comes from a poor family but is, nevertheless, determined to achieve an education and status in life. Supported by his father, Jojo, at quite a young age the author tells us, decided to pursue an education and to use his knowledge to contribute to the development of his society. Two things are worth noting in Jojo's desire for education. First, his journey to the West is not based on economic improvement despite his poverty. Mobility was predicated on the search for education. Second, his pursuit of education is not a drive for individual success but rather is to be used for the benefit of his society. Jojo is not an economic migrant, nor is he seeking self-gratification.

Jojo's story can be explored in the context of the history of West African migration narratives that have always been centered on the figure of the been-to, the student from West Africa who travels abroad for higher education and returns home after the completion of studies to contribute to national development.[35] This is part of the literary tradition of the West African novel, and works like *Fragments, Two Thousand Seasons, Our Sister Killjoy,* and *The Dilemma of a Ghost* depict this trend. Returning to the homeland is the justification for departure. However, it is also made clear that return is not a red-carpet welcome, for the been-tos quickly realize they are now outsiders in their homeland and cannot adjust to its norms and values. Reintegration becomes a struggle. *No Longer at Ease* and *The Interpreters* are indicative of this phase of development in the West African novel. In the early sections of *The Other Crucifix* and prior to Jojo's departure, Uncle Kusi and his granddaughter intentionally devote time to imploring Jojo to return home and contribute to nation-building. He tells Jojo, "Don't stay too long in America. They will turn you into a eunuch. Come back home. I'll find a place for you in my business. Someday, you and I can rule this country, Jojo. You have the intelligence. And that booming voice of yours is just perfect for politics."[36]

Complementing Uncle Kusi's vision is Jojo's own statement about his journey to the United States: "Here's where I'd earn my education, work

---

35 For a more detailed chronology of the development of the postcolonial flâneur and its connections to colonialism and the global economy, see Alexander Greer Hartwiger's "The Postcolonial Flâneur: *Open City* and the Urban Palimpsest," *Postcolonial Text* 11, no.1 (2016): 1–7. See also Pieter Vermeulen's "Flights of Memory: Teju Cole's *Open City* and the Limits of Aesthetic Cosmopolitanism," *Journal of Modern Literature* 37, no. 1 (2013): 40–57.

36 Kwakye, *The Other Crucifix*, 6.

no more than two years for practical training and return to help the country of my birth. Marjorie was waiting. Uncle Kusi was waiting. Ghana was waiting."[37] Uncle Kusi and Jojo's reflections introduce two major constructs pertaining to migration: home and return. It is clear that home for Jojo is a physical location, a geographical and cultural setting in the continent, that embodies his heritage, history, and identity and is predicated on relationships with others within that society. The psychological gesture implied in Uncle Kusi's and Jojo's reflections is that Ghana will always be home to Jojo. This suggests that America, on the contrary, will never be home to him, regardless of its promises and possibilities.

Despite the focus on return in early West African literature, *The Other Crucifix* breaks this tradition by depicting the nonreturning been-to, who after the completion of his studies, chooses to stay abroad rather than return home. This action of Jojo is significant in understanding the complex situations in which migrants find themselves and the choices they are forced to make. Given its centrality to my argument of return, I devote time to analyzing it. Yitah and Okyerefo note that "Kwakye's novel is one of a few that portray, as central characters, immigrants to the West who do not return to Africa. . . . The protagonists remain abroad and endure hardships and setbacks, either because their downward social mobility renders them unable to fulfill roles and expectations back home, or because [they] hope to attain victory over adversity and create a new identity for themselves."[38] Critics like Yitah and Okyerefo have in this way explored the novel's framing of the construct of home and belonging. In their paper "Migration, Cultural Memory and Identity in Benjamin Kwakye's *The Other Crucifix*," they define home and the migrant's relationship to it in this way: "Home as it was in Ghana may not exist for Jojo in America; instead, home is replaced by cultural memory which helps to re-situate the migratory subject, but is also necessarily affected by the tensions between competing identities in the origin and in the destination."[39] Their definition of home affirms the irreconcilable differences between the two societies and the continual struggle of the migrant to combine the two.

Exclusion as a consequence of flight is further demonstrated in the grandfather's address and exploration of the constructs of belonging and identity, as well as their intersection with home and return. Uncle Kusi's game of chess and instructions to Jojo as a player become a metaphor of return and a template for accomplishment of the dream. He instructs Jojo on different moves the chess player can adopt to outwit his opponents. This requires

---

37   Kwakye, *The Other Crucifix*, 8.
38   Yitah and Okyerefo, "Migration, Cultural Memory and Identity," 91.
39   Yitah and Okyerefo, "Migration, Cultural Memory and Identity," 82.

60 ❧ CHAPTER TWO

"will, patience, and awareness," and, moreover, "knowledge, intelligence, and focus;"[40] but these attributes must be predicated on a golden rule, "to start with [the] end game. Begin at the end." Uncle Kusi's piece of advice is a metaphorical configuration of migration as a game of chess with rules for success. If Jojo is to win, he needs to know the rules and adhere to them. He must take his opponents' weaknesses into account and exploit them; failing to do so will allow his own vulnerabilities to be exploited to his detriment. It is "better to know where you intend to end. You can hardly go wrong if you combine that and the knowledge you acquire from those who've played it before and your own experience. Even if you don't win, you'd play the game better."[41] The successful migrant begins the journey with a path to return, a map of the backward journey, and an intention to return home.

The grandfather's gesture to belonging and identity are revealed in his address. He boldly declares that Jojo will never belong to the land of white people. Using the mirror as a symbol of reflection of identity, he emphasizes that Jojo will never see his reflection when he looks into the human mirror around him. Displacement, physical and psychological, and the cultural, social, and economic struggles to integrate are reinforced in migrants' inability to see themselves as rooted in this new environment. Migration for Jojo will always remain a struggle to overcome the consequences of physical and psychological displacement and to integrate in the face of racial and cultural differences. These differences are historicized in the legacies of slavery, colonialism, and white nationalism.

The diasporic experiences of Jojo raise questions pertaining to the American dream and his decision to stay at the end of his studies. Framing the conversation in the context of cultural retention or memory versus cultural amnesia, Jojo, upon his arrival in America, insists on cultural memory through maintaining connections to his home, family, and culture. He journeys mentally back home to reconnect with spiritual and cultural values. He notes, "I wanted to remember," "I wanted to never forget," and "I made my mind take a trip to any market" in Accra as evidence of his determination to fulfill his promise of returning to Ghana.[42] His decision to stay at the end of the novel is evidently counterintuitive to his pronouncements in the early sections of the novel. In the aforementioned paper by Yitah and Okyerefo, I recognize their attempt at dealing with this question of Jojo's stay by exploring the concept of the "remnant consciousness" of the migratory subject that puts him in a position to "reconcile these competing and

---

40 Kwakye, *The Other Crucifix*, 6.
41 Kwakye, *The Other Crucifix*, 7.
42 Kwakye, *The Other Crucifix*, 17–18.

UNFULFILLED DREAMS ❧ 61

seemingly irreconcilable identities."[43] They suggest that Jojo's decision represents his "attempt to resolve the tension between the anxiety of losing his original identity and his desire to create a new one" and that "as Jojo begins to put down new roots and to define himself according to the truth of his marginality, America also becomes a space for his identity-in-transition, an identity that becomes a matter of choice rather than tradition."[44] I argue that although he attempts to justify his residency by noting that "even under the siege of things foreign, Ghanaians have a way of domesticating things to make it their own,"[45] the narrative conveys a different impression, or reality, of his decision.

In the opening section of the novel, Jojo cites the American Declaration of Independence as something that attracts migrants to America. He cites the beginning of the second segment of the document: "We hold these truths to be self-evident, that all men are created equal, that they are endowed by their creator with certain unalienable rights, that among these are life, liberty and the pursuit of happiness."[46] The underlying principle is that America is the place where dreams can be pursued, and so migrants are determined to cross all kinds of barriers in pursuit of their dreams. Jojo's experience turns out to be something quite different.

In analyzing Jojo's migrant experience in America, I begin with an examination of the title of the novel, which depicts the ambivalence of migration in its fusion of the possibilities and limitations of the dream. It is in the context of biblical allegory that this ambivalence is best realized. From a biblical standpoint, the crucifix reveals the crucifixion of Christ, and it brings up memories of the cup—the agony of Christ on the cross. However, in the context of salvation, the cup becomes a necessary ingredient for man's redemption and reconciliation to God (and hence its possibilities). The message is that eternal life is costly, as it comes with pain and sacrifice.

In deploying the symbolic significance of the crucifix on the experiences of the migrant, there are interesting parallels between the crucifixion and migration. The other crucifix in this instance is the personal cross of the migrant; it is the cup that he has to drink from in order to begin a new life—the resurrected life anticipated in the Promised Land, the New Canaan. This agonizing situation—a combination of racism, social isolation, and cultural alienation— constitutes the other cross the migrant has to bear and on which he will be crucified. Like the crucifixion of Christ, there is a promise: it is the death of the old life of the migrant and the birth of the new. Like

---

43 Yitah and Okyerefo, "Migration, Cultural Memory and Identity," 82.
44 Yitah and Okyerefo, "Migration, Cultural Memory and Identity," 83.
45 Kwakye, The Other Crucifix, 18.
46 Kwakye, *The Other Crucifix*, 8.

62 &❧ CHAPTER TWO

Christ, also, the migrant is the sacrificial lamb that must undergo crucifixion for the benefit of his or her people and society to which he or she must
return. Undertaking the cross for the peoples' redemption, the migrant
becomes Christlike. What is clear here is that there is a cost to migration,
as there is a cost to salvation—a profound sense of self-sacrifice laced with
physical and psychological trauma and sharpened by the migrant's otherness
in the contexts of racial prejudice, social alienation, and economic strangula-
tion. The question one needs to answer at the end of this journey is whether
the cost matches the outcome and whether the journey was worth the cost
of the dream.

The question of cost is important to Kwakye, and that is why he opens
the novel with a question: "Was my arrival in the US a day to curse or
bless?"[47] Jojo wonders. This self-reflection and introspection are the lot of
the migrant. It never goes away or comes to an end. The migrant lives with
it, constantly nagging at the conscience and relentlessly demanding answers.
Jojo says, "I have to step back a little to resolve that memory from increasing
obscurity and the blitz of my successes and failures, hopes and regrets."[48]
In the context of Robert Frost's poem "The Road Not Taken," Jojo, from
the benefit of hindsight, assesses the cost of his journey to the United States
and his decision to stay at the end of his studies. As the author takes us
through the plot, the reader encounters the in-between lived experience in
the context of culture, history, and politics.

Jojo's encounter with the ugly side of immigration starts on day one at
John F. Kennedy International Airport, the port of entry into the United
States for most migrants from West Africa. The questions, "Are you going
back home or are you going to be like those who stay after they're done
with school?" and "Where are you going, n-----?"[49] that come from the
immigration and customs officers, respectively, indicate an unpleasant
truth: despite the proclamations of liberty and freedom in the American
Declaration of Independence, not all migrants are welcomed in the United
States. The immigration officer is resentful of any attempt by Jojo to integrate into American society in the future. The custom officer's question
speaks to Jojo's otherness, indicating his contempt for Blackness. A significant aspect of Jojo's experience in America demonstrates the implications of
living as Other.

As part of the restrictions the migrant encounters in flight, Jojo has to
cross multiple borders in America. The first is linguistics. In America, his
speech and accent are markers of his otherness. He is the ethnicized other,

---

47 Kwakye, *The Other Crucifix*, 1.
48 Kwakye, *The Other Crucifix*, 1.
49 Kwakye, *The Other Crucifix*, 7.

and he comes to realize that Africans occupy the lower end of the racial hierarchy. Jojo's struggle to communicate with the officer at the airport is the beginning of the many hurdles he will have to surmount. In chapter 1, he tells us:

> The airport seemed so big I didn't know where to go to connect to the next flight. After repeated attempts in very slow English, I managed to communicate my problem to an airport official who directed me, in English I found difficult to understand, to the appropriate gate. It'd get better, I said. These are not native English speakers. Once I arrive in America, native speakers will understand me and I them.[50]

This struggle to communicate is part of a larger problem of language, variation, accent, and dialect that define identity and that he will come to recognize. In trying to understand the reason for the breakdown in communication, he reflects on his apparent difficulty in communicating in English with nonnative speakers in Zurich. However, in this situation, the difficulty was astounding since he was communicating with native speakers in America. What he fails to realize at this step of the journey is that in the United States, accent is not only an indication of otherness in terms of linguistic variety but also an index of the humanity of the speaker. Accent, a simple linguistic marker of geographical origin and evidence of linguistic variety of standard English, is the basis for discrimination and a constant reminder of the otherness of the migrant. It is not only a burden migrants carry right through to the end of their stay, but it is also anchored in the series of mental and physical adjustments they have to make.

The article "Internationalism and Academics" in *The University Review* is Jojo's first encounter with systemic racism. The article notes: "The University celebrates the admission of a freshman class of thirty international students from Asia, Africa, Europe, and South America. We need not indulge in much imaginative thinking to know that this desire to increase the presence of international students comes, for the most part, at the expense of lowered academic excellence."[51] The core of this argument is the otherness of international students, suggestively people of different ethnicities and cultural orientation and their supposed intellectual inferiority to Americans. Jojo's shock is due not to the blatant racism displayed in the article but to the fact that the university can legitimize dehumanization of international students in the guise of academic discourse.

The amplification of Jojo's otherness would be made explicit in the conundrum he finds himself in: the in-between of his position among white

---

50   Kwakye, *The Other Crucifix*, 4.

51   Kwakye, *The Other Crucifix*, 83.

64 ❧ CHAPTER TWO

and African American students. While he is subjected to racist abuse from white students, he is treated with cool indifference and distance by African Americans. He comes to realize that racial identity is not only integral to belonging but is also critical to survival and success in the United States. How he comes to navigate the complexities of the in-between, the duality of his Africanness, and his historical connections to African Americans, as well as his human connections to whiteness, will be proof of his success or failure in America.

In a telling moment of introspection in one of the fraternity parties to which he was invited, Jojo tells us of his struggle with his racial identity:

> But my *otherness* seemed to weigh on me: my manner of speech, the penchant of so many either to ignore me completely or show overt curiosity, the use of slang and phrases I didn't know, the request to repeat my words. . . . For the first time, I saw myself more sharply in terms of colour as a contrast to others and became self-aware of it in a native way I'd never known before. For the first time I sensed what it must feel like to be one of a kind among others, and not just read about it—the nagging sense of separateness that is not proclaimed but finds its place somewhere in the psyche even deeper still: somehow spiritual, so debilitating, so passively wounding, so dangerous, yet so oddly empowering and even enriching.[52]

The passage brilliantly sums up the ambivalence of migration in terms of its limitations and possibilities, a tension that requires careful analysis if one is to understand the cost of migration. Jojo points out this ambivalence in both the debilitating power of racism to wound the psyche of the migrant and its ironic potential to empower and enrich his experience. This struggle to understand, navigate, and reconcile these two opposites is never completely accomplished. In fact, the narrative suggests that it is a never-ending process in the life of the narrator. It is a spiritual wound that is never healed, a psychological turmoil that is never calmed, and a heaviness that is never lifted from the shoulders of the migrant. The task of balancing the opportunities for socioeconomic advancement with the devastating effects of racism constitutes the burden of carrying the other crucifix.

Accordingly, right from the start of his time in the United States, Jojo begins to see signs of his expectations being reversed. Two symbols are critical to understanding this sense of reversal: the bridge to the house of William Redford, Jojo's international advisor, and his urge for sexual gratification from white women. During his first visit to Redford, Jojo describes the bridge leading to the Victorian mansion as sturdy from a distance but shaky when standing on it. It is rickety and squeaks with every move engendering fear of

---

52   Kwakye, *The Other Crucifix*, 31.

collapse and "an uncomfortable urge to turn back."[53] If William Redford is the bridge to cultural integration, then the challenges are glaring. The bridge is shaky and rickety, and continued use of it threatens safety and security. Crossing the bridge and getting to the other end, figuratively the accomplishment of the dream, will be fraught with challenges. The contrast between appearance and reality is clearly depicted. The significance of the bridge as metaphor lies in the two different perspectives of its path to the realization of the dream. From the outside, the bridge to accomplishing the dream seems sturdy, but in getting close to and then upon it, the dreamer realizes the danger posed by crossing and reaching one's destination. The last phrase, "an uncomfortable urge to turn back," short and direct in its finality, sums up Jojo's experience as a migrant—one of fear and anxiety—but also conveys the dichotomy between the "urge to turn back" and return to the homeland or to continue walking on the rickety bridge in the hopes of getting to the other end. Benjamin Kwakye addressed this dichotomy in his presentation "African Migrations" as part of the Lecture Series of the African Literature Association in 2021.[54] As Kwakye hints in the novel, this is a decision that calls for deep introspection and reflection; as he notes, it cannot be critically explored or "measured in days or weeks or even months, but by the depth of many years accumulated, tasted, tested, weighed, felt, loved, rejected, hated, accepted."[55] At the end of the day, he takes comfort in the fact that, even if regrettable, it was an experience worth having. As he notes: "Perhaps that isn't bad after all—a life without regret implies a perfect life or one without ambition, lived too glibly, without trial and growth. But, at the same time, a life filled with regret is a sad one, even depressing, perhaps."[56]

Jojo's urge to have sexual relations with a white woman needs some attention. At the beginning of the novel, he tells us of his love for Marjorie, his girlfriend, betrothed to him at an early age, and with whom he has pledged blood covenant to marry. He tells us of his promise to Marjorie and counts on their relationship as another reason to return to Ghana at the end of his studies. Yet, within a month of his arrival in Ghana, Jojo is desperate to have sex with a white woman. While the narrative shows Ed's efforts to set him up with an American student, one cannot gloss over Jojo's sexual fantasies

---

53   Kwakye, *The Other Crucifix*, 24.

54   In his virtual address to members of the African Literature Association as part of its Lecture Series on "African Migrations," Saturday, December 4, 2021, Benjamin Kwakye notes that, among other things, the story of JoJo Badu is intended to interrogate the belief that elsewhere is the best, that the grass is greener in the West, and that everything is worth sacrificing to give living in another country a shot.

55   Kwakye, *The Other Crucifix*, 26.

56   Kwakye, *The Other Crucifix*, 2.

66 ❧ CHAPTER TWO

for Joan, Chloe, and later, his relationship with Norah Turner. The context for understanding Jojo's aspirations for sexual gratification is found in his otherness, based on racial invisibility, and his need for acceptance—albeit a flawed conception of belonging.

In chapter 5, Jojo talks about his otherness and its impact on his psyche. Struggling to make sense of his racial identity in order to find his place in a new environment, Jojo is looking for a means of acceptance and belonging. Initially, he lamented being excluded by his peers through their act of cool indifference toward him. He sees this as an attempt to make him invisible—a presence that is nonetheless an absence. This threat of invisibility displaces Jojo and erodes his sense of self. To gain acceptance in the community, he tries both the white fraternities and the African American parties. He is rejected by both of them. In this situation, Jojo's humanity is also called into question. In his mind, an intimate relationship with another being, or more crucially, the being that defines him as other, serves to restore his dignity and acceptance of his humanity. Given the intimacy of a sexual relationship with the other—in this case, a white woman—is the proof of the acceptance he seeks. While this flawed conception of belonging provides a rationalizing basis of sexual intimacy for Jojo, it highlights the extent to which social alienation has affected his psyche. He fails to see not only his affirmation of his own racial inferiority but also the objectification of women in his attempt to reclaim his human dignity through sexual relations. He fails to recognize that a validation of human dignity based on sexual intimacy with the opposite sex is problematic and potentially dehumanizing.

Jojo's sexual fantasies about white women illustrate the extent to which race and racism can go to define social relationships in America. Negotiating racial and ethnic identity is perhaps one of the biggest challenges confronting African migrants. As Ava Landry reminds us of the impact of making African migrants in the diaspora the racial and ethnicized other, Jojo's experience testifies to the fact that America's conception of Blackness shapes Black existence. For Jojo, race problematizes sexuality and belonging and complicates history and culture, especially in relationships between Africans and African Americans. While the narrative makes efforts to deconstruct historical biases and inaccuracies and strives to expose stereotypes associated with blackness, one is not sure of what actually is accomplished. Given the divergent histories and experiences of the two groups of people despite their shared ancestry, the gulf between Dwayne and Jojo, for instance, is never bridged. Jojo confirms that "after so many years, and all we'd experienced together, Dwayne and I still faced that vexing chasm."[57]

---

57   Kwakye, *The Other Crucifix*, 128.

The cultural and racial stereotypes associated with Blackness and perpetuated by the dominant group depict another dimension to Jojo's frustrations. The articles in *The University Review* are cases in point. In the op-ed penned by Owens purporting to be the view of an anonymous African student on campus, the article reads:

> Africans are frustrated because they do not quite fit in with white students. At the same time, they can find no sanctuary among American Negroes because the latter, for one reason or the other, tend to deprecate their African counterparts. A number of Africans feel that black Americans relegate them to second-class status. Says one African student, "American blacks don't like us because we represent everything that they don't want to be, everything the society has taught them they have to run away from. In fact, I find more white than black American students interested in my background in Africa. Some of them even continue to blame us for selling their ancestors into slavery. Perhaps I simplify. It is a complex relationship, but one thing is for sure: it is not an easy relationship.[58]

The article depicts the stereotypes, cultural stigma, and racial bias, based on historical inaccuracies and misunderstandings, that Africans and African Americans have to navigate to bridge the cultural gap between them. The negative representation of Blackness in the media, the grotesque disruptions of history, and the codification of these disruptions as valid in the academy are alarming. These perspectives of Blackness have become institutionalized and systemic, and they represent the huge task of deconstruction and reconfiguration of history that needs to be done. The psychological effect of these figurations of Blackness on Jojo were clear. He tells us: "It appeared I was a ghost living in a land of flesh and blood, confined to the fringes, sometimes loved, sometimes disliked; now welcome, now feared. In my own skin, which I found so comfortable, I was perplexed by it all."[59] More frustrating to him is that his membership in the Alpha fraternity, envisaged as the last attempt to bridge the gap between him and Dwayne, turns out to be a dismal failure and ends up deepening the divide between them.

Fiona and Jojo's relationship adds another layer of complexity to the complications of Black identity in America. Since this relationship is critical to my argument of return, I devote time to analyzing it. Their relationship depicts the construction of identity framed around individual and collective perceptions of it. It is apparent that Jojo sees Fiona more as Ghanaian than American. But it is clear that Fiona sees herself as more fully American. Jojo's gravitation toward Fiona stems from his perception of cultural affinities with

---

58 Kwakye, *The Other Crucifix*, 38.
59 Kwakye, *The Other Crucifix*, 122.

68 ❧ CHAPTER TWO

her. His relationship with Fiona symbolizes his attempt to reclaim lost values in his ethnic identity, occasioned by time and distance. The dilemma in this approach to identity construction is that Jojo's perception of ethnic complementarity with Fiona is anchored in a location and culture antithetical to his present abode. Moreover, Fiona does not share the same view of ethnic identity as Jojo. She holds her Ghanaian identity at a comfortable distance. Jojo is seeking acceptance on a shaky cultural foundation, and the narrative amplifies this idea in emphasizing Fiona's linguistic and biological features as more American than Ghanaian. She speaks English with an American accent, her hair is straight, and her nose is thin. She is familiar with white students on campus and represents an otherness that is more relatable to them, less threatening and more acceptable to the dominant group than Jojo's.

However, Fiona exists as an amalgamation and juxtaposition of identities, and she struggles to negotiate commitment to either or both of them. While Fiona and Jojo find solace in each other's identities and can appreciate each other's differences, they have to decipher the significance of their otherness in the larger society and for their understanding of their own way of life. Fiona and Jojo can define their identity on an individual basis, or do they see themselves as part of a collective Ghanaian identity to which they belong and that takes precedence over individual sense of self? The tension between the two modes of conception underscores the shaky foundation on which their relationship is built and highlights the uncertainties it poses for the future. This tension is first seen in the anxieties surrounding their dating. Interestingly, Jojo is more nervous about Fiona's possible rejection of him than being rejected by any white girl. This is because Fiona's rejection would constitute a rejection of his Ghanaian identity. At the same time, a rejection of Fiona by Jojo would imply a rejection of that aspect of her identity, which even though held at a comfortable distance, is recognized as critical to Jojo's love for her. As the plot reveals, Fiona "had thought her African–ness was what would win her admiration, not the American–ness, which she would have liked to see rejected, just as much as she would have liked to reject it" during her school and undergraduate days in Ghana.[60] When Fiona decides to leave and return to America, she tells us: "It was like leaving the presence of an unfamiliar grandmother, hardly seen, not known, hardly missed."[61] If Jojo is to stay in the United States and feel a sense of belonging, it is important not only that he reclaim his Ghanaian values implicit in the Fiona relationship; it is also critical for Fiona to navigate the competing identities of African (Ghanaian) and American.

---

60   Kwakye, *The Other Crucifix*, 146.

61   Kwakye, *The Other Crucifix*, 148.

A significant aspect of Kwayke's exploration of the migrant experience in *The Other Crucifix* is its gesture to return and the implications of staying in America at the completion of Jojo's studies. Given the main argument concerned with return in this book, I use sections of *The Other Crucifix* to tease out the complications of the migrant's return, as well as the sacrifices he or she makes in choosing to stay. The experiences of Fiona's parents in Ghana and Jojo in America provide two interesting frames to critique return. While the context may differ slightly for both George, Fiona's father, and Jojo regarding the return to the ancestral homeland and the birth land, George's experience offers a basis for critiquing Jojo's decision.

George's experiences in Ghana parallel Jojo's experience in America. While both may consider the prospects of cultural integration as the bridge to belonging, George realizes that "home is not always where the heart desires to be, after all."[62] Citing colonial history and its influence in shaping the experiences of Africans and African Americans after independence, George laments the disillusionment he witnessed in Ghana. He recognizes the toll that time and distance have taken on possibilities of cultural integration and grieves the disruptions to a spiritual connection with Africa. George's and Jojo's culture shock are two sides of the same migration coin. George's struggle to negotiate the competing identities of African (historical and cultural, which he longs to reclaim) and American (social, which he has lived) constitutes his identity crisis. In America, he was the "oddball amid an ocean of whiteness," while in Africa, even though "Ghana allowed him in, . . . he remained at an unshakeable level . . . American."[63] Like George in Ghana, Jojo will always be seen as Other in America. This is crucial to Jojo's understanding of the significance of racial and cultural identity to belonging. When Kwame Nkrumah was overthrown in 1966 and African Americans were scapegoated as complicit in his death, George moved back to the United States with his family. The significance of his story should be clear to Jojo as well—he would be better served by returning to Ghana than staying in the United States. Even though Fiona offers the possibility of reclaiming cultural identity and establishing a basis of belonging, the narrative gestures more to the difficulties of its accomplishment rather than the possibilities

Given the many complications associated with Jojo's struggle for integration, it is difficult to come to terms with his decision to stay. Apart from the fact that his action seems contrary to his initial goals, it contradicts the experiences of racial prejudice and discrimination that he encounters during his stay. It also contradicts his pledge to Uncle Kusi and his grandfather to return and contribute to nation building. On the other hand, his education,

---

62 Kwakye, *The Other Crucifix*, 143.
63 Kwakye, *The Other Crucifix*, 144.

70 ❧ CHAPTER TWO

marriage to Fiona, starting a family, and his naturalization as an American citizen can be seen as evidence of success. His choice of residency in America should therefore not come as a surprise. Regardless of the many obstacles in his path, he continues to push relentlessly until he accomplishes his dream. Like the migrant on the other crucifix, he bears his cross well and with resilience and, at the end, opens up a pathway for his family and other migrants. As he reflects on his struggles at the end of the novel, he tells us that he longs for a day when America can "bridge oceans and histories as diverse as skin colour, or as irrelevant,"[64] and considers his journey as one of renewal for "all is renewed and my life starts again."[65]

Notwithstanding, there is evidence to suggest that Jojo's decision to stay might not have been the right one. At the completion of his undergraduate studies and law school, he goes out in search of employment. After sixty-three interviews, he finally receives an offer. Even though race, or more precisely his Ghanaian ethnicity, is never mentioned as the reason for his rejection, the reader cannot fail to perceive Jojo's otherness in the whole process. He tells us:

> But in my case was the added surprise, it seemed when I walked into the room and spoke with an accent to which the interviewers weren't accustomed. I remember one interview in particular when I had to sit through request upon request to repeat what I'd just said. I recalled interviewers who asked me to repeat my name several times and still mispronounced it, or pulled faces when I said it. I remember interviewers who asked me why I didn't want to go back to my country; interviewers who lost interest in me the moment I walked into the room. But I endured it all because I was desperate for a job. And after all that, to receive only one offer . . . what such near unanimous rejection does to a man's ego needs no repeating. I'd watched friends with anywhere from five to fifteen job offers struggling to make a choice.[66]

It is clear that Jojo's racial and cultural identities were the cause of his rejection. His name and accent, markers of his Ghanaian ethnicity, were unfamiliar to the interviewers and considered inappropriate or sub-standard for employment in America. The pain of racism, and the shame of overt discrimination are evident. Even though Jojo demonstrates class and resilience in enduring the insults, he acknowledges the toll it took on his psyche. Prior to this interview, he had to settle for a job of stacking hay in a barn after repeated unproductive telephone conversations with potential employers. In

---

64 Kwakye, *The Other Crucifix*, 178.
65 Kwakye, *The Other Crucifix*, 218.
66 Kwakye, *The Other Crucifix*, 216–17.

this situation of open hostility and prejudice, one wonders what it would take Jojo to succeed in this society.

The problem becomes more acute in the resistance of the dominant group to validate Black success. At one of his job interviews, Jonathan Rich, a potential employer, was amazed at Jojo's credentials. His amazement stems from long-held beliefs in the inferiority of Black people and their cognitive abilities. While he admits that Jojo has "done well," he cannot fathom the means by which, nor hide his surprise at the fact that, he graduated from a university. And yet, despite this realization, he insists on referring to him as "boy" and denies him employment because he is not an American citizen or permanent resident, even though Jojo cannot get anyone to sponsor the change of his immigration status.

In addition to this attitude of dismissal, there is the contempt shown to migrants when they succeed, even by those one would expect to be on their side. When Jojo informs his former college roommate, Ed Palmer, of his admission to law school, Ed remarks sarcastically that he is still waiting to hear from the law school because he is "not from Africa or anything . . . [and is] competing against a different pool" of applicants.[67] The implication is that Jojo's admission is based on the college's preference for diversity in the student body and not on individual merit. White perception of Black success is prejudiced by their low expectation of Black intelligence, and this devalues black accomplishments. Moreover, it seems to question whether such accomplishments are based on merit.

Jojo's marriage to Fiona could suggest a different reality when brought under scrutiny. On one level, it is possible to see his marriage and the birth of his two daughters as evidence of success. Hence, his decision to stay is illustrative of sacrifice and devotion to his family. However, the careful reader would argue that the foundation of his marriage does not quite merit this interpretation. In fact, a careful analysis of his relationship with Fiona suggests underlying tensions between them, and it is evident that racial and ethnic differences are part of this tension. Fiona makes it clear that in spite of her dual identity, she prefers her American culture over her Ghanaian identity. The revelation that Fiona never considers marriage to an African even as a remote possibility is concerning. Further, the comparison she draws between Jojo and her ex-boyfriend suggests a struggle to reconcile two opposing identities. It is apparent from this incident that the foundation of their marriage is shaky.

The first threat to the stability of their relationship comes at the time when the gender roles are reversed and Fiona gets to be the breadwinner. Jojo's fear of depending on his wife, possibly stemming from a cultural

---

67   Kwakye, *The Other Crucifix*, 165.

72 ❧ CHAPTER TWO

sensitivity to gender relations, underlies the anxieties in their marriage. To him, dependency indicates a shift in power dynamics and is unsettling. The shift in power dynamics is also noticeable in Jojo's naturalization as an American citizen. It should be pointed out that this path to citizenship was made accessible to him because of Fiona's status as an American citizen. His naturalization is thus a consequence of their marriage and another indication of his dependency on his wife. More important is the issue of identity that this process unveils. While naturalization offers Jojo the opportunity to stay and be employed, it comes at the cost of possible erasure of his Ghanaian identity and its values. In a situation where cultural retention is the frame for Jojo's identity, American citizenship represents erasure. Citizenship for him comes at the expense of cultural heritage, as he has to rescind his Ghanaian nationality in the process of naturalization as an American citizen. As he tells us, "The day I surrendered my Ghana passport, I felt as if I had killed a part of my identity and acquired a new one. I wept."[68] Alongside this sense of cultural erasure is the feeling of entrapment that comes with his lack of employment. In what seems to be a moment of confession to the reader, he reveals to us: "I felt trapped for the first time since I'd known Fiona. I needed to do something, and it had to be done soon; otherwise, I feared what might happen to us."[69]

Jojo's fears about the future of his marriage are based on emotional and practical considerations. He remarks, for instance, that getting married to Fiona would grant him permanent residency in the United States. However, the process comes with a caveat, as residency would be offered if they stayed married "until immigration made its final decision," and "if [they] divorced, [his] application would be rejected."[70] As Jojo reflects on the power dynamics this creates, he says of himself: "Reduced to its minimum, she held the power of returning me to Ghana at a time when I couldn't return."[71] The decision to marry Fiona and stay in the marriage goes beyond emotional considerations, for even if the need arises for them to go their separate ways, he could not afford it. Is he compelled out of necessity and not love to stay in the marriage? Is his decision to stay based on the fear of being seen as a failure upon returning home without economic success? As he himself tells us, "How could I return home broke? What would I tell my family? I had come to America to stack hay?"[72] In rationalizing his marriage, he tells us the foundations of the marriage are already in place and there is nothing

---

68   Kwakye, *The Other Crucifix*, 159.
69   Kwakye, *The Other Crucifix*, 161.
70   Kwakye, *The Other Crucifix*, 157.
71   Kwakye, *The Other Crucifix*, 157.
72   Kwakye, *The Other Crucifix*, 157.

he can do to change course, even as he reveals his fears over Fiona's power. One gets the impression of resignation in spite of the glaring apprehensions. On the other hand, political conditions and home are not favorable for return. The cold-blooded murder of Uncle Kusi at the hands of "a group of drunken soldiers [who] had miscarried their orders [to arrest him] and shot him" did not provide any motivation for return.[73] Sithole's speech detailing the crippling effects of apartheid on the Black population in South Africa was another reminder of the political instability and corruption back home. Consequently, Jojo loses confidence in Ghana and chooses to stay. He concludes: "Was this the country to which I wanted to return after graduation? Check. A man has died. A dream had died. It seemed time for new beginnings. America had openings. Not yet checkmate."[74] Using terminologies from the game of chess that Uncle Kusi taught him, Jojo reverses the goal of return that he and Uncle Kusi have set out to accomplish from the start of the journey.

The dominant feeling that pervades his experiences in the United States is one of exclusion, social alienation, and fear. His encounter with racism and its impact on his sense of self cannot be rationalized away. He tells us: "In those days I still struggled not to think in terms of skin shades, but time and time again I couldn't escape it."[75] He takes comfort in his ability to adapt to changing circumstances and compares this ability to death and resurrection. While we can focus on the resurrection and the possibility of new life, his scepticism is revealed when he notes that "each time I died and lived, the death and resurrection left me with an altered soul, not necessarily bad or worse, just different; sometimes stronger, sometimes weaker."[76] In this reflection, Jojo highlights a significant truth about migration: its most deadly power is in its ability to alter the soul of the migrant. It is in the realm of the spiritual and psychological that the most devastating effects of migration are registered.

Consequently, even though externally it appears that Jojo is successful and has accomplished part of the dream, the dominant impression from his journey is the pervasive influence of race and ethnic discrimination on his life. It dogs his every step and cannot be overlooked. At the end of the novel, Jojo still can't answer the question he asks at the beginning of the novel, whether his coming to America was a curse or blessing. He notes that he considers himself "a continuing sojourner, who had triumphed over pitfalls and would face more in the foreseeable future" and that he "was not sure [he] could

---

73   Kwakye, *The Other Crucifix*, 111.
74   Kwakye, *The Other Crucifix*, 112.
75   Kwakye, *The Other Crucifix*, 173.
76   Kwakye, *The Other Crucifix*, 173.

adequately answer the question presented: whether the day of [his] arrival in the US was to be blessed or cursed."[77] His rumination that "with two children and a loving wife, I was convinced my future in America held much promise" is an instance of cold comfort.[78] His accommodation of Dwayne's theory of instincts comes across as an unconvincing attempt to further rationalize his uncertainties. The lasting impression of the journey is the sense that, despite Jojo's optimism, he has a huge mountain to climb if he is to derive any sense of fulfillment from the journey.

---

77 Kwakye, *The Other Crucifix*, 217.
78 Kwakye, *The Other Crucifix*, 217.

Part II
Arrival

This section of the book deals with the second phase of the migration process. It explores the pain and suffering of migrants upon arrival in the West. For the purpose of analysis, I divide this phase in the migrant's experience into two components and use three novels to explore them in two chapters.

Chapter 3 focuses on the disillusionment that comes with the realization that the grass, after all, is not greener on the other side and draws from specific incidents in the narrative such as police surveillance and raids and the arrest, detention, and deportation of the narrator to highlight the precarity that defines illegal migration in France in *Blue White Red*. I use *Harare North* in this chapter also to extend the picture of suffering by focusing on a group of illegal migrants from different countries in West and Central Africa living in horrible conditions in Brixton, England. The events in *Harare North* heighten the migrant's suffering because they not only depict the dehumanizing experiences of its characters and their psychological frustrations but also lead to insanity and death for some of the characters.

In chapter 4, I use *Behold the Dreamers* to extend the conversation on the suffering of undocumented migrants. The chapter explains the anxieties and fears that translate to psychological depression and violence. Through examining the life of the Jongas, a migrant family from Cameroon, the narrative demonstrates the psychological toll that undocumented residency can take on the lives of migrants. At the end of the novel, the protagonist acknowledges return as a better alternative to the suffering abroad and returns to Cameroon with his family. Despite the relief that comes with this move, the narrative stresses some underlying tensions in the family. *Behold the Dreamers* provides a neat segue into part 3 where the complications of return are explored. As in part 1, the dominant picture that emerges in both America and Europe is the precarity of migrant life.

Chapter Three

Disillusionment and Death

Alain Mabanckou's *Blue White Red* explores the circumstances that necessitate the flight of the protagonist from the Republic of Congo and his subsequent disillusionment when confronted with the realities of illegal immigration in France. Mabanckou uses irony and satire to condemn the greed and avarice that lure illegal migrants to Europe and exposes the ignorance and gullibility of African societies. In the examination of the life of the narrator in Paris, Mabanckou sends a clear message to Africans contemplating departure about the dangers of illegal migration.

At the opening of the novel, the narrator is in solitary confinement. The narrator, unnamed at this point in the story, is reflecting on his past and tells us of the psychological torture of being in detention awaiting deportation. Using memory as a structural device of plot construction, the author depicts the precarious lives of illegal African migrants in Paris. Further, in the narrative, he references numerous and continuous raids by both the police and immigration officers and the arbitrary arrests and detention of undocumented migrants in unsanitary facilities.

The voice of the unnamed narrator is personal, introspective, and reflective. Its subdued tone registers the honesty with which he assesses his situation in the context of the deep psychological struggle he is going through to make sense of his location. He reflects on the decision to migrate to France and questions the moral rightness of flight, even with the best of intentions. His mood shifts from justification to lamentation. Finding himself in this space between resignation and hope, the voice hints at the motivation for continued struggle despite the odds. He takes on the responsibility of providing for his people and sees migration as a burden that well-meaning individuals undertake on behalf of their families. He feels entrusted with a mission that he has to accomplish at all costs. Herein lies not only the motivation for departure from the home country but also the reason to stay and continue to struggle; the mission to alleviate the suffering of the loved ones must be accomplished at all costs. This is the burden of the migrant, a burden that is a product of history and the cultural values of their society. In the struggle to accomplish this motive, innocent people are deceived,

78   &   CHAPTER THREE

lured by the gleam and the deception of fraudsters, who traffick them to Europe and abandon them to a hostile society where they are caught in a conundrum: stringent migration laws that make it impossible for them to acculturate and the expectations in their home countries that make it equally impossible for them to return, lest they be judged as failures. This in-between space puts the narrator in a position of vulnerability and opens him to exploitation and abuse.

The novel's depiction of migrants' experiences overlaps with their reasons for departure. Since the struggle to survive in Paris is crucial to understanding the plight of the narrator, it is important to spend some time exploring the reasons for his departure from the Congo. Dominic Thomas notes the legacy of history as contributory factor to flight:

> The period following African independence from colonial rule was devoted to the daunting task of nation building, and now that some fifty years have elapsed since that process began, young people often find themselves alienated, disenfranchised, and with limited professional opportunities. As such, they are compelled to seek out employment prospects outside of their country of birth and invariably move toward the relatively more prosperous regions outside of the African continent.[1]

Continuing on the motivations for departure, Thomas asserts, "Economic, political, and social asymmetries account for transitions in migratory patterns within countries and continents and beyond strict national/continental borders."[2] The socioeconomic status of sub-Saharan countries put them in a position of the disadvantaged, and this necessitates and highlights the "unidirectionality of human mobility toward those economically prosperous geographic zones in the European Union."[3]

While contemporary African migrants might be justified in their pursuit of a better life in the West, the current body of literature that can be labeled "migration literature" speaks to a different migrant experience of the West. There is an abundance of literature devoted to the reversal of expectations of the migrant and the resulting disillusionment that accompanies this state of events. The reasons for this are many and varied. Thomas contends that "developments in migratory patterns have also coincided with the shifting frameworks of twenty-first-century economic, social, and political realities, which have yielded increasing control and legislation. Migrants now find themselves in additionally precarious circumstances, forced to confront racial profiling and arbitrary police round-ups and avoid detention centers

---

1   Thomas, "African Migration and African Dandys," xii.
2   Thomas, "The Global Mediterranean," 140.
3   Thomas, "The Global Mediterranean," 140.

and deportation procedures."[4] In his article "The Global Mediterranean: Literature and Migration," Thomas states: "Indeed, if migration has emerged as a key geometric coordinate of globalization today, so too has the concern with *controlling* the planetary circulation of human beings (labor forces, asylum seekers, refugees) particularly when it comes to the African continent."[5] The racialization of migration, especially where Black bodies are concerned, and the barriers they have to overcome to succeed, are indicative of their othering, social alienation, and economic exclusion.

The literature of migration from the African continent is becoming increasingly activist in voicing both the conditions that necessitate departure and the precarity of life that awaits the illegal migrant upon arrival in the West. As Thomas further notes, "Today, there exists a wide range of works by authors from both north and south of the Sahara (and from numerous other geographic locations) addressing postcolonial circumstances, exhibiting a particular concern with the plight of migrants, asylum seekers, and refugees."[6] Alain Mabanckou's *Blue White Red* is a case in point. The desire for economic advancement, coupled with the disillusionment in post-independence African societies, has pushed thousands of young men and women to the point of desperation, and as Thomas adds, the result "has been an exponential rise in the death toll of vulnerable economic migrants attempting perilous ocean crossings in order to reach the southern landmarks of 'Europe' that are Lampedusa, Gibraltar, Sicily, the Canary Islands, Ceuta and Melila (the last two being Spanish enclaves on the 'African' continent)."[7] Though the journeys of the main protagonists, Massala-Massala and Moki, are not across the ocean, the evidence indicates that the conditions that have necessitated departure have not changed much in the migrants' home countries: whether the migration is by air (as in the disastrous attempt of the two stowaways, Koita and Tunkara, mentioned in the introduction) to reach Belgium in the disaster with Brussels Airlines in 1991 or through the Mediterranean Sea in 2023 when Africans were forced to flee the continent. It is certainly plausible to read Mabanckou's novel on this level as a scathing commentary on the conditions at home that force innocent young people to take such desperate and perilous journeys to the West, many of them unaware of the living conditions that await them as illegal migrants.

However, not all critics or writers from Africa share this perspective on migration. In her article "Lark Mirror: African Culture, Masculinity, and

---

4   Thomas, "African Migration and African Dandys," xii-xiii.
5   Thomas, "The Global Mediterranean," 140.
6   Thomas, "The Global Mediterranean," 143.
7   Thomas, "The Global Mediterranean," 144.

80 ❧ CHAPTER THREE

Migration to France in Alain Mabanckou's *Bleu Blanc Rouge*," Wandia Njoya asks a very important question: "Is life in Africa so poor and desperate that it is worthwhile to endure the treacherous hazards of migrating to Europe, and the possibility that one may live in poverty or worse, be deported?"[8] This question is not only at the heart of Mabanckou's novel but also the thread that connects the novels selected for study in this monograph. As Njoya quotes Senegalese writer Boubacar Boris Diop: "People are ready to sacrifice their lives to leave their homeland, but where is the willingness to serve that country, to invest a life there, at least in the interest of future generations?"[9] Njoya adopts a theoretical framework, based on the metaphor of the lark mirror as a hunting device from Odile Cazenave, with which to read the novel and, in essence, illegal migration as "that which is pleasing and deceitful, to describe the determination of African migrants to seek their fortunes in France despite the legal and economic hurdles they face."[10]

Given the centrality of departure to the condition of the migrant in Europe, I explore the significance of Njoya's questions and Thomas's assertions by raising two questions of my own: Why is Moki so attractive to his people, and why is Massala-Massala so easily deceived? I use these questions to address the core of Njoya's argument concerning the lark mirror by seeking to engage the reasons for which the decoy, in spite of the deaths of numerous birds, will continue to be attractive to many more. Thomas attributes departure to mythology in Francophone African culture, in this case, that of the Congolese. While acknowledging that "post-migrant narratives have provided disquieting accounts of the social conditions in Europe," he also questions "what motivates individuals to emigrate," and asks "what are the *push* factors?"[11] He cites the myth of a French paradise as motivating factor for departure, especially when juxtaposed, by implication, with an African or local hell. He notes in support of this myth a long list of contributory factors: "weak economics, limited employment prospects, sub-standard governance, dysfunctional nation-states, poor environmental conditions, and industrialized offshore fishing practices."[12] These conditions have underlined and amplified the "symbolic value of France (and its capital city Paris in particular) [and have] informed the Francocentrist quests of young African protagonists for generations."[13]

---

8   Njoya, "Lark Mirror," 338.

9   Njoya, "Lark Mirror," 338.

10   Njoya, "Lark Mirror," 339.

11   Thomas, "The Global Mediterranean," 148.

12   Thomas, "The Global Mediterranean," 148.

13   Thomas, "The Global Mediterranean," 149.

Njoya disagrees with this view and advances a historical framework to understand departure. She argues that access to and adoption of Western lifestyle are defining rites of passage for young Africans in Francophone Africa. This rite is represented in the image of La Sape (Society of People of Ambience and Elegance) and locally manifested in the lifestyle of celebrities and icons such as Kofi Olomide and Papa Wemba. From this, Njoya argues that departure stems from "the human need to assert one's identity as an individual and as a man in his society, and whose fulfillment since colonialism has been pegged to the acquisition of a Western lifestyle and access to consumer goods, as opposed to being founded on the values and history that affirm African societies and that are embodied in African traditions."[14] Without extending the debate on the colonial legacy and Western capitalist influences to African migration, I posit a different reading of Mabanckou's novel. While I acknowledge Njoya's theorizations and analysis of French colonial influence in shaping the mindset of prosperity in the West, I hesitate to say that Mabanckou endorses that view. I contend that to do so is to miss the irony in the presentation of Moki, Mabanckou's central character. It is apparent that Moki's migration to France was "inspired by French literature and magazines which his father brought home from the hotel at which the latter worked,"[15] as Njoya rightly noted; but I argue against justifying this as Mabanckou's perspective. To so justify is to conflate the voice of Moki with Mabanckou, and this is deeply problematic. In many instances in the novel, Mabanckou not only distances himself from Moki and the actions of his compatriots; he also ridicules their exaggerated performances and laughs at their pretensions to French civilization and culture. Equally important is the recognition that Mabanckou satirizes Congolese society and spotlights its willful and self-destructive materialism. Moki's success, while stemming from his status as Parisian, also hinges on the gullibility of society and their willingness to be deceived. Therefore, while Moki's migration, in the words of Njoya, "stands as a reminder to the community that migration to France is a milestone for initiation into adulthood and respect for African men,"[16] I question whether this perspective on rite of passage is misplaced. I do so on the basis that the situation in France is a reversal of this perspective, and so, reading the novel as a counter-narrative to this conception of manhood is more productive. Mabanckou is urging Africans to re-evaluate some of the mythologies associated with culture, rituals, and ceremonies and is calling attention to the legacies of French colonialism that warrant at the least

---

14   Njoya, "Lark Mirror," 340.

15   Njoya, "Lark Mirror," 340.

16   Njoya, "Lark Mirror," 343.

82 ❧ CHAPTER THREE

a reconfiguration in order to decenter French values prescribed as the norm and recalibrate African attitudes to an embrace of its traditions. I use this structural frame to analyze both the deception of Moki and the gullibility of society.

Part 1 of the novel, "The Country," depicts life in the narrator's home country before departure and highlights a crucial aspect of illegal migration: the lure of the West made concrete by the demonstration of lavish opulence by fraudsters who return to the homeland as wealthy celebrities. Moki's persona, especially the flaunting of his supposedly acquired wealth, provides the motivation for others in the village to search for greener pastures in Europe. The figure of the Parisian is the symbol of success and the yardstick by which all others are measured in the village. To aspire to the level of the returned migrant is to embody the drive and aspiration to succeed. Moki's image of splendor is so compelling that unsuspecting villagers are willing to risk everything to achieve it. The assumption is that, even if life in Europe is fraught with challenges, it could be overcome through hard work and determination. In any case, acquiring the wealth and status of Moki is a risk that is definitely worth taking. More importantly, without risk taking, it is apparent that there are few alternative paths to success. As the narrator reflects on life before Moki gave him the opportunity to travel to Paris, he states: "I was nothing but a shadow. A shadow is nothing by itself. It needs a presence and a virgin surface on which to print its outline."[17]

Nicknamed the Parisian, Moki demonstrates a lifestyle that is proof of his transformation from poverty to wealth. The construction of his father's house is part of the evidence of his opulence. In one of his trips back home, Moki resumes construction of the building by hiring "a dozen masons who were enticed to work by getting paid in advance and in amounts that make our mouths water."[18] He personally supervises the work and demonstrates so much generosity toward his workers that the village thinks "he even spoiled them" by picking them up by car in the morning and driving them to their homes at night, giving them tips, and congratulating them for every work done.[19] At the completion of the building, an immense white villa with green doors and shutters stands majestically in the village. The villa concretizes the rationale for flight. It depicts the dichotomy between poverty and riches.

The image of the Parisian grants Moki a celebrated status and prominence reserved only for successful migrants and access to facilities previously denied him. This "sense of the dichotomy of these two worlds grew sharper when

---

17   Mabanckou, *Blue White Red*, 22.
18   Mabanckou, *Blue White Red*, 24.
19   Mabanckou, *Blue White Red*, 24.

Moki installed electricity and a water pump on their lot."[20] Given the fact that houses with electric lighting and access to potable water are rare, "the villa acquired an added status of providence in addition to its prominence, as it became the only source of light and potable water to the village."[21] In addition, there "were more surprises" for the village, as scarcely a year after the construction of the house, "we saw two Toyotas arrive. Moki had chartered and sent them from France so his family could make a profit off them as taxis. That protected the family from utter destitution."[22] The celebrated prominence is also acquired by the relatives of the successful migrant. Moki's father, a previously humble and relatively unknown figure, is transformed into a celebrity to the point where he is hastily nominated to the presidency of the village council. In recognition of his growing influence, and the reverence people bestowed on him, he "wasted no time in adopting the latest fashions."[23] Hence:

> He cast aside all his traditional clothing and preferred to wear clothes straight from Paris. From that time on, he wore gray trousers made of virgin wool, well pressed with sharp pleats. No belt, but tricolor suspenders (blue, white, and red), a white dress shirt, a black fedora, and the kind of good black shoes you wear to church. Suddenly he looked like the American blues singer John Lee Hooker. He strolled around the neighborhood, chest out, head held high, both hands in his pockets.[24]

The excerpt operates on two levels: the image of Moki's father as the reward of parental duty on the one hand and the subtle but biting comment on materialism on the other. Depicting the contrast between appearance and reality, the excerpt illustrates society's attraction to the external manifestations of prosperity and the celebration of material wealth. It raises questions about the norms and values of society and interrogates the vainglory that comes with material acquisition. Without any consideration for the source of Moki's wealth, his father became a local celebrity. Mabanckou demonstrates the elitism that often comes with material acquisition, especially condescending behavior toward those considered socioeconomically inferior, and ridicules the almost infantile display of his possessions. As we learn from the narrator, "You really need to see him on his bicycle. He rode slowly, stopping to greet everyone he met at an intersection. Without any prompting, he gave everyone the latest news on Moki."[25] The father's ridiculous valorization of

---

20 Mabanckou, *Blue White Red*, 25.

21 Mabanckou, *Blue White Red*, 25.

22 Mabanckou, *Blue White Red*, 26.

23 Mabanckou, *Blue White Red*, 29.

24 Mabanckou, *Blue White Red*, 29.

25 Mabanckou, *Blue White Red*, 29.

84 ✜ CHAPTER THREE

everything French is a grotesque demonstration of the Francophone attachment to France to the point of caricature. He not only uses suspenders in the national colors of France but also explains a distorted version of French history to the locals at the council meeting. We learn that he "was capable of reciting to the village council the names of all the kings and presidents sequentially from the Second Empire of Napoleon III up to the present, without faltering."[26] In such moments, "Loyalty sparkled in his eyes, a blind loyalty deeply rooted in the depth of his soul."[27]

In the elaborate preparation for Moki's visit, Mabanckou ridicules society's preference for the attractions of the West. Moki's father embarks on a charade-like cleaning campaign of the house and courtyard to the point where "not a single leaf from the mango tree was left on the ground."[28] Moki's return is conceived as a village festival, and every member of the extended family is required to be present: "One family member's success was not the business of one or two people. It had to benefit the entire clan in the broadest way possible."[29] Hyperbolic in its depiction, the celebration satirizes the open display of reverence for material wealth.

As earlier mentioned, the image of the Parisian is crucial to understanding the motivations for illegal migration. The connections between the two are worth exploring. The opening lines of "The Country," the title of part one of the novel, are critical to my analysis. Mabanckou writes:

IN THE BEGINNING, there was the name. A Humdrum name.
A two-syllable name: Moki . . .
At the beginning, there was that name.
Moki is standing in front of me. I see him again. He's
talking to me.[30]

An obvious parody of the biblical Creation story in Genesis, the excerpt demonstrates the elevated position of the Mokis, the successful migrant. A Christ-like figure, Moki assumes the qualities of savior and redeemer in the eyes of his people. In this image of the redeemer, he is respected and revered. Moki not only leads people to their destiny; he also is destined to function in this capacity. This is the burden he carries; this is his role in life—one ordained by God from the moment of creation. A few lines later, the narrative records, "He was the one who created me in his own image. His manner of living bankrolled my dreams."[31] The extension of the Creation

---

26   Mabanckou, *Blue White Red*, 28.
27   Mabanckou, *Blue White Red*, 32.
28   Mabanckou, *Blue White Red*, 31.
29   Mabanckou, *Blue White Red*, 35.
30   Mabanckou, *Blue White Red*, 19.
31   Mabanckou, *Blue White Red*, 22.

story to Moki's creation of the thus-far unnamed narrator calls attention to Moki's godlike status. Moki has the power to create followers after him and in his likeness. The effect of the parody is clear: the vanity of a society that likens material acquisition to salvation and the blasphemy inherent in raising the fraudster to the level of the godhead. In the parody, Moki is the creator, and Paris is paradise. The deception of society cannot go unnoticed.

Moki's transformation is also worthy of comment. His appearance is striking: "The first thing we noticed was the colour of his skin. Nothing at all like ours, poorly cared for, devoured by the scorching sun, oily and as black as manganese. He was extraordinarily white."[32] Part of the appeal of the Parisian is the light skin he acquired in Paris. This not only serves as a contrast to the dark skin of his countrymen but also puts him in an elevated position of celebrated otherness. He is like the white man; he lives in the white man's country. And he has brought home evidence of the white man's wealth. It turns out, as the narrator tells us, "Later, in France, I learned that he applied hydroquinone products to his entire body."[33] While Moki's deception cannot be more painfully realized, the idea that greed in society lays the grounds for deception cannot be overlooked.

At the distribution-of-gifts ceremony for his extended relatives, Moki's status as a been-to is established. The ritual of handing over trifles as cheap trinkets to relatives, who have waited for days for his return, illustrates the absurdity of the situation. Moki thrives not only on the ignorance of the people but also on their greed and materialism. Their willingness to believe his lies is uncanny: the obsequious relatives are willing to go through a humiliating process just to receive "a little something from France" and would give "thanks, in the first instance to the Parisian's father, and then to him, while wishing him good luck."[34] The greed of society is further extended into the desire to imitate the Parisian. The imitation is conducted on the basis of blind deception. It is hilarious to the point where the young people of the country "knocked themselves out in their irreversible blindness to ape Parisians [and] made do with cheap products made in Africa like Ambi Red and Ambi Green."[35] The result was disastrous, as the "imitators got slapped with allergies, red spots, and blood clots on their faces."[36] One wonders about the extent to which the narrator is prepared to go against his better instincts and judgment.

---

32 Mabanckou, *Blue White Red*, 38.
33 Mabanckou, *Blue White Red*, 38.
34 Mabanckou, *Blue White Red*, 37.
35 Mabanckou, *Blue White Red*, 38.
36 Mabanckou, *Blue White Red*, 38.

86   CHAPTER THREE

More than the distribution of gifts, the meeting at the buvette gives a more accurate picture of the people's gullibility and the deception of Moki. Their failure to recognize his tall tales, false sense of importance, and superficial fortune is a satire of society's blind attraction to the West and susceptibility to manipulation and lies. Moki's life in the village was one of elaborate performance; the pace of his walk, his mannerisms at the table, his dress, and his speech all indicate the cruel brilliance of his cunning and pretense. He affects the manners of high society in Paris and has pretensions to refinement and culture. He dabbles in French history and feigns knowledge of literature. He imitates the sophisticated and learned, and through grandiose but parodied elegance, he succeeds in creating a clout of respect and admiration around himself and uses this to deceive his audience. The irony lies not only in the gap between Moki's appearance and reality but also in the inability of the people to perceive the phoniness of the performance being enacted right in front of them. The gap between the yarn that Moki spins for his audience and their susceptibility to his pretensions accounts for a huge part of his success. The following monologue of Moki's in one performance at a buvette is instructive:

There were a lot of us walking Indian file with our Solex mopeds along Independence Avenue at Pointe-Noire. We weren't called *sapeurs* yet, but *fighters*. This latter term unfortunately had a pejorative side. It inspired brutality, combat, while all we demanded of ourselves was refinement, elegance, and beauty. From *fighters* we went to being called *playboys*. But all that sounded too English or American. Today we are *sapeurs*, and so much better. Far from putting out fires, we love ambience, the beautiful lifestyle, and we admire beautiful creatures such as those surrounding me here. Is it because the word *sapeurs* is going out of style little by little that we are now called *Parisians?* Clothing is our passport. Our religion. France is the country of fashion because it is the only place in the world where you can judge a book by its cover. That's the truth, believe me.[37]

Any sensitive adolescent can see through Moki's performance. Using trifles and decorative language to hoodwink the audience, Moki succeeds in getting away with such absurd statements as France being the only place where a book is judged by its cover. The excerpt suggests that society's attention to the superficial puts it in a position of vulnerability. Unscrupulous fraudsters like Moki can exploit this societal weakness to the fullest. Their belief in Moki's knowledge of French authors simply because he namedrops writers like Guy de Maupassant, Andre Gide, Albert Camus, Victor Hugo, Lamartine, and Alfred de Vigny, "even though [he] failed his baccalaureate

---

37   Mabanckou, *Blue White Red*, 55.

DISILLUSIONMENT AND DEATH 87

in literature twice,"[38] is revealing of society's gullibility. He recites bits and pieces of poetry and fiction from famous French writers and pretends to be an expert on their works. He concocts elaborate stories of his theatrical performances in France whose credibility is as thinly veiled as the absurdity of the stories he tells. The narrator comments on how Moki keeps telling these same stories every year, and yet the people's enthusiasm for these tales never abated: "The Parisian had officiated his annual mass. He will do it again next year. With the same audience and same newcomers. He would omit a detail here, add an anecdote there. Silence was the sign that the crowd was with him."[39] Society is not only superficial; it is willfully ignorant and blind.

The narrator's status as a would-be Parisian throws him into the limelight. As he tells us, "People didn't look at me in the same way anymore. I was no longer a native. I was a Parisian."[40] In accordance with this elevated status, Adeline, a girl with whom he had sexual relations thirteen or fourteen years earlier, perceives his status as an opportunity for socioeconomic advancement and declares that she is carrying the narrator's son. His uncle who normally would resist giving out loans to relatives, gladly consents to buy his plane ticket, while the shopkeeper, who typically would not give out his merchandise on credit, was more than willing to allow the narrator's father to "choose whatever [he likes and to] come back to [him] to sign the receipt" after he makes his selection. Upon receiving his housing certificate, the narrator says, "People wanted to see it, palpate it, smell it," while he not only "lived in permanent terror of losing it" but also the "anguish dwelled in [his] unconscious to the point that it tossed the landscape of [his] dreams upside down."[41] Moki finally returns to the village and, together with the narrator, who has a tourist visa, flies out to Paris. As Moki tells him, "We'll see when you get here how to prolong your stay; the important thing is that you get into France."[42] Here lies the catch, the crux of Moki's deception: for once the narrator overstays his visa, he is at the mercy not only of Moki but also of the immigration officers.

The contrast between the charade and reality is shocking as the narrator comes to realize Moki's deception. The realities of life for illegal immigrants in Europe are captured in the section of the novel titled "Paris" and functions as the stage where Moki's mask is unveiled, for here the narrator comes to see him for what he truly is. For the first time, Massala-Massala is able to penetrate the mask, the veneer of success, and comes face-to-face

---

38   Mabanckou, *Blue White Red*, 55.
39   Mabanckou, *Blue White Red*, 57.
40   Mabanckou, *Blue White Red*, 67.
41   Mabanckou, *Blue White Red*, 65.
42   Mabanckou, *Blue White Red*, 65.

88 ❧ CHAPTER THREE

with the truth about Moki's double life. He recognizes what the reader had long determined—that Moki is fake, his success story is one elaborate performance, and Massala-Massala has fallen for the antics of a trickster.

John Patrick Walsh provides an insightful reading of the opening of the novel that unveils a narrative structure that serves as a foregone conclusion even before the reader is taken on the journey. Walsh notes that the opening line of the novel indicates a failed attempt at migration and actually foreshadows a failure of arrival in Europe. He contends that both verbs [*arriver à*, to manage, and *s'en sortir*, to pull through] shifts between the idiomatic and the literal, "to arrive" and "to get out," indicates a semantic slippage, suggesting that "the illegal migrant 'arrives' in Paris, his physical destination, but never 'manages to pull through': the dream of inhabiting the mental territory of *Parisien*—a long-term project—turns out to be a hopeless illusion."[43] Walsh points out the reversal of the migrant's expectations and further remarks: "Alone in his cell, Massala-Massala can only contemplate the unsurpassable distance between an imagined geography and an incarcerating reality. The story of migration and return at the heart of Bleu-Blanc-Rouge is about the conflict between the idea of Paris as imagined by the Congolese protagonist and the experiences that do not live up to the dream."[44] This conflict between imagination and reality is summed up as an image of entrapment and death by Wandia Njoya, earlier mentioned. She also references this image when she notes "the inevitability of migration, the inexplicable attraction to certain images, the manipulation of these images to entrap migrants, and the ambush awaiting them" is illustrative of the suffering of the characters depicted in the novel.[45]

Also, in the Paris section of the novel, Mabanckou gives us a detailed portrait of the anguish of the narrator in solitary confinement. The preface is taken from an excerpt in Abdellatif Laâbi's *Le spleen de Casablanca*:

It seems that the gates of hell
border those of heaven.
The great joiner designed them
in the same coarse wood.[46]

The excerpt from Laâbi when deployed in the context of migration depicts two sides of the immigration coin, heaven and hell, as two sides of the same process. On one side, there is the path to opportunity, and on the other side, there is the road to anguish and a living hell. It appears that Paris is at the intersection of both gates or pathways, and based on one's immigration

---

43   Walsh, "Mapping Afropea," 96.
44   Walsh, "Mapping Afropea," 96.
45   Njoya, "Lark Mirror," 345.
46   Mabanckou, *Blue White Red*, 80.

DISILLUSIONMENT AND DEATH &♥ 89

status, one can enter through either the gates of heaven or the gates of hell. Given the temporary nature of Massala-Massala's tourist visa, the indications are that he would be redirected to the gates of hell within a very short time.

The image of disillusionment here, depicted as hell, is reflected in the thought processes of the narrator. It reveals his frustrations occasioned, first, by the shock that comes with the unveiling of the realities of Moki's situation and, second, by his detention in solitary confinement as he awaits deportation. In his cell, he struggles to hold on to memories of the past, and as he puts it, to "resist easy abandonment, abdication, and resignation."[47] In anger at his gullibility in believing Moki, Massala-Massala tells us how he "spent hours flagellating [himself] to punish these limbs, this head, these eyes, these ears that led [his] good judgment astray" and made him susceptible "to [his] fate."[48] In grim determination to survive, he pledges to "find a passage, a way out of this abyss" so that his spirit is "not derailed on the slope of regrets."[49]

For the first time in the story, the unnamed narrator tells us his name: Marcel Bonaventure. However, he quickly informs us that Bonaventure is not his real name; it is his pseudonym. A few lines later, he tells us that he also used the name Eric Jocelyn-George at some point in Paris. Naming is crucial to identity, and the switch from Massala-Massala to Marcel Bonaventure is critical on a number of fronts. First, it constitutes a departure from his historical and cultural identity, one that constitutes erasure. Second, it shows a split personality, given the multiple identities he bears. Later, he discloses that Massala-Massala is the "name carried by my father, my grandfather, and my great grandparents. I thought the name was eternal, immutable. I thought the name reflected the image of a past, of an existence, of a family history, of its conflicts, its rights, its grandeur, its decadence, and its dishonor."[50] The erasure of identity is the beginning of the physical and symbolic separation from his homeland. The chances that Marcel will find a way back home are slim.

It is important to note that one of the first acts of Massala-Massala in his attempt at integration is his name change. Njoya rightly notes that this attempt to regularize his status corresponds with the gradual loss of identity and agency. Hence, "The problem with these identities is not in their variety. . . . [Rather,] Massala-Massala's names refer to different people, and more importantly, people whom he does not know and who are imposed by

---

47   Mabanckou, *Blue White Red*, 83.

48   Mabanckou, *Blue White Red*, 83.

49   Mabanckou, *Blue White Red*, 83, 85.

50   Mabanckou, *Blue White Red*, 84.

90 & CHAPTER THREE

the institutional demands of staying in France."[51] Because his name "differs from the names acquired in France . . . it situates him in the history of his family and society in Congo," which by their erasure, has rendered this history "valueless by the immigration laws that necessarily require Africans to assume varied identities if they are to remain in the country."[52] Njoya beautifully sums up the predicament of naming, identity, and historical erasure as follows: because the name Massala-Massala links the protagonist linguistically, biologically, historically, geographically, and spiritually to his community, its irrelevance within France's borders artificially detaches the young man from his cultural roots. Notwithstanding, she argues that "worse, the detachment also denies his community transcendence of its historical and geographic borders."[53] For her, transcendence is crucial "because without it, both the individual and the community are imprisoned in the here and now, and lack the global perspectives necessary to give coherence to their present."[54] This compulsion for erasure is not only Massala-Massala's but also that of his compatriots.

Recognizing Moki's deception and confronted with culture shock, Massala-Massala's disappointment gradually turns into bitterness. In regret over his blind trust in Moki and alarmed at the precarity of his situation, Massala-Massala laments: "I was getting over my bewilderment. The shock of reality gnawed away at me. Moki, for better or worse, made an effort to console me, sensing that I was sinking into disillusionment. There was nothing more he could do. I was annoyed with him for not being more explicit about a certain number of things. About the essentials, *I certainly wouldn't have made the same decision.*"[55] (Emphasis added.) The weight of the regret on the narrator's mind is heavy. His confession, italicized in the excerpt, underscores this regret.

As the dust gradually settles, Massala-Massala comes to realize that Moki's scheme to get him into France is part of a larger syndicate of collaborators, later labeled the "white pipeline." He comes to recognize his physical and psychological dependence on Moki, and in spite of his anger and resentment, he has little alternative but to comply. Evidently, he "was hanging on Moki's willpower and, as [he] realized later, on the will of others in that milieu."[56] His acceptance of his dependence on Moki stems primarily from his realization of the culture of materialism back home and the image of

---

51 Njoya, "Lark Mirror," 351.
52 Njoya, "Lark Mirror," 351.
53 Njoya, "Lark Mirror," 352.
54 Njoya, "Lark Mirror," 352.
55 Mabanckou, *Blue White Red*, 86.
56 Mabanckou, *Blue White Red*, 87.

DISILLUSIONMENT AND DEATH   91

success that Moki has cultivated. In spite of his willingness to expose the reality of Moki's life, Massala-Massala comes to accept that very few, if anyone, would believe him back home. Instead, he would be seen as a failure and making excuses for his lack of success by blaming his benefactor. For this, he would be subjected to humiliation. Moki is aware of this mindset and uses it to his advantage. He brushes aside Massala-Massala's threat to disclose the truth about his life in Paris because he knows his countrymen back home will not believe Massala-Massala.

In this conundrum, Massala-Massala is resigned to fate and driven to silence. He notes, "I didn't send letters home anymore. Like everyone else around me. This way, they said, we manage the suspense back home" and then proceed to "learn how to live differently" through projecting success by perpetuating the myth of the grass being greener on the other side.[57] Through letters written back home, the migrants perform the dream. As Massala-Massala tells us, "If I wanted to write, the letter had to recount all the good things I thought about Paris. Moki would correct me. He would never miss an opportunity to squeeze in, here and there, a superlative more bombastic than my own."[58] In perpetuating the deception through empty verbosity, Massala-Massala becomes the image and likeness of his creator, Moki. The letter framed and hung on the wall that serves as the template from which he and his compatriots copy to write their own letters of "delight and happiness" is further indicative of Moki's replication in the framing of their people back home.[59]

Quite to the contrary, the novel exposes the dehumanizing conditions in which the undocumented African migrants are forced to live in Paris. Recognizing the fact that the "final judgment will be back home [and] they're waiting for us back there; it's unthinkable to go home empty-handed. Who would commit such a suicide,"[60] the undocumented ones resign themselves to a life of crime, first, to survive and, second, to keep the dream alive and perform some semblance of its accomplishment to friends and relatives back home. They are forced to live as squatters rather than return home and be humiliated as failures. Massala-Massala's description of the inhuman conditions in dilapidated buildings approved for demolition in which they are forced to live can be compared to a similar situation in *Harare North*, where illegal migrants from Zimbabwe are forced to live in Brixton as squatters in horrible conditions. The congestion in the building that Massala-Massala has to live in and the limited space for sleeping are described as piles of

---

57   Mabanckou, *Blue White Red*, 88.
58   Mabanckou, *Blue White Red*, 88.
59   Mabanckou, *Blue White Red*, 88.
60   Mabanckou, *Blue White Red*, 91.

92 &♦ CHAPTER THREE

bodies on the floor "like cadavers tied to a mass grave" necessitating the need to "keep . . . gesticulations and farting to a minimum."[61] It is a situation where "stretching out length-wise or spreading your legs and hands" attracts a "sharp dig of an elbow or knee."[62] Massala-Massala's situation is in reality a microcosm of the suffering that African migrants from various parts of the continent go through in France. He describes the market in Château Rouge, a popular rendezvous for undocumented African migrants, as a Tower of Babel where groups of Africans speak patois and sell fake electronic items to unsuspecting clients. He points out the regular police raids and the constant scramble for cover.

The lifestyle of the key players in this Tower of Babel is worth depicting. There is Boulou, the self-styled "real estate specialist," who finds accommodation for squatters in unoccupied apartments.[63] Benos is the hi-fi technologist who "knew all about the latest technologies in hi-fi and household appliances and walked around with a big bag full of catalogs [and] if someone ordered something from him, he would deliver the merchandise to their home the next day. No paperwork to be signed. Or even seen. Or known of."[64] There is Sote, the workhorse, who steals personal checks from mailboxes, and Prefet, who specializes in preparing false identity cards and residency papers as French citizens for illegal migrants. The lives of these migrants unveil a world of crime where threats to their existence, including death, are only a heartbeat away from them. The landscape of illegal African migrants in the diaspora depicts a mirage of shadowy and shady characters living on the fringes, flirting with crime, violence, and death, and wasting their lives in inhuman conditions abroad. Like Chikwava in *Harare North*, Mabanckou uses migrant suffering to demonstrate the drawbacks to illegal migration. While the novel points out the stringent immigration laws in France as a possible reason for migrant crime, the narrative is clear in emphasizing that the activities of Prefet, Sote, and Boulou cannot be condoned. For instance, Sote is the "specialist in mailboxes [who makes] his way around remote provinces where certain banks still trusted the mail with their client's checkbooks."[65] Boulou sells unoccupied apartments to eligible squatters, draws up fraudulent occupancy contracts for them, and profits off their need for housing. Again, while the novel references the difficulties Africans have obtaining visas to Europe, the narrative is clear in condemning the actions of these characters.

---

61 Mabanckou, *Blue White Red*, 91.

62 Mabanckou, *Blue White Red*, 91.

63 Mabanckou, *Blue White Red*, 98.

64 Mabanckou, *Blue White Red*, 98.

65 Mabanckou, *Blue White Red*, 102.

DISILLUSIONMENT AND DEATH   93

Massala-Massala's experience in Paris lends credence to the argument of return. With a fake identity card bearing the name Eric Jocelyn-George, which matches his fake photo ID and the name of the checkbook holder, he attempts to use the checkbook to purchase orange coupons of monthly passes on the metro for resale on the black market at Château Rouge. Massala-Massala is approached by potential clients (actually plainclothes detectives) who had been surveilling him and Prefet throughout the day. The Black detective lures Massala-Massala to a side street where a colleague in a police car is waiting. He is arrested without struggle and taken first to the squatter building in search of his accomplices; then when the search turns up nothing, he's sent to the Seine-Saint-Denis jail. He is "cloistered in a cell in the A wing, B building, fourth floor" and "condemned for complicity in fraud, identity theft, forgery, and use of forgeries."[66]

After two years of incarceration, Massala-Massala is released from solitary confinement, and he finds himself onboard a chartered airplane for deportees to Africa. The flight, he tells us, "will make stops in several African capitals: Bamako, Dakar, Kinshasa, and finally Brazzaville."[67] The deportees, enough to fill an airplane, from the three African former French colonies in Africa—Mali, Senegal, and Congo—point to the number of illegal migrants held in detention in France and, perhaps, all over the world.

Confronted with the grim reality of a failed return to his country of origin, Massala-Massala contemplates suicide but eventually decides on return. He informs us that he "chose to confront another reality . . . to see this through to the end. [He] would go home."[68] Mabanckou is not naïve or simplistic to the challenges of return, for he does confirm the possibility of Massala-Massala becoming "the laughing stock of the neighborhood."[69] With this, he prepares himself mentally for the challenges he will encounter but also takes comfort in the fact that "everything is possible in this world of ours."[70] There is still hope for the returned migrant at home.

James Arnett and Angela Wright's "Paul's Letter to the Congolese: Allegory, Optimism, and Universality in Alain Mabanckou's *Blue White Red*" offers a reading of Mabanckou's novel as an intervention into the perils of African migration. Read through the lens of biblical allegory, the author draws from two parables—the Prodigal Son and the Lost Sheep—to situate the plight of the illegal migrant and explore the question of return to the homeland. If Massala-Massala is read as the prodigal son, then the novel

---

66 Mabanckou, *Blue White Red*, 135.
67 Mabanckou, *Blue White Red*, 141.
68 Mabanckou, *Blue White Red*, 142.
69 Mabanckou, *Blue White Red*, 142.
70 Mabanckou, *Blue White Red*, 147.

94 ❧ CHAPTER THREE

illustrates the futility of the search for becoming and undermines the notion of France as the Promised Land. Massala-Massala squanders his "inheritance" in similar ways to the son; and even though his return is forced through deportation, he returns to the "father," here interpreted as the homeland, and is warmly received.[71] The novel is a warning against this quest and an invitation to all the prodigal sons of Africa in the West to return home.

Brian Chikwava's *Harare North* continues the theme of suffering in the migrant experience abroad. In this novel, the author critiques the experience of illegal Africans, especially that of the unnamed narrator from Zimbabwe seeking political asylum in England along with his friend, Shingi. One significant aspect of the novel is the detailed and methodical focus on the mental and psychological states of the migrants, in addition to the cultural, economic, and emotional struggles to survive. *Harare North* is crucial to the notion of precarity for it depicts the death of Shingi and the mental breakdown of the narrator at the end of the novel.

The unnamed narrator, who is also the protagonist of the novel, is seeking asylum in Brixton, England, nicknamed Harare North by his countrymen. He is trying to raise $5,000 as ransom money for crimes he is accused of having committed by the militia that works for President Mugabe.[72] He doesn't provide explicit details of his involvement in the crimes for which he is accused but frames the occasion as one of unfounded accusations. Notwithstanding, given the role of the militia in brutalizing political opponents of the Mugabe regime, the reader suspects some degree of involvement by the narrator. He seems to be more concerned with covering up his tracks than in disclosing the details of the encounters. He is an unreliable narrator and cannot be taken at his word.

The narrator arrives in London in the shadows of a dark past and carries with him a burden of secrecy that he struggles to keep, symbolized by the cardboard suitcase he brings to London. The emotional weight of the past is more dogged and indelible in his consciousness than he is willing to accept so that when we see him at the end of the novel carrying the empty

---

71 Arnett and Wright, "Paul's Letter to the Congolese," 239.

72 The Mugabe regime, especially in the late 1990s, is reputed for its assault on political opponents and the campaign of violence conducted by vigilante groups and militia on behalf of the state. These groups wielded unwavering power and used violence as innocent citizens deemed traitors of the ZANU-PF party. In *History of Africa* 4th edition, Kevin Shillington writes: "Spontaneous political violence by ZANU-PF zealots against the main opposition party, and any other critic of the government, had reached such a height around the 2008 parliamentary and presidential elections that in the election that followed in 2013, little direct incitement to further violence was needed to ensure Mugabe and ZANU-PF an overwhelming victory."

DISILLUSIONMENT AND DEATH 95

cardboard suitcase on his head and walking naked in the streets of London, we recognize the toll the past has placed on the present. Compounded with the trauma of the present, he goes through a process of mental breakdown and loses his mind.

As mentioned earlier, it is on the level of psychological introspection that the novel best operates. The foray into the minds of the characters is revealing in its depth and artistry. The novel avails itself of its craftsmanship in the use of this method of character depiction. From the graphic but methodical process of mental derangement, Chikwava exposes the grim realities of life of the illegal migrant in Europe and, in subtle ways, interrogates the reasoning behind departure from the home country in the very first place. Delphine Fongang alludes to this predicament when she opens her essay in this way: "No matter how far one travels to escape the socio-economic and political malaise in Africa, one soon realizes that the diaspora is neither an accommodating nor welcoming space. Dreams of a safe haven, filled with opportunities and economic stability, are shattered by cultural and racialized ideologies that keep many migrants at the margins. It is this phenomenon that Brian Chikwava effectively demonstrates in *Harare North*."[73] Fongang goes on to elucidate the struggles of the unnamed narrator and his fellow migrants from the African continent to succeed. She cites the mental breakdown of the narrator at the end of the novel as indicative of "the ambivalent duality of consciousness" and infers that "Chikwava's story is not only one of triumph and success, but characterized by psychological trauma, cultural isolation, and socio-economic adversity that hinder the narrator from achieving economic empowerment and fulfillment in the diaspora."[74] She describes the experiences of illegal migrants as defined by "fragmentation and traumatic alienations" due to the fact that it is becoming "harder and harder to enjoy economic empowerment and cultural inclusion, leaving some migrants estranged and alienated in metropolitan spaces."[75] Given the "displacement of Africans from Africa to various metropolitan spaces of the West," Fongang notes that displacement reveals "how migrants struggle to adapt to cultural difference as racialized subjects."[76] She summarizes this struggle to survive as fraudulent activities including blackmail, extortion, and deception, concluding that such activities "reveal the economic desperation many migrants face in various European-American metropolitan spaces. The will to survive trumps any culpability on the part of the migrant. Chikwava clearly shows that the diasporic space is a complex web of economic challenges, with the

---

73 Fongang, "Cosmopolitan Dilemma," 27.

74 Fongang, "Cosmopolitan Dilemma," 28.

75 Fongang, "Cosmopolitan Dilemma," 28.

76 Fongang, "Cosmopolitan Dilemma," 28–29.

96 &♦ CHAPTER THREE

desire for survival a constant struggle."[77] I agree with Fongang's theorization on racial otherness and the cultural displacement of Africans in the diaspora.

Harare North is unique in the questions it raises on the cost of migration and the extent to which the illegal migrant is willing to go to accomplish the dream, a dream that for an undocumented migrant is largely elusive. The novel seems to question the extent to which illegal migrants are willing to sacrifice their minds and bodies to achieve a near-impossible dream. As the reader watches the gradual but inevitable process of the protagonist's mental deterioration, the erosion of human dignity is laid bare as spectacle.

The combined experiences of the narrator, Shingi, Tsitsi, Aleck, and Farayi call into question the feasibility of the dream for illegal migrants and expose the naïveté around which the dream is conceptualized back home. From the perspective of the narrator, and indeed that of many migrants, escape to Europe offers a guarantee of economic success. What turns out to be true is that the dream is not even achievable for many Westerners who are citizens of the countries that are highly sought after by migrants. The narrator was so sure that he would make five thousand dollars in a short time and return to Zimbabwe a successful migrant that he was stunned by the reversal of expectations. He comes to realize that life in Brixton deeply exacerbates the precarious life he was fleeing from in Zimbabwe. In Brixton, he cannot afford basic necessities of food, shelter, and clothing that he had back home. He lives in a squatter house with constant threats of police raids. Unemployed, hungry, and destitute, he scavenges for rotten leftovers in dumpsters. He lives in fear of arrest and deportation, if not incarceration. To add to this, he is compelled to send money back home almost on a regular basis to alleviate the sufferings of relatives and friends. A slow process of mental deterioration ensues that leads to his insanity. The spectacle of him, naked and carrying an empty suitcase on his head on the streets of London, is devastating. Throughout the process, Chikwava emphasizes a crucial aspect of his message: while the West potentially offers some form of opportunities for physical safety and economic advancement, it can come at a huge cost. And the price that migrants are called upon to pay, particularly undocumented migrants, may be far greater than any opportunity available to them.

Upon his arrival in London, the narrator quickly realizes that time and culture have transformed previous relationships and that hospitality in accommodating a friend is not to be taken for granted here. Paul and Seckai could not continue to accommodate him after a while. With a complete reversal of the tradition at home by which strangers are welcomed, the narrator has to deal with these and other elements of the culture shock he will

---

77   Fongang, "Cosmopolitan Dilemma," 31.

DISILLUSIONMENT AND DEATH &❧ 97

encounter throughout his stay in Brixton. Without income or a source of employment, he moves out of the house and into a squatter house with a former schoolmate, Shingi, in another part of town.

Shingi is willing to accommodate him, but staying with him will come at a cost. The house has been approved for demolition by the county officials, and Shingi and other migrants from Africa are occupying the house as squatters. Similar to the situation in *Blue White Red*, the squatters are undocumented migrants in danger of being arrested by the police. They, like Marcel and his compatriots, could either be deported or incarcerated in a county jail. Living in the squatter house also comes with an economic cost. The first to occupy the house, Aleck is the presumed landlord and exploits his fellow illegal migrants by renting out individual rooms to the squatters with payment due at the end of the month. Given the protagonist's precarious situation, he needs to find employment and quickly if he is to continue staying in the squat. Without residency or a work permit, he can only get "grafts," badly paid manual jobs that illegal migrants are compelled to do in order to survive and in dangerous working conditions. The threats to physical safety are high, and reports of bodily injuries are common. Without medical insurance, the lives of the workers are at risk.

Compounding this situation is the unscrupulous employers who exploit the vulnerability of the illegal migrants and their status as undocumented workers by hiring them to work in the most inhumane conditions and for paltry sums of money. Exploitation of migrant labor is part of the suffering of the undocumented in Western societies. Chikwava presents a layered system where Aleck's exploitation of the squatters becomes a mirror image of the exploitation in the larger society. The spotlight is on the hypocrisy of the British government that robustly condemns illegal migration but benefits from the exploitation of migrant labor. It is the wickedness of a society that pledges its allegiance to human rights and yet can subject vulnerable and destitute migrants to the most dangerous and inhumane working conditions. As the larger society exploits the migrants, they in turn exploit each other. Aleck exploits his fellow squatters, and the narrator blackmails Seckai. A vicious system of exploitation ensues, and the undocumented are at the center of it.

A critical aspect of the migrants' staying at the squatter house is the toll it takes on their mental health: this is perhaps the most poignant message of the novel. In *Harare North*, a combination of factors leads to the mental deterioration and eventual insanity of the protagonist: the brutal murder of Shingi, the use of drugs and alcohol, the threat of police raid and the possibility of homelessness, lack of employment and the basic necessities of food and clothing, and the pressure for remittances to relatives and friends. The squatter house amplifies the horrible conditions under which illegal migrants

98 &♦ CHAPTER THREE

are forced to live in England. The conditions indicate the depths of precarity that characterize their situations as they realize that even the basic necessities of life they took for granted back home they cannot have in England. They have to rummage for rotten food in trash bins in order to eat, and in winter, they have to put up with the cold because the house cannot be heated. As the narrative unfolds, a sense of impending doom hangs over the story. The characters move as if in a trance, and the narrative content and structure reflect the emptiness of their lives. The broken, short, and incomplete sentences, uncompleted thoughts, broken dialogs, and difficulty in fully articulating their thoughts indicate the mental stress they are enduring. The dialog registers the prevalence of the symptoms of trauma, while partial loss of cognition points to an impending mental breakdown. The narrator's initial delusions of grandeur—represented by his belief in his superior abilities to beat the system—his hallucinations and nightmares, his obsessive-compulsive determination to kill the imagined rat, his unnecessary and brutal killing of the squirrel, and the continued imagined conversation with Shingi's cousin all depict a compelling picture of the deterioration of the human mind. The naked man with the empty cardboard suitcase on his head in the streets of London completes the picture of mental derangement.

Through relating specific incidents in the lives of individual characters, the author sheds light on the dangers of illegal migration. It is important to remember that the decision to flee from Zimbabwe is not without merit. The novel's background is the political turmoil of the Mugabe regime in Zimbabwe in the late 1990s. It foregrounds the social and political unrest, violent and oftentimes deadly, that put thousands of Zimbabweans to flight. The brutal Zimbabwe African National Union-Pacific Front (ZANU-PF), in its delusionary construct that every political opponent of the party is an enemy of the state, created an environment of trepidation where peaceful citizens are perceived as enemies of the regime, are brutally assaulted, or disappear in mysterious circumstances. The novel hints at the campaign of violence conducted by the state militia, the Green Bombers, who are recruited from the president's supporters to enforce the infamous land distribution reforms. Coupled with police brutality, extortion, and political oppression, a huge percentage of the population sought political asylum in other countries. Brixton, nicknamed Harare North because of the number of Zimbabwean migrants living there, was one such destination for fleeing Zimbabweans. Their encounters and interactions with migrants from other parts of Africa give a snapshot of the illegal side of the African diaspora in England.

Since improvement in the migrant's economic status is one of the primary reasons behind illegal migration, Chikwava addresses the prospects of this rationale for migration. As noted, the life of each migrant tells a specific aspect of the illegal migration story. The narrator's story begins with his

DISILLUSIONMENT AND DEATH ❧ 99

quest for employment, the means by which he hopes to make five thousand dollars to pay for his freedom back home. Given his undocumented status, there are two types of grafts, or temporary work, available to him: BBC graft, which is readily available but demeaning, and menial graft, which is labor intensive, badly paid, and dangerous. He tells us that "BBC graft [is available] for £8 per hour. Immediate start, and it's in Croydon."[78] Further, he notes, "BBCs—British Buttocks Cleaners—[are African illegal migrants] looking after old people that poo their pants every hour."[79]

On the other hand, there are menial jobs like the Wimbledon and Finsbury Park grafts looking for laborers that pay "£2.45 per hour. Eight hours per day. Five days per week. That makes £98 per week. But after they do emergency tax code it come to about £68."[80] As he tells us, the emergency tax code is a way for unscrupulous employers to swindle illegal migrants out of their already meager pay. After expenses, including thirty pounds rent to Aleck and refund of money to Shingi for basic amenities, there is practically nothing left of the sixty-eight pounds. Thus, he laments that "with this kind of graft, now I see there is big danger that you can work until you grow horns and still you won't catch US $5,000."[81]

Chikwava contrasts this implicitly with the economic situation back home in Zimbabwe and leaves the reader to deduce the better of the two situations. As the narrator tells us of the economic instability of the Zimbabwean economy, particularly the state of the local currency in relation to the dollar, the exchange rate keeps increasing, for example, 1.80 to 1.89 in one week, and perhaps 2.5 in a few months, so that "if you wanted US $5,000 you have to find £2,777.78."[82] The inability to reconcile the battered economy in Zimbabwe, in part due to the stranglehold of the dollar on it, and the labor-intensive grafts in exploitative and dangerous working conditions in England, leaves the narrator in a conundrum.

Another layer of economic instability is that the grafts are temporary and can be terminated without notice by the employer and for no apparent reason. At these grafts, "You spend them weeks shifting mud with shovels and sweat beads come out of every pore in the body because you is putting out heaps of effort while your buttocks point to high heaven and migrant flesh start to stink around you as shirts and underpants get damp."[83] With the graft at the contractor's plant yard in Finsbury Park, the employer was

---

78   Chikwava, *Harare North*, 65.
79   Chikwava, *Harare North*, 41.
80   Chikwava, *Harare North*, 49.
81   Chikwava, *Harare North*, 50.
82   Chikwava, *Harare North*, 40.
83   Chikwava, *Harare North*, 49.

100 &❧ CHAPTER THREE

looking for workers for a drain repair project, and as the narrator tells us, "workers who is prepared for challenging work; excavating and stripping them old drain pipes out of the earth, laying new ones, and going down pipes to remove blockage when necessary. All for £2.40 per hour, take it or leave it."[84] The exploitation is blatant; but perhaps it is in the disregard for human life and the safety of the workers that the cruelty of the employers is manifested. What stands out as interesting is that even the narrator, in all his desperation and simplicity, can still see the disregard for human dignity in the scheme. As he correctly notes, "I have not been in London long time but me I can smell big con from miles."[85]

Amazingly, the employers still design additional ways and means of fleecing the already swindled migrant workers. For instance, all workers without work permits, and that would be the overwhelming majority of them, would need ID cards from the company to make them eligible for work. The company provides these ID cards for an additional cost of three hundred pounds, which is taken from their pay. The ID cards not only are fake, but they also will transform the workers into indentured servants because at the rate of £2.40 per hour, it will take months to repay three hundred pounds, and during that time, they will be providing free labor to the company. It is a situation of indebtedness from which the illegal migrants may never free themselves. Recalling the wise words of his late mother, the narrator reflects on his predicament: "If you don't want millipedes to come back [to your doorstep] you also have to throw away the straw broom that you use to sweep it away."[86] The unfortunate reality is that not many undocumented migrants can afford to throw away the millipede and the straw broom. With Shingi's papers, the narrator finds a job at Tim's Fish Bar, working 11:30 a.m. to 5:30 p.m., Mondays to Fridays, "washing things and cleaning floor." While he is able to earn his first decent wage here, he has to confront the racism associated with his origin, accent, and lack of proficiency in English. Repeated taunting from the kids in the neighborhood while on duty and from Tim over his accent, the narrator becomes disillusioned and is eventually fired from his job to begin another cycle of hardship and dependency.

Within this overall narrative structure of the narrator's story, there are other embedded stories of the experiences of the squatters. For the purpose of analysis, I take each in turn. It is clear that the economic troubles of the migrants are pushing them into a life of crime in order to survive. I cite the case of Suleiman, Tsitsi, Farayi, and Aleck as justification for this assertion.

---

84 Chikwava, *Harare North*, 51.

85 Chikwava, *Harare North*, 51.

86 Chikwava, *Harare North*, 52.

DISILLUSIONMENT AND DEATH &❧ 101

Suleiman's encounter with the bus driver over a fake bus pass is notable. Stopped and questioned by the bus driver as Suleiman is trying to board the bus with a fake pass, he loses his nerve and runs. As he comically scurries for a hiding place, the incident reveals the sad reality of life as an illegal migrant. While not rising to the level of violent crime, the issue at stake here is human dignity. In the contrast between the two sets of people, the "quality people in nice clothes," and the "mud-shifting boy" running to safety, the disparity in status is clearly registered.[87]

Tsitsi's story provides another lens through which to read the life of the illegal African migrant in the diaspora. When we first meet her, the seventeen-year-old mother and girlfriend to Aleck is one of the occupants of the squatter house. The narrator describes her as "a small girl with sharp look in she eye, nose as small as chicken poo dropping and face drawn tight over small skull."[88] He further tells us that "she comes from small village in Mashonaland East Province" in Zimbabwe. Tsitsi is a runaway from a tyrannical aunt and is married to a doctor, who the narrative suggests fathered Tsitsi's baby. For this act, Tsitsi was thrown out of the house by her aunt. With an expired visa, a fatherless son, and no place to live, she seeks refuge at the squatter house with Aleck. The narrator remarks that Tsitsi's story is one of many from young girls brought over to London by relatives to "babysit, cook great mountains of meals, make she host's bed every morning, even touching them things that should have been taboo for she to even see—things like the father of the house's underwear that is full of them skid marks."[89] At the squatter house, she cooks the meals for the occupants in lieu of rent. Her story of domestic and sexual exploitation again mirrors the realities of the larger society. Tsitsi's struggles as a teenage mother are revealed by her breastfeeding moments with the child. This moment foreshadows the menstruation scene later in the story. The narrator describes the breastfeeding scene:

> I have finish picking them glass so I follow she into lounge. She go to Shingi's bed. She tiny skeleton fold neat as she sit on the bed, crossing she legs and holding the baby close to she bosom. With one hand she pull she blouse up. She don't wear bra; she left breast jump out and hang like talisman. It look bigger than the other. She bring she baby closer, bending she back. Baby catch it like thief. I stand leaning against the wall watching.[90]

---

87 Chikwava, *Harare North*, 50–51.
88 Chikwava, *Harare North*, 29.
89 Chikwava, *Harare North*, 31.
90 Chikwava, *Harare North*, 32,

102 &» CHAPTER THREE

The picture of the mother, herself a child, trying to feed her hungry baby is portrayed. Like the narrator, the reader watches in amazement and sympathy. At the end of the process, he tells us: "When she finish feeding the baby she unfold she legs. As she gets onto she feet, there is sound of ripping cloth. She turn around to look and there is one clean new slit running down she dress, from the bum all the way down and through hemline."[91] This incident is troubling in its revelation both of the struggle to survive in a life of poverty as the ripping dress suggests and its symbolic exposure of Tsitsi's private parts. The unveiling of her buttocks is a revealing of her premature motherhood and the lack of preparedness for such a task. The ripping dress also foreshadows the menstruation scene, and again, Tsitsi's lack of preparedness and understanding of the challenges of adulthood are depicted. The narrator describes the scene in this way: "He turn around now and chase after Tsitsi. As Tsitsi ran for the ball me I see now there's disaster on she bum: it look like she have been sitting on head of goat that has just been cut off—blood on she dress. She have hit the moon, I know straight away."[92] What is on full display here is Tsitsi's innocence and immaturity. Little prepared for womanhood and sexually exploited by her aunt's husband, she was equally not ready for motherhood when the baby arrived.

Interestingly, in both the breastfeeding and menstruation scenes, Tsitsi gives little consideration to the gaze of the opposite sex in such intensely private and gendered moments in her life. While her disregard could indicate the trauma stemming from the psychological abuse of her aunt's husband and the domestic violence of Aleck on her, it is almost as if she is putting up for public view the abuse she has suffered at the hands of the opposite sex in society. She is offering them a mirror to see themselves and to confront the consequences of their actions. Whatever the interpretation of these moments, what is clear is that Tsitsi is traumatized by her past and the struggles to raise her fatherless baby. She is forced by her circumstance to go into the baby scheme, where "for £50, any woman can take Tsitsi's baby to Lambeth Housing Department and play out to be single mother, fill them forms and take baby back to salon as soon as she have been interview."[93] Later, we witness the incident when, screaming and running down the stairs, Tsitsi "burst into [the squatters'] room with limp baby in she hands. The baby have vomit blood while asleep and now she don't know if it only pass out or she has already dead."[94] The baby was taken to hospital where he was revived. Incidents like this attest to Tsitsi's trauma

---

91 Chikwava, *Harare North*, 32.
92 Chikwava, *Harare North*, 157.
93 Chikwava, *Harare North*, 61.
94 Chikwava, *Harare North*, 98.

DISILLUSIONMENT AND DEATH 🐟 103

and allow society, particularly her exploiters, to witness the consequences of their exploitation and abuse of her.

With Farayi, a similar story of the migrant's hope, reversal of expectations, and disillusionment is depicted. A former teacher at the mission school, he shares a room with Shingi and has been with Aleck longer than all the other squatters. The narrator tells us that Farayi "have graft at Tooting where recruitment agency put him to do photocopying and stationery for NHS."[95] We also learn that his papers are not in order, so he lives in London as an undocumented migrant. His undocumented status makes it impossible for him to seek medical assistance at the government hospital, and we learn from the narrator that at one time, "Farayi once fall sick with some terrible bug and everyone is thinking is it the bird flu. . . . Farayi cough like chicken and shake under his blankets. . . . [He] don't want to go to the hospital because he have already become illegal."[96] Eventually, he leaves the squatter house in fear of a suspected impending police raid after Aleck leaves.

Aleck's story is not much different than those of the other squatters. Landlord of the house, frequently increasing the migrants' rent, he is also Tsitsi's boyfriend, and there are indications of the prevalence of domestic violence in their relationship. Aleck's claim to landlordship of the house is exposed when the narrator discovers the postcard from Mirjam and Ed with an Indian stamp on it. As previous squatters, they wrote to Aleck informing him that since they might not return to England it is up to him whether he stays or moves out. Aleck was the caretaker of the squatter house previously "owned" by Mirjam and Ed. We learn later that Aleck's job is not at Tooting, but that he is "picking old people's *kaka* off beds and then coming here walking around like he is district administrator coming every time to collect money even when we have nothing."[97] Aleck is a British Buttocks Cleaner. After a physical confrontation with the narrator that leaves Aleck with a bloodied tooth, the occupants of the squat wake up one morning to find out that Aleck is gone. He never returns to the squatter house. His absence sends a wave of panic through the squat, for the occupants fear that all he needs to do is "to stop at nearest phone box, call them police and tell them about nest of them illegals who is occupy this house. Then he simply jump into sea of 10 million Londoners."[98] The squatters evacuate the house in a panic. They are now forced to live on the streets, away at different spots during the day and finding some safe spot to sleep during the night. Eventually, with the exception of Farayi, they return to the squat. Aleck evidently never makes the dreaded call to the police.

---

95 Chikwava, *Harare North*, 34.
96 Chikwava, *Harare North*, 95–96.
97 Chikwava, *Harare North*, 118.
98 Chikwava, *Harare North*, 133.

104 &❧ CHAPTER THREE

With Shingi's brand new graft at Winchester, things significantly improve at the house. But as Shingi tries everything to start a relationship with Tsitsi, the narrator does everything he can to discourage him. This period of respite is short lived as Shingi's health begins to deteriorate. The narrator suspects that Shingi is living with HIV after his time in prison. It is at this time that Shingi meets the tramps Dave and Jenny, whose addiction to drugs will change his life forever. It is also around this time that Shingi takes to sleeping with prostitutes, especially one particular Polish girl.

Tsitsi leaves, and the dynamics of the squat change considerably. Dave and Jenny move into the squat, while the narrator moves into Tsitsi's room. Dave, Shingi, and the narrator go dumpster diving, rummaging for food in trash bins behind a Marks & Spencer. Dave justifies dumpster diving by telling them, "Lots of good food—cans of baked beans, beer, sausages, expired foodstuffs—can be found there waiting for us."[99] Worse than dumpster diving, Dave introduces Shingi to hard drugs. We learn from the narrator, "Last week there was syringe in the lounge. Then there was another in the kitchen. Yesterday one was lying on staircase. Now there is even one inside toilet bowl. And evenings now end with everyone curled up on floor of Shingi's room like they is dead."[100] In another instance, we also learn that "in the evening there's heaps of vodka bokkles going around and everyone on Shingi's room sound loud and pathetic. By midnight Dave is lying on floor like dead, Shingi have pass out on his bed and Jenny is lying in pool of vomit in bathroom."[101] This is the beginning of the end of the squatters. The reader watches helplessly as their lives unravel. The combination of alcohol and drugs takes a huge toll on their mental and physical health. In the context of the precariousness that already characterizes their existence, it isn't surprising that they come to a disastrous end. Cutting off all forms of communication with family back home and now fully addicted to marijuana and narcotics, Shingi deteriorates mentally and physically. The spectacle of him "doing deep belch, making animal grunts, breathing deep and loud and groaning . . . [as] he's getting the shakes,"[102] which are withdrawal symptoms from narcotics, is deeply disturbing.

In the concluding sections of the novel, Chikwava details the psychological toll of illegal migration on the undocumented. Through a series of incidents and the use of symbolism, he depicts the gradual breakdown of the narrator's mind. The psychological trauma is clear, and its symbolism is manifested in the prelude to and foreshadowing of this derangement. One such incident is the brutal killing of the squirrel by the narrator: "I take

---

99   Chikwava, *Harare North*, 167.
100 Chikwava, *Harare North*, 170.
101 Chikwava, *Harare North*, 171.
102 Chikwava, *Harare North*, 175.

DISILLUSIONMENT AND DEATH &❧ 105

out my screwdriver, put my foot on squirrel's head to pin him down, position my screwdriver right behind the head; on the spine. The screwdriver go through the neck right onto the grass and wet ground below. The squirrel don't feel anything. No pain, no movement except them front paws that shiver like the squirrel now go spastic. Blood squirt everywhere."[103] In its graphic details, the incident depicts a deeply troubled mind, possibly on the brink of snapping. The cold and sadistic brutality with which he snuffs out the life of the animal calls attention to the descent of the mind into insanity, especially since the violence of the scene is out of proportion to anything the animal could have done. On the contrary, the narrative points out that the animal was in need of care, as it was suffering from a broken back. The episode depicts the wanton disregard for life stemming from an unbalanced mind. In a dark and twisted way, this scene prefigures the murder of Shingi, and in both cases, the violence is totally unprovoked. Shingi and the squirrel are handicapped and in need of help but instead are targeted and brutally killed by individuals whose state of mind is largely unstable. Like the squirrel squirting blood everywhere, as the narrator tells us, "Shingi soaked, his trousers heavy with the blood of big mama [the tramp that attacked him], he holds onto them and hobble into shadows of tall buildings. That's the last I saw of him."[104] Subsequently, we learn that Shingi was lying in a coma in intensive care and the hospital pronounced him a "hopeless case."[105]

From this point, the narrative focuses on the gradual mental deterioration of the narrator. In the absence of the other squatters, his isolation is heightened, and the alienation he feels deepens his fear of the police. Unemployed and without any source of income, he continues to struggle to secure basic necessities. Faced with the demands for financial assistance from relatives back home and the effects of the drugs on his mental well-being, he goes into a state of fragmented consciousness. The potential for mental derangement heightens after Shingi's death. The symptoms are clearly manifested in the meaningless walks in the park, time spent sitting aimlessly under Waterloo Bridge, and loitering in Brixton Tube Station. He isolates himself from Dave and Jenny when he returns to the squat and smokes and daydreams. The narrator conducts his daily routine in a trance, and the narrative itself takes on a trancelike quality in reflection of the meaninglessness of his actions. He does not shower for days, and a noticeable animal smell is palpable around him.

In further demonstration of this process of mental deterioration, the narrator continues to focus intensely on small meaningless tasks that he performs and that have no clear significance. He repeatedly goes to the toilet,

---

103 Chikwava, *Harare North*, 184.
104 Chikwava, *Harare North*, 185–86.
105 Chikwava, *Harare North*, 195.

106 &⊷ CHAPTER THREE

looks over the photos in Shingi's album, and smokes marijuana. The disjointed incidents reflect a fragmented mind. In time, he begins to lose memory of his daily routine. He tells us, "I woke up and realise that I had fall asleep."[106] While he slips into a gradual loss of consciousness, one part of his mind is alert to his situation and keeps nudging him to search for employment. He develops a split personality, where, on one side of his consciousness, he gets dressed up and goes out to look for employment. But on the other side of his brain, as he tells us, "Shingi is still in my head, so me I go window-shopping to get him out of my head first."[107] As he walks around the city looking for a job, he becomes aware that he is "dizzy" and on some occasions, "suddenly absent-minded, stray[s] into clothes shop fizzing over with them people."[108] In one of the clothing stores, he sees his reflection in the mirror and for the first time cannot tell whether he is normal or abnormal. His mind is unable to make the distinction. The erosion of the rational is the death knell of the conscious mind.

Returning home one evening from one of his walks, the narrator imagines he sees Shingi's fat rat running across the floorboards and suspects that the Romanian family that lived next door is out to get him. Given the onset of hallucinations and delusions of persecution that the narrator is exhibiting, it is not surprising that he performs the most outrageous tasks to get rid of the imagined rat. He takes his screwdriver from under his pillow and proceeds to undo all the floorboards to get to the rat. In the process, he throws away Shingi's belongings with those of Dave and Jenny. While this action denotes another stage in the process of mental deterioration, it symbolically highlights a rejection of the dream—the realization that material acquisition cannot replace human dignity and worth. He throws out the material possessions of Shingi and the emotional props—cigarettes, drugs, and syringes—from Dave and Jenny as an act of relinquishing the dream.

The narrator's psychological and mental deterioration parallels the physical deterioration of the squatter house. He tells us: "From the rubber P-trap, which have swell and is covered by fungus, water drip down onto the floor of the cupboard, which have also start to rot; there's heap of bread that Shingi have been putting there to feed the rat. Now mushrooms is growing everywhere."[109] He develops insomnia and fever. In a state of psychological transfer, he sees the rat as the source of his troubles and sits up all night with his screwdriver and clawhammer to kill it.

---

106 Chikwava, *Harare North*, 206.
107 Chikwava, *Harare North*, 205–6.
108 Chikwava, *Harare North*, 207.
109 Chikwava, *Harare North*, 214.

DISILLUSIONMENT AND DEATH &. 107

As the days go by, he informs us that "I walk around the house with the screwdriver and claw hammer, my boots make clattering sound on them floorboards."[110] One night, he imagines he sees the rat and quickly attacks it:

> Tuesday night. I am almost nodding off when the rat appear at kitchen doorway. I throw spanner and catch him on his bum. He fly into the air, come down on the floorboards, try to scurry away but his behind look like they is broken so that he remain on the same spot like the squirrel that I kill in the park. I think I have maybe break his spine or something. When I get up to finish him off, he recover and slip into some hole that I can't fit into. But I know that I have deal fatal blow and expect the smell of rotting body in them coming days.[111]

His inability to distinguish between reality and fantasy—the supposed handicapped rat with a broken spine and the one that recovers and scurries away—is symptomatic of hallucination. The reader realizes that the narrator did not deal the rat a fatal blow because he cannot find a body nor is there any smell of a decayed body in the house.

The narrator's commitment to finding the rat never wavers, and as the narrative unfolds, his mind gives way to illogical reasoning and fantasies. He realizes that if he can take the kitchen floorboards apart, he can find the rat at the bottom. As he works in vain to find the rat, his level of desperation and anxiety increases, and so too does his determination to find the rat. The elusive search for the rat parallels the dream of the illegal migrant. The chances of illegal migrants accomplishing their dream in Brixton are as high as the narrator's chances of finding the imagined rat. The idea of the illegal migrant accomplishing the dream in England is as delusional as the insanity of ripping away the kitchen floorboards to find the imaginary rat. Evidently, as the narrator rips the floorboards apart, he is figuratively ripping apart his cognition and physical well-being. He tells us of his worsening diarrhea and alopecia. Nevertheless, his commitment to the task never wavers, and it is in this commitment, the narrative suggests, that the conundrum is fully manifested, and the undoing of the illegal migrant is demonstrated.

The novel exposes the power of the dream to hold dreamers captive to their situations. It is the desire to achieve the dream that turns out to be, ironically, the instrument of the dreamer's destruction. In spite of the overwhelming obstacles to achieving the dream, dreamers are never dissuaded. In this way, they are complicit in their own destruction. The ripping of the floorboards is a symbolic process of self-destruction, a stripping of the physical, mental, and human faculties of the narrator. The narrative suggests that this is the insanity of the dream and the pathological process it

---

110 Chikwava, *Harare North*, 246.
111 Chikwava, *Harare North*, 216.

108   & CHAPTER THREE

engenders—the unrelenting belief that the grass is greener on the other side and that it has to be pursued regardless of the cost. As the reality begins to dawn on him, the narrator says, "You always know more than what you believe in but always choose what you believe in over what you know because what you know can be so big that sometimes it is a useless weapon, you cannot wield it proper, and when you try, it can get your head out of gear and stop you focusing."[112]

In the novel's final pages, the narrator walks through the streets of London with his cardboard suitcase on his head. He engages in imaginary phone conversations with Shingi's cousin, but the narrative blurs the line between reality and fantasy. This blurring of the lines between the two can be read as indicative of his mental breakdown. As he walks through the streets, the unsuspecting reader ponders his destination and the logic behind his actions. But, as the novel progresses, rhetorical and discursive clues are provided that hint at the process of mental breakdown. These clues are noted in the woman with the baby who moves away hastily from his table at the cafe, the repeated appointments and cancellations with the supposed cousin of Shingi, his disclosure of AIDS without evidence, and the security guard that prevents him from entering the library. Suddenly, the narrative provides the much-awaited clarity: "I walk towards Oxford Street. I am in vigilant mood and not walking on them pavements, but right in the middle of the streets, on the white line, with suitcase on my head while traffic flowing past me in different directions."[113] From this point, he loses his trousers, then his shirt, and then he is completely naked roaming the streets with the empty cardboard box on his head. The process of mental breakdown, like the systematic stripping of the floorboards, is now complete. Mind and body are destroyed in the pursuit of the dream. Delphine Fongang explains the narrator's psychological breakdown as the climax of the trauma experience in migrancy and isolates the financial and cultural barriers as constituting his predicament leading to his mental deterioration and eventual insanity. She pinpoints the empty suitcase he carries as symbolic of "the emptiness of his life and how little he has accomplished in London. There is neither money to secure his freedom back home, nor a return ticket to his most cherished homeland. He is in a psychological dilemma, cut between two worlds (London and Zimbabwe), and neither a member of any."[114] The combination of psychological trauma, material dispossession, and social exclusion ends up driving the narrator insane.

---

112 Chikwava, *Harare North*, 43.
113 Chikwava, *Harare North*, 225–26.
114 Fongang, "Cosmopolitan Dilemma," 35.

Chapter Four

Psychological Depression

This chapter focuses on the psychological depression and violence that come with unfulfilled dreams. Imbolo Mbue's *Behold the Dreamers* is crucial to exploring this aspect of the migrant experience upon arrival abroad. The novel tells the stories of two families: Jende and Neni Jonga, African migrants from Cameroon; and Clark Edwards, a wealthy Wall Street banker in the United States, and his wife, Cindy. The intersection of the stories of these two families comes when Jende is hired by Edwards as his personal chauffeur. Jende's employment creates an invaluable opportunity for cross-examination of each other's situations. Jende is given a window seat into the workings of the capitalist system in America. In this way, he is brought face to face with the dynamics of a system that he will have to navigate if his dream is to be accomplished. In working with Jende, Edwards comes to see the realities behind the operation of the immigration system in his own country. In this way, he understands the restrictions of the system that produces migrant labor from which he benefits. As the story unfolds, Jende realizes that his perception of the dream was misconstrued and that capitalism was a stumbling block to its achievement. He sees the realities of the capitalist system in the lives of Clark and Cindy and recognizes the contrast between the superficial attractions and the profound realities. Jende concludes that the cost to achieving his dream is too high and returns home with his family at the end of the novel.

In the opening sections of the novel, Mbue focuses on the dream of the migrant. By dissecting the story of Neni and Jende, she provides a framework for defining both dream and dreamer. Neni's story is a clear illustration of the conflict between the dream and the systems that work to thwart its achievement. At the opening of the novel, she is celebrating a year and a half of residency in New York City. She is depicted as living the American dream, satisfied and fulfilled, even at this early stage in her journey. Living with her family in New York, working as "a home health aide through an agency that paid her in cash, since she had no working papers," and having matriculated as a student "for the first time in sixteen years, studying chemistry at Borough of Manhattan Community College, she envisages a bright future

110   CHAPTER FOUR

since "for the very first time in her life, she had a dream besides marriage and motherhood: to become a pharmacist like the ones everyone respected in Limbe."[1] In order to achieve this dream, "she had to do well in school, and she was doing just that—maintaining a B plus average. Three days a week she went to school and, after classes, walked the school hallways with her bulky algebra, chemistry, biology, and philosophy textbooks, glowing because she was growing into a learned woman."[2]

Mbue paints a picture of a woman who lacked opportunities back home but is determined to make the best of the available opportunity she finds in America by breaking the cycle of marriage and motherhood that defines women's lives in Cameroon. In this excerpt, Mbue frames migration as an act of becoming—a process by which an individual through available opportunities is transformed by the accomplishment of his or her dreams. She depicts Neni as someone willing to go the extra mile to accomplish those dreams. She is determined and capable of succeeding if offered a level playing field. Neni has the will and the potential to accomplish her dreams. What she needs is a society that can afford her the opportunity to put her aspirations into practice. The sense of fulfillment she demonstrates is indicative of the aspirations of African migrants in the diaspora, an aspiration that is bound with ambition and anchored in hope. As the narrative records: "She was going to make herself proud, make Jende proud of his wife, make Liomi [the Jongas' son] proud of his mother. She'd waited too long to become something, and now, at thirty-three, she finally had, or was close enough to having, everything she'd wanted in life."[3]

The Jongas' search for becoming is the motivating factor behind their migration. Yet, in spite of the promises and initial satisfaction, Mbue hints at the transience of the moment. Neni, no doubt, has made tremendous progress toward living her dreams, but it isn't clear whether this new environment would be her home, inasmuch as she wants it to be home. At the same time, though she is employed as an aide health worker, she is not officially allowed to work in the country, a fact manifested in the method of payment for her service. Her visa status as visitor makes her ineligible for a work permit and permanent residency in the country. The stability that the current moment promises is shaky. The indications are that the fulfillment of the present moment can come to a crashing halt by virtue of the Jongas' immigration status. Despite the promise, the threats to stability and continued residency are clear.

---

1   Mbue, *Behold the Dreamers*, 14.
2   Mbue, *Behold the Dreamers*, 14.
3   Mbue, *Behold the Dreamers*, 14.

PSYCHOLOGICAL DEPRESSION 🙾 111

Augusta Atinuke Irele focuses on this contrast between the migrant's expectations and desire for becoming and the constricting realities of migrant experience upon arrival in the host country.[4] While her analysis reinforces Neni's belief in the lack of opportunities available for social and economic advancement in Limbe, including the stigma of poverty and the oppressive authoritarian control of her father, Irele also points out that the expected freedom and growth in the United States might be exaggerated and, therefore, illusory. The disappointment is more shocking to Neni, given her images of imprisonment in Cameroon against that freedom in America. Irele points out that "the United States, cast from a distance, and even early in Neni's migrant experience remains a utopic space in which she can enjoy experiences that are inconceivable in Cameroon."[5] Thus, she concludes, "as the narrative progresses, the United States loses its glossy facade and Neni watches herself and her family transform into unrecognizable victims of the challenges of contemporary life in United States' large metropole."[6]

Jende's story provides another facet of the dream. Staying on an expired visitor's visa and with a family to provide for, Jende is desperate for employment. Three years earlier, he had walked out of the consular office in Yaounde, Cameroon, with a three-month visitor's visa upon the invitation of his cousin, Winston. It was clear from the outset that Jende was an economic migrant who sees migration to the United States as the path to economic advancement. His happiness upon receiving a visa to America is anchored in the hope of material success, to claim "his share of the milk, honey, and liberty flowing in the Paradise-for-strivers called America."[7] In Jende's dream is embedded both the reasons for departure from the homeland—"a future of poverty and despondency"—and the desire for economic success and returning home as "green card—or American passport-bearing conquerors."[8] As with Neni's dream, Mbue is careful to expose the illusion or grandiose expectations behind the dream—the notion of America as an earthly Paradise, a land flowing with "milk, honey, and liberty," from which everyone is invited to partake. This is the concept of the grass being greener on the other side and the abundance of resources open to all that require only migrants' presence for their own share of it. This dream of material success requiring only the presence of the migrant is the naïve perception of Jende. Its delusion is made worse by its impact on return, and the expectations of those left behind, that migrants should return as conquerors waving

---

4   Irele, "Dystopian Dissonance," 15.
5   Irele, "Dystopian Dissonance," 15.
6   Irele, "Dystopian Dissonance," 15.
7   Mbue, *Behold the Dreamers*, 19.
8   Mbue, *Behold the Dreamers*, 19.

112 ❧ CHAPTER FOUR

American green cards and passports with pockets full of American dollars. Anything to the contrary is considered a failure and is bound to attract shame and humiliation. As in *Harare North* and *Blue White Red*, this is part of the reason why the characters depicted in the novels prefer the continued struggle to integrate over the humiliation of a failed migration.

It would be wrong to frame Jende's dream as simply based on economic advancement, for embedded in the dream is the human desire to become: and in this way, his dream mirrors that of Neni. Here, the Jongas' experience offers another window to engage the reasons for their departure. As with Massala-Massala in *Blue White Red*, we see overlaps in the migrant experience of departure. In a conversation with Clark on the reason for his departure from Cameroon, Jende explains: "'Because my country is no good, Sir,' he said. 'It is nothing like America. I stay in my country; I would have become nothing. My son will grow up and be poor like me, just like I was poor like my father. But in America, Sir? I can become something. I can even become a respectable man. My son can become a respectable man.'"[9] Poverty and the quest for opportunities for a meaningful existence are at the core of the migrant's motivation for departure. Jende further reinforces the social barriers that exclude the ordinary citizen from the pathways to success in his country in this way: "For you to become somebody, you have to be born somebody first. You do not come from a family with money, forget it. You do not come from a family with a name, forget it. That is just how it is, sir. Someone like me, what can I ever become in a country like Cameroon? I came from nothing. No name. No money. My father is a poor man. Cameroon has nothing."[10] Jende unveils the systemic exclusion of the poor from achieving their dreams. Without connections, a family name, and wealth, the path to upward mobility is nonexistent. The plausibility of achieving the dream is reinforced in the novel by the story of Barack Obama, the son of an African studying in America and a white woman, who goes on to become the first Black president of the United States. The implication is that the dream is realistic. Here, again, Mbue is careful to point out the naïveté in this perception, that is, if the accomplishment of Obama is used as a yardstick to measure the feasibility of the dream for all people, especially migrants. From Clark's questions to Jende, Mbue suggests that Obama's story might be the exception rather than the rule and that the systems of immigration and capitalism might work very differently for African migrants than for an American born in the United States with ancestral connections to Africa.

---

9   Mbue, *Behold the Dreamers*, 39.
10   Mbue, *Behold the Dreamers*, 40.

Julian Walker points out the flaw in Jende's perspective of becoming in the two countries—Cameroon and America—in his stereotypical framing of the latter as not only the antithesis of the former but, in this regard, also the solution to the lack of opportunities in his homeland: "Jende's problematic comparison between Cameroon as a place of lost opportunities and America as a location of hope displays the United States as a place in which the Jongas not only long to belong, but as the only place where 'belonging,' from Jende's perspective, is possible.[11] He parallels a negatively connoted notion of a strict societal hierarchy in Cameroon and the notion of belonging, of upward social mobility in the United States."[12] Jende's position at this point is critically important because it sheds light on the shift in his perspective at the end of the novel when he decides to return home and implement the American dream in his native Cameroon, a situation that Walker defines as "translocating the American Dream."[13]

From Walker's postulate, *Behold the Dreamers* focuses on the limits to migration and the possibilities of attaining the American dream. He argues that the actualization of the dream is based on a number of variables, including and more specifically "citizenship and residence permission,"[14] all of which are outside of the migrant's control. Jende's situation is precarious, for in his position, his dream "of becoming someone, of belonging, is ultimately tied to, first and foremost, his precarious status as 'illegal' immigrant and his dependency on his employer Clark Edwards."[15] The precarity of life in the West as an illegal immigrant and the fragility of the dream are demonstrated. As Walker concludes, it is "the nightmare of losing opportunities and material security once promised by the ideal of the American Dream that continues to haunt the Jongas. The text unmasks the lure of the capitalist USA and the accompanying brain drain of African localities as a horrible trade-off."[16]

In bringing the realities of life as an illegal migrant to Jende and Neni, Mbue focuses on the immigration system itself and points out the limitations of the immigration system for migrants. A critical aspect of this reality is the dismissal of Jende's application for asylum. Bubakar, Jende's lawyer, informs him of the rejection of the application and the referral of the case to an immigration judge. The application was based on a concocted story of persecution that emphasized the risk to the life of the applicants if they were to

---

11   Walker, "Bringing the Wisdom of Wall Street to Limbe," 236.

12   Walker, "Bringing the Wisdom of Wall Street to Limbe," 236.

13   Walker, "Bringing the Wisdom of Wall Street to Limbe," 242.

14   Walker, "Bringing the Wisdom of Wall Street to Limbe," 237.

15   Walker, "Bringing the Wisdom of Wall Street to Limbe," 237.

16   Walker, "Bringing the Wisdom of Wall Street to Limbe," 242.

114   &   CHAPTER FOUR

return to Cameroon. While the reader is aware of the barriers that immigration laws can potentially erect to migrants, the falsification of the persecution story to earn Jende a stay in the country and the corruption of Bubakar are illegal and unlawful. Despite this, Bubakar describes the immigration system as wicked and its officials as bastards, while noting that "some of them . . . don't want people like me and you here."[17] Bubakar's statement is a fitting characterization of the immigration laws, especially in the racialization of its procedures for refugee and asylum status in the last ten years in the United States. The exclusionary nature of the system, especially in its treatment of people of color, gives further credence to Bubakar's characterization of discrimination.

Compounding this state of helplessness is the atmosphere of violence and death that characterize the relationship between Black people and the police in America. The Jongas' sense of insecurity is heightened by the killings of Black men by the police, and their status as illegal migrants exacerbates the threats to their safety. This fear seriously erodes feelings of belonging. As Bubakar advises Jende, he should "always stay close to the gray area and keep [himself] and [his] family safe. Stay away from any place where [he] can run into police. . . . The police is for the protection of white people. . . . Maybe black women and black children sometimes, but not black men. Never black men."[18] In this precarious situation, the Jongas' future rests on one potential possibility: the enactment of "an Immigration bill like the one Kennedy and McCain were fighting for will [hopefully] pass Congress and the government will give everyone papers: Then your *wahala* will be over."[19] In the meantime, they have to contend with fighting for their status. As Bubakar tells Jende, "I know people who've been fighting Immigration forever. In that time, they've gone to school, married, had children, started businesses, made money, and enjoyed their lives. The only thing they cannot do is go outside the country."[20] For Neni, who always "wanted to be in control of her own life, and now, clearly, she wasn't, and simply thinking about the fact that someone else was going to decide the direction of her future was enough to intensify her headache, leave her feeling as if a thousand hammers were banging on her skull. This helplessness crushed her, the fact that she had traveled to America only to be reminded of how powerless she was, how unfair life could be."[21]

---

17   Mbue, *Behold the Dreamers*, 57.
18   Mbue, *Behold the Dreamers*, 74.
19   Mbue, *Behold the Dreamers*, 74.
20   Mbue, *Behold the Dreamers*, 72.
21   Mbue, *Behold the Dreamers*, 62–63.

PSYCHOLOGICAL DEPRESSION ❧ 115

This situation of helplessness fully reveals the hardships that characterize the Jongas' experience. Neni and Jende must balance the demands of work and the requirements of the school system in order to get an education. Balancing the hours required to earn enough money for the sustenance of the family, oftentimes from menial and low-paying jobs and with the hours required for school and study, is taxing. Working odd jobs to provide for the family does not stop with the immediate family of the migrant. They are called upon to provide for their families back home. Jendi recalls his financial commitments to his brother's family and was grateful for Cindy's assistance with five hundred dollars. As he ponders Cindy's willingness to help, he marvels at "how this business of sending money to relatives back home worked and how some relatives had no consideration for those who sent them money because they thought the streets of America were paved with dollar bills."[22]

The Jongas' predicament is further depicted in the slow but forceful realization that America doesn't have answers for and cannot solve all their problems. As Neni comes to realize, "America doesn't have the best of everything,"[23] and with the complex American culture that the migrant has to navigate, most times tinged with racism, life in the West can be very challenging. It is in such moments that nostalgia surfaces, and the migrant begins to question the rationale for departure and assess the cost to migration. Faced with the culture shock in the United States during his first days in the country and struggling with the isolation that comes with living in New York City, Jende would listen to Neni over the telephone as she tells him of her plans for the week. The conversation would leave him "*craving everything he wished he hadn't left behind. During those times, he told her, he often wondered if leaving home in search of something as fleeting as fortune was ever worthwhile*"[24] (emphasis added). In these moments of introspection, Jende comes to miss the little things they never considered important while in Cameroon. He begins to develop nostalgia for his homeland.

The narrative structure of Mbue's work is especially suited to an unveiling of the realities of life in the West, a reality that Jende, by virtue of his position as chauffeur to Clark, and Neni, as handmaid to Cindy, come to realize firsthand. In pairing the two families, Mbue constructs a parallel structure for exploration of their experiences in the context of both the possibilities and the misconceptions surrounding the pursuit of wealth and happiness in America. In spite of the power differential in the two families, the narrative works to deconstruct previous notions and perceptions of family welfare that

---

22   Mbue, *Behold the Dreamers*, 86.

23   Mbue, *Behold the Dreamers*, 89.

24   Mbue, *Behold the Dreamers*, 96.

each family initially has. The parallel lives of the two families are depicted in the mirror images of each other: they initially long to become the reflection of what they are seeing, but as the narrative unfolds, it becomes apparent that they would gladly exchange each other's reflection. Jende sees his future self in Clark, while Clark sees his struggling past in Jende. Jende, meanwhile, longs to become like Clark and would work harder to accomplish his level of material success. But as he continues to stare at Clark's reflection in the rearview mirror—from the vantage point, literally and figuratively, that his job as chauffeur offers—Jende comes to recognize that images are not indicative of the realities of the objects or situations they reflect. Through this structure, Mbue interrogates not only the feasibility of the American dream but also its meaning for its pursuers—both citizens of the United States and migrants from across the globe. Through the life of Clark and Cindy, Jende and Neni come to realize that wealth is not happiness and that far from providing the stability and love people assume come with it, on the contrary, it undermines trust and happiness and opens the family to a life of destruction. They see that material success is only one aspect of the dream and that its retention is perhaps the hardest part. Clark's struggle to retain his wealth is depicted as both self-destructive and inimical to family unity. It is a paradox, therefore, that while the Edwardses have achieved economic success, they would have gladly traded it for the peace and love that come with the simple lifestyle of the Jonga family. The façade may be beautiful and attractive, but beneath it all, there are layers of dysfunction and unhappiness, defined by an alcoholic wife, a cheating husband who sleeps with prostitutes, and a disobedient son, who wants nothing to do with his family. The capitalist system, as depicted here, makes it clear that economic success comes at a cost in the same way as resettlement through the immigration system comes at a certain expense to the migrant. In the proximity of both families, and through the connections between capitalism and the immigration system, they come to see the pros and cons inherent in their dreams and a realization of the limitations of both. While the two systems may be different, they are both defined and underpinned by the same search for wealth and happiness, as well as their elusiveness. Importantly, the Jonga family should learn from the lives of the Edwards family in the same way as the Edwardses should learn from the Jonga family. As Jende states earlier in the novel, "In Limbe, we live simple lives, but we enjoy our lives well."[25] While he is initially running away from this life, he comes to realize that he and the Edwardses would give all they have for the peace that comes with this simple lifestyle. In the process, both Jende and Clark recognize that the small things in life give us the biggest joys and that wealth or fortune might not be one of those things.

---

25   Mbue, *Behold the Dreamers*, 38.

PSYCHOLOGICAL DEPRESSION ❧ 117

The capitalist system and its role in the pursuit of happiness is central to the plot of the novel. Mbue uses it as the backdrop to locate the American dream. Given its ties to the capitalist system, the dream is then accomplished or lost in the context of the complexities of the system. Lehman Brothers is presented as the epitome of capitalist success, and so its operation is indicative of the possibilities of capitalism. In this accord, the author uses the collapse of the company and its reverberating effect on Wall Street in 2008 to emphasize the temporality of material wealth and, by implication, the transience of a dream that is built upon it. This fact of ephemerality Jende had initially pondered in one of his telephone calls to Neni—the realization that the economic aspect of the dream is fleeting and therefore unreliable. Its instability interrogates the rationale for its pursuit. Further, the miserable life of even those, like the Edwardses, who are deemed to have achieved it, especially in the struggle to retain their wealth, questions the meaning behind it.

Mbue makes clear in the depiction of the Edwardses that all that glitters is not gold. In their relationship with Clark and Cindy, Jende and Neni have insights into the cost of capital success. Neni comes to recognize the signs of loneliness in the neglected wife as she listens to Cindy's plea over the phone for her husband's company. She sees Cindy's fears and insecurities concerning her husband's preference for younger women and the inevitable outcome of losing him. By looking at Cindy's reflection in this mirror, Neni sees her own image and equally recognize the fear and insecurities that come with migration and the immigration system. Like Cindy, she dreads the inevitable outcome of losing Jende not to younger women but to the psychological torture of a failed migration attempt, as the narrative comes to demonstrate. Both Cindy and Neni suffer abuse from their husbands, on both emotional and physical levels. The characters reflect each other's situations with echoes of similar and contrasting images since the two situations are mirror images of each other. In the end, Cindy's troubled past and present isolation lead her to alcohol and drugs as a coping mechanism, and she eventually dies of an overdose. Beneath the promise of resettlement and the gleam of capitalist success, the reader sees two deeply unhappy women struggling to keep their lives together.

In Jende's case, he comes to see the demands on family that capitalism makes on the entrepreneur and the sacrifice they are forced to make in order to achieve economic success. He notes the terrible choice Clark had to make between his family and his career, as well as the consequences of choosing the latter. He sees in Clark the perpetual strife and physical and spiritual toll that the making and preservation of wealth take on people in the American capitalist system. It is a struggle not only to achieve wealth but also, and more importantly, to keep it. He ultimately concludes that, in spite of the veneer of accomplishment, Clark is a slave to his assets, and he is spiritually and physically imprisoned by them. He tells Jende that "unless you make a certain kind of money in this country, life can be brutal."[26] The reader wonders what amount of money qualifies as the "certain kind of money" and what it would take to get it. The pressure to make and retain a specific amount of money as guarantee of happiness is illusory and destructive. It robs individuals of their soul and deprives them of the happiness of friends and family. Jende comes to realize that even though it is good to provide for one's family, such a provision cannot come at the expense of their happiness. For Clark, since his pursuit of money is taking a huge toll on his family—as he rarely has any time for them—the disintegration of the Edwardses is a foregone conclusion. It is in Clark's joy at the little things of life, as in watching the sun set, that Mbue drives home the true meaning of life and fosters Jende's realization of what he took for granted back home in Cameroon—the peace and happiness that come with a simple lifestyle. In his poem that he reads to Jende, Clark demonstrates his desire to return home. This contemplative move reflects his growing preference for this kind of simple life. The novel suggests that his son, Vince, has embraced this idea of a simplified existence, and this sets him on the path to staying abroad in India.

This separation of father and son is a structural device to alert Jende to the contrast between his own relationship with his son, Liomi, and Clark, with Vince. The implication of the contrast is for Jende to appreciate the bond he has with Liomi, in spite of the challenges he faces in raising his family in America. Similarly, Neni comes to recognize that she should not take for granted her relationship with her husband. In learning of rape, abuse, and trauma from Cindy's childhood memories and the details of her present condition—the neglect from her husband, her addiction, and her depression—Neni is appreciative of the gift of a united family, and despite instances of Jende's abuse, she is in a position to see the contrast between the acquisition of wealth and the stability that comes with reciprocal love. Neni is in a position to realize that a family doesn't need to be wealthy to be happy, that neither money nor friends can substitute for happiness, and that the simple life, something akin to the vision that Vince articulates, cannot be traded for capitalist fortune.

In a scathing comment on the capitalist system in America, Vince gives us his view of the negative transformation that comes with capitalist success:

> Look at my parents—they're struggling under the weight of so many pointless pressures, but if they could ever free themselves of this self-inflicted oppression they would find genuine happiness. Instead, they continue to go down a path of achievements and accomplishments and material success and shit that means nothing because that's what America is all about, and now they're trapped. And they don't get it![27]

---

26   Mbue, *Behold the Dreamers*, 148.

27   Mbue, *Behold the Dreamers*, 103–4.

PSYCHOLOGICAL DEPRESSION   119

It is interesting that Vince defines success in terms of happiness and does not equate material acquisition with it. Vince's definition offers Jende a mirror to assess his own perspective on success and to reconfigure his definition of the American dream as material aggrandizement. The narrative shows that the Jongas go through a process of introspection in which they question the view that material wealth is the foundation to a fulfilled life. Vince's rejection of this view of the American dream essentially interrogates one of the Jongas' fundamental motivations for departure and illustrates a misunderstanding of the operation of the capitalist system and its impact on the process by which migrant dreams are realized.

In addition, Vince depicts capitalism as a cold-hearted syndicate of ruthless predators that thrive on the exploitation of the masses. He describes it as a system of bondage with "people going around living meaningless lives, because it's what they've been conditioned to think is good for them. Walking around completely mindless of the fact that they're living in a society ruled by a cold-blooded cabal."[28] In aspiring to free himself from the bondage of capitalism and its materialistic hold on the people, Vince aspires, as Jende notes, "to become a whole new person."[29] The transformation required is total—a spiritual and physical break from the grip of materialism engendered by capitalism.

The pressures of the capitalist system are also seen in the relationship between Jende and Neni. Compounded with the immigration system and the threat of deportation, the Jonga family deteriorates. In December, after the birth of their daughter, Timba, at Harlem Hospital, a letter arrives from immigration: "On the basis of being admitted to the United States in August of 2004 with authorization to remain for a period not to exceed three months and staying beyond November 2004 without further authorization, it has been charged that he is subject to removal from the United States, the letter reads. He was to appear before an immigration judge to show why he should not be removed from the country."[30] The date for the court appearance is set for the second week of February.

In this precarious position, Jende becomes vulnerable to exploitation—in this case, from the lawyer, Bubakar, who sees in Jende's plight an opportunity to make money. Apart from financial exploitation, Jende experiences signs of trauma and depression. He has nightmares that illustrate his anxieties over their possible deportation. Both Jende and Neni each had nightmares that neither spoke about the next morning: Jende of being forcefully removed from the country, and Neni, of returning to Limbe, a desolate and deserted place. Added to their fear of return is the complicated situation of

---

28   Mbue, *Behold the Dreamers*, 105.
29   Mbue, *Behold the Dreamers*, 105.
30   Mbue, *Behold the Dreamers*, 224.

120 ❧ CHAPTER FOUR

the children—what to do with Liomi, who they "would never take . . . back to Limbe. If they took him back, he might no longer be the happy child he is and was before coming to America. He might become angry, disappointed and hostile, forever resentful toward his parents."[31] While Liomi would miss the opportunities America has to offer, Timba's situation poses a significant difficulty because, unlike Liomi, she is an American citizen. What it would mean for her to grow up in Cameroon is a question about return that the Jongas have to seriously consider.

Jende and Neni have two different perspectives on how the situation is to be handled. Neni believes the family should continue to hope and, if necessary, fight for legal status. She takes refuge in religion and could be heard singing songs about "having a very big God who was always by her side and another about Jesus never failing even though the man of the world would let her down."[32] Neni will do whatever it takes, especially for her children, to remain in America. As she tells us, "Timba was going to enter Limbe one day as a proud Cameroonian-American returning to see the land of her ancestors, she told herself. Not as a child of failed asylees tossed out of the country like food that has turned sour."[33] She castigates Jende for what she sees as pride in not doing whatever it takes to stay in the country, while to Jende, it makes more sense to take what they have and return home.[34]

The contrast in perspective on staying and returning is clear, and as the days go by, the rift between the two begins to take a toll on their relationship and mental health. Neni could see the physical and mental transformation in Jende ever since he received the letter from immigration. In one of the scenes where Jende returns from work and is distant from his wife, Neni describes the scenario:

> He glared at her and returned to his potatoes and spinach. She pretended the look wasn't half as nasty as he'd intended it to be. She had to forgive him easily these days or her marriage would be doomed. She just had to, because he hadn't been the same man since the day the letter for the deportation hearing arrived. The weight of the letter was crushing him, she could see; he was now a man permanently at the edge of his breaking point. . . . It was as if the letter of his court appointment had turned him from a happy living man to an outraged dying man intent on showing the world his anger at his impending death.[35]

---

31   Mbue, *Behold the Dreamers*, 227.
32   Mbue, *Behold the Dreamers*, 227.
33   Mbue, *Behold the Dreamers*, 227.
34   Mbue, *Behold the Dreamers*, 231.
35   Mbue, *Behold the Dreamers*, 235.

PSYCHOLOGICAL DEPRESSION ❧ 121

The psychological torture Jende experiences ultimately finds an outlet in violent outbursts of emotion directed at Neni and for the slightest of offenses. On one such occasion, Neni discusses her immigration status with the pastor of the local church she attends. In fury, "fuming and breathing heavily," Jende berates her for disclosing private family matters to outsiders. Neni is convinced of the rationale behind keeping family matters private, but in her desire to seek assistance from people in the community, especially those Americans she believed "wanted to keep good hardworking immigrants in America," she had told the pastor about their plight. As Jende rages on, Neni contemplates:

> It will be futile reasoning with a raging man, so she decided to sit quietly with her head bowed as he unleashed a verbal lashing, as he called her a stupid idiot and a bloody fool. The man who had promised to always take good care of her was standing above her vomiting a parade of insults, spewing out venom she never thought he had inside him. For the first time in a long love affair, she was afraid he would beat her. She was almost certain he would beat her. *And if he had, she would have known that it was not her Jende who was beating her but a grotesque being created by the sufferings of an American immigrant life.*[36] (emphasis added)

The life of the illegal migrant has transformed Jende into a person his wife hardly recognizes. The fear is deep, the insecurities are certain, and the trauma is palpable. The Jonga family, like the Edwardses, is on the brink of disintegration. Though for two different but related reasons, the Jongas and the Edwardses are brought into proximity, and a process leading to the realization of the dangers of the pursuit of the dream is unveiled.

Jende's writings in his personal journal provide a canvas for the realization of misperceptions of American society. His entries are symbolic of the mapping of the journey or path to self-destruction in two ways: an external mapping or landscaping of Clark's journey and an internal or psychological mapping of Jende's own recognition of this process of disintegration. In mapping out the landscape of Clark's journey, Jende is symbolically mapping his coming to terms with his perspective on the material and begins to question his expectations of the dream. He comes to see firsthand the stripping down of the Edwards family and provides an avenue for an engagement with the lure of the material and its capacity for destruction. The collapse of Lehman Brothers is also symbolically the collapse of the fabric of the Edwardses' marriage, one built on material acquisitions rather than on solid spiritual foundations of love. Clark's journey is a mirror image of Jende's path to potential self-destruction. The mindscaping of Clark's journey offers

---

36   Mbue, *Behold the Dreamers*, 237.

122 ᔍ CHAPTER FOUR

Jende an opportunity to change direction and recalibrate the expectations of the dream. Return to the homeland was one such aspect of this process of recalibration.

Jende's position as Clark's chauffeur takes on a new level of complication as he finds himself between husband and wife. While he is morally bound to tell the truth about Clark's infidelity to Cindy, he also recognizes that Clark is the source of his economic sustenance, and exposing him could come at the expense of his job. In this conundrum and in an attempt to please everyone, he succeeds in displeasing both Clark and Cindy and is eventually dismissed by Clark. His dismissal does not surprise him. In fact, he anticipated the move long before Clark makes the announcement to him. On the day of the dismissal, as Jende takes out his briefcase from the car and prepares to meet Clark, he makes a last attempt to ensure that none of his personal belongings are left behind. He looks in the glove compartment: "He'd always been diligent about that; nothing he'd tossed in there and forgotten to take out. Keep everything he owned, even his garbage, in his briefcase; even though he spent hours a day, practically lived in it all day, he was constantly aware that it wasn't his car and it would never be."[37] The car is a metaphor for the migrants' relationship with the new environment they find themselves in. There is the sense that regardless of the number of years they stay in the migratory country, it will never become their home. In Jende's case, immigration laws conspire with capitalist exploitation to make him "constantly aware" of his position as outsider and the impossibility of belonging to this society. In Clark's ruthless dismissal of him, one gets the feeling of the truth in his statement: "You will punish me and make my children suffer for doing what you told me to do?"[38] Clark's dismissal of Jende constitutes the abuse of the vulnerable migrant, and it highlights the immunity that defines the actions of those in high echelons of power in society. The life of the undocumented and the abuse to which the migrant is exposed are laid bare. And herein lies the cold-heartedness of the capitalist system—its capacity to use and dispose of the vulnerable with impunity. The chances of undocumented migrants successfully overcoming these barriers are very slim, indeed.

The full import of the negative transformation that comes with the consequences of losing one's job in a capitalist system is most fully realized in Jende's agony and abuse. Mbue describes Neni's thoughts of her husband after his dismissal: "The Jende who had returned home to her on the night of the firing was a husband pitilessly bowed by life. She had suspected something was wrong that night, but she did not deem it right to push an exhausted man to talk so she let him be. He went to bed without eating,

---

37   Mbue, *Behold the Dreamers*, 249.

38   Mbue, *Behold the Dreamers*, 252.

PSYCHOLOGICAL DEPRESSION   123

saying nothing to her except that he'd had a bad day and was very tired."[39] Jende's dismissal comes at a time of excruciating anxiety over their immigration status and the threat to deportation that it poses. The loss of the source of the family's income will have a direct impact on the family's welfare. After the court appearance and the postponement of a verdict on his asylum application, Jende seeks employment in two restaurants as a dishwasher. While this offers some guarantee of a steady income, the underlying exploitation of the undocumented through the capitalist system of daily wage labor comes through.

Feeling the weight of her husband's desperation, his silence, and helplessness, Neni decides to take action against Cindy who she believes is responsible for Jende's dismissal and the suffering of her family. First, she pleads with Cindy to intervene and have Clark rehire Jende, and when she refuses, Neni resorts to a threat of blackmail—to expose the photo of Cindy taking drugs and alcohol. In fear of exposure, Cindy hands Neni an undisclosed amount of money. The ethical implications of Neni's actions cannot be glossed over, and as Jende later tells her, it is unacceptable to use the threat of blackmail to get what one wants. That said, it would equally be unreasonable to gloss over Cindy's lack of consideration for the Jongas and the consequences of Jende's dismissal on his family. What the incident demonstrates is the outpouring of emotional frustration by two women angry at each other and desperate to protect their families at all costs. Even though they may be coming from two different angles—Neni, the desperate wife trying to secure her family's welfare, and Cindy, the desperate wife trying to protect her family's reputation—the underlying intention is the same: protecting their families by every means possible, whether the ruthless dismissal of a dutiful worker or the threat of blackmail of a caring employer and family friend. Neni's and Cindy's actions are best interpreted against the cold-hearted capitalist system—they have become as cold-hearted and individualistic as the system. In the process, both women are objectified, and this demonstrates the power of the capitalist system to dehumanize people. The instinct to survive is the primary consideration, and moral codes of conduct are given secondary consideration.

However, in spite of the pressure to conform, Jende is trying to keep his principles in place. Even though he is desperate and fully aware of the financial consequences of their current situation, he recognizes the need to preserve the codes of conduct that define ethical human relationships. Even when he seems to change his moral position after the argument with Neni, it is apparent that his action has more to do with pleasing his wife and putting an end to the quarrel than a justification of his stance. As he tells her, "We're

---

39   Mbue, *Behold the Dreamers*, 254.

124 &❧ CHAPTER FOUR

not those kinds of people. . . . You don't have to do something like this! . . . This has nothing to do with being African!"[40] Jende's position is critical to understanding the authorial voice in the narrative and an engagement with the moral rightness of his stance when he eventually makes the decision to return home. The narrative suggests that Jende is more level-headed and given to clear thinking than Neni, who is impulsive and headstrong. This is important because when Jende comes to insist on the need for them to return to Cameroon, the implications are that the authorial voice implicitly supports his decision. Neni's defiance and defense of staying in America would then come across as illogical against the thoughtful and constructive argument of Jende.

Neni's flawed judgment is revealed a few chapters later in her decision to apply for a green card through an elaborate scheme that involves a divorce with Jende, a marriage to her cousin, who will file on her behalf to stay in the country, and a remarriage to Jende. Natasha, a fellow church member and friend to Neni, comes across as the voice of reason when she asks Neni: "Why would you want to divorce your husband and risk your marriage for papers, Neni? Is America that important to you? Is it more important to you than your family?"[41] Natasha's questions are meant to question the rightness of Neni's stance. As she further tells Neni, "I think you ought to step back a little bit, ask yourself why you're [so desperate to stay in America]."[42] As Neni blurts out that maybe she is becoming another person, Natasha replies, "Let me put it this way: Are you happy with who you are becoming?"[43] That said, Neni's position is not to be dismissed so easily either. Her desperation to stay in America reflects a reality beyond just the desire to stay. It is the fear of returning home as a failed migrant. It is the fear of returning to those conditions that precipitated flight in the first place. It is the uncertainty of how they would be received and what it would take to reintegrate into a society that was once familiar but has become so different from what it was. It is the anxiety of the unknown and the unpredictable nature of return.

Five weeks after Neni takes the money from Cindy, the woman dies at her home in New York City. The reality of the circumstances surrounding Cindy's death should offer Neni a basis for a moral evaluation of the pursuit of material wealth. The death begins the process of deconstruction of the dream and coming to terms with its many pitfalls. It is the beginning of the realization that accomplishing the dream might not be everything in life and that it has its drawbacks. Cindy's death is intended to provide a rationale

---

40 Mbue, *Behold the Dreamers*, 272.

41 Mbue, *Behold the Dreamers*, 284.

42 Mbue, *Behold the Dreamers*, 329.

43 Mbue, *Behold the Dreamers*, 351.

PSYCHOLOGICAL DEPRESSION ❧ 125

for the Jongas to return home. At the death of Pa Jonga in Cameroon, the stakes grow higher in the choice to return or to continue to stay in America. Despite efforts to save him, Pa Jonga dies of complications from either malaria or typhoid fever. Jende's sadness over his father's death is deeply agonizing and illustrates the plight of the undocumented migrants who cannot go home to attend the funeral rites of loved ones because they do not have the required immigration papers. Their loved ones are buried in their absence. The scene with Neni, after Jende returns from work on the day Pa Jonga dies, reveals the agony that has come to define their lives. The trauma from his father's death proves too much for Jende, and in the following days, he is in the hospital suffering from chronic backache. As it turns out, the pain was precipitated by the psychological trauma of his father's death and the many stressors in his life.

In the face of these struggles, Jende settles on his decision to return home. He tells Neni, "I am ready to go back home. . . . I want to go back to Limbe. . . . I don't want to stay in this country anymore."[44] As he tries to rationalize his decision with Neni, Jende interrogates the pursuit of the dream in the process. He reveals to her: "I don't like what my life has become in this country. I don't know how long I can continue living like this, Neni. The suffering in Limbe was bad, but this one here, right now . . . it's more than I can take."[45] Jende's recognition of the realities of their situation and the comparisons to his homeland are the beginning of self-realization and the turning point in the migration process. Interestingly, Jende squarely predicates his decision to return home on his unhappiness with America, the same lack of happiness that broke Cindy's heart, pushed Clark into infidelity, and took Vince to India. Like Cindy, Jende has come to realize that fortune is not synonymous with happiness, and besides, happiness is not achieved by one's presence abroad. Happiness for Jende becomes a spiritual disposition that yearns for a simple life back home. And for that, one does not need to go through agony in America to be happy. Thus, when Neni characterizes his unhappiness as circumstantial and stemming from the death of his father, Jende clarifies: "But it's not only my father's death. It's everything that's happened. I lost my job. My *papier* situation. This work, work, work, all the time. For what? For a little money? How much suffering can a man take in this world, eh? How much longer . . . ?"[46] Jende is pointing out the demands of the capitalist system on the life of the individual; the same complaint that Clark makes to Cindy as he struggles to keep his fortune. The grind is not only in the struggle to make money but also in the

---

44 Mbue, *Behold the Dreamers*, 305.
45 Mbue, *Behold the Dreamers*, 306.
46 Mbue, *Behold the Dreamers*, 306.

126 ❧ CHAPTER FOUR

labor to keep it. In his reflection on the impact of the Wall Street collapse on their situation, Jende goes back to his initial conclusion that wealth is not everything in life.

Julian Walker sees Jende's decision to return in the context of "translocating the American Dream," gesturing to the point that while it is crucial for the dream or some aspects of it to be accomplished abroad, it should be lived or made manifest in the migrant's home country.[47] I agree with Walker's interpretation of Jende's return, regardless of the challenges that he will encounter: "Although the novel paints a dark and strenuous picture of immigrant life in the United States, the Jongas' return to Limbe does not break with the ideals that the American dream promotes. Even though Jende acknowledges that his dreams of becoming someone within the United States' economic system remains unachievable, he cannot escape the American dream and his reverie. The American dream, the dream of becoming someone economically, travels with the Jongas back to Limbe."[48] Walker's interpretation does not dismiss the challenges associated with return. But it does articulate the point quite profoundly that the possibility of living the dream in the migrant's homeland is more realistic than continuing to endure the precarity of life as an illegal migrant in the West.

At the next court hearing and at the advice of Bubakar, Jende petitions the judge to close the deportation case in exchange for his voluntary departure from the country. He opts to leave within ninety days to return to Cameroon. With this arrangement, neither Jende nor Liomi can return to the United States. Neni can in the future "if she formally [withdraws] from BMCC and [leaves] by a certain date after the international students' office [terminates] her record in SEVIS. The embassy would probably give her another visa in the future."[49] Timba, the child born in America, can always come back because she is an American citizen.

As disappointing as this arrangement might seem to Neni, and indeed to Jende as well, it is in the words of his cousin Winston that the wisdom of Jende's decision can be found: "Even if Jende got papers, Winston went on, without a good education, and being a black African immigrant male, he might never be able to make enough money to afford to live the way he'd like to live, never mind having enough to own a home or pay for his wife and children to go to college. He might never be able to have a really good sleep at night."[50] Winston's view corroborates Jende's previous position to Neni that "America is not all that; this country is full of lies and people who like to

---

47   Walker, "Bringing the Wisdom of Wall Street to Limbe," 236.
48   Walker, "Translocating the American Dream," 242.
49   Mbue, *Behold the Dreamers*, 327.
50   Mbue, *Behold the Dreamers*, 322.

PSYCHOLOGICAL DEPRESSION   127

hear lies. If you want to know the truth I'll tell you the truth: This country no longer has room for people like us. Anyone who has no sense can believe the lies and stay here forever, hoping that things will get better for them one day and they will be happy. As for me, I won't live my life in the hope that someday I will magically become happy. I refuse to!"[51]

Regardless of the finality of his position, Neni was determined to continue her "battle to help her husband recognize the folly of is conviction,"[52] and so, when she continues to argue her position, he unfortunately resorts to violence:

> She didn't see the slap coming. She merely found herself stumbling backward and falling on the floor from the force and shock of it, her cheek burning as if someone had rubbed hot tar on it. He was standing over her, his fists clenched, screaming in the ugliest voice she'd ever heard. He was calling her useless and idiot and stupid and a selfish woman who would be happy to see her husband die in pain all so she could live in New York. She jumped up, her cheek still throbbing.[53]

As the argument continues, the situation deteriorates. Neni confronts Jende over his actions, demanding to be beaten: "So he did. He hit her hard. One vicious slap on her cheek. Then another. And another. And a deafening one right over her ear. They landed on her face even before she was done asking for them. She squealed, stunned and pained; she fell on the ground wailing."[54] In spite of her pain, Neni comes to the following realization when the narrative emphasizes: "Neni Jonga fell asleep with tears running into her pillow, convinced her husband had beaten her not because he didn't love her but because he was lost and could find no way out of the misery that has become his life."[55] Jende remains in a state of torment until he feels relief through Neni's action: "The relief came only later that night, when Neni looked at him and, with tears in her eyes, said how glad she was that his ordeal might soon be over."[56] Jende is a product of the cruel immigration system, and the violence against Neni was emotional transfer of his fear, feelings of entrapment, and loss.

As the Jongas prepare to return, they have to contend with the many complications that return to Cameroon poses to the family. Decisions involving every aspect of their lives have to be made. There are certainly

---

51   Mbue, *Behold the Dreamers*, 333.
52   Mbue, *Behold the Dreamers*, 333.
53   Mbue, *Behold the Dreamers*, 333.
54   Mbue, *Behold the Dreamers*, 334.
55   Mbue, *Behold the Dreamers*, 335–36.
56   Mbue, *Behold the Dreamers*, 337.

128 ᔬ CHAPTER FOUR

challenges to relocation, but they are not insurmountable and are for a worthy cause. Return will be painful and will require a lot of sacrifice; it will also be defined by initial doubts and even disorientation, but it is sensible, worthwhile, and potentially fulfilling. Neni exemplifies the anxieties surrounding return, and one must accept the fact that her anxieties are quite legitimate. And so as the date of their departure draws near, she cries without provocation, feels no excitement at the thought of reunion with family and friends, and is apprehensive at the thought that "she might never be happy in Limbe as she'd been in New York."[57] In addition, she worries that "she might have too little in common with her friends, being that she was now so different from them, being that she has tasted a different kind of life and being transformed positively and negatively in so many different ways, being that life had expanded and contracted her in ways they could never imagine."[58] The reality of Neni's apprehension lies in the fact that she is a different person returning to Cameroon from the one who left some six years ago. What that difference means is scary to contemplate, difficult to predict, and uncertain as to how it would be received. This is cause for genuine concern.

The children pose another layer of complication. As Neni contemplates return, she "wavered between joy and sorrow—joy for the beautiful things Cameroon would give them; sorrow for the things it wouldn't. . . . In Limbe, Liomi and Timba would have many things they would not have had in America, but they would lose far too many things" as well.[59] It is in striking a balance between the two that the value of return will be seen. Needless to say, it is not as simple as working out a binary and making some sacrifices here and there. It involves a critical process of navigating the cultural values that were once familiar to the parents and are totally strange to the children. Fatou, another of Neni's friends also contemplating return, notes this conundrum: "After twenty-six years, she was ready to stop braiding hair for a living and go back home, but the decision wasn't hers alone to make. And even if Ousmane, her husband, wanted to go back home, her children were Americans who had never been to their parents' homeland. All seven of them, the three in their twenties and four teenagers, wanted nothing of living in West Africa. Some of them didn't even consider themselves African."[60] While relocation to the continent might be easier on the part of the parents, the children born in the diaspora would have a hard time navigating the cultural differences between their parents' homeland and their places of birth.

---

57   Mbue, *Behold the Dreamers*, 360.
58   Mbue, *Behold the Dreamers*, 360.
59   Mbue, *Behold the Dreamers*, 361.
60   Mbue, *Behold the Dreamers*, 357–58.

PSYCHOLOGICAL DEPRESSION &❧ 129

With USD $18,000 in their possession, Jende believes the American dream, so to speak, can be best lived back home in Cameroon. As Neni thinks of his plans, he thinks: "With the new exchange rate at six hundred CFA francs to a dollar, he would be returning home with close to ten million CFA francs, enough to restart their lives in a beautiful rental with a garage for his car and a maid so his wife could feel like a queen. He would have enough to start a business, which would enable him to someday build a spacious brick house and send Liomi to Baptist High school."[61]

It is worth noting that Jende's dreams are not illusory or unachievable. In fact, in the context of his native Cameroon, they make sense. It is tempting to correlate Natasha's sermon and Clark's words during the farewell visit with Jende's decision to return. Natasha preaches about "the treatment of the weary stranger in America [and] decried the contemporary American definition of weary stranger as illegal alien."[62] Drawing from Genesis 18, she uses the story of Abraham and the weary strangers to indict the immigration system in America, and for a society that purports to have been founded on Christian principles, the sermon cannot be more telling.

At his farewell meeting with Clark, Jende is pleased to see how much happier Clark looks after the loss of a good proportion of his material wealth. He notes that Clark "finally seemed a genuinely happy man,"[63] and it appears almost as if letting go of the material is the basis for true happiness. While this perspective toward life validates Vince's ideology, it also concretizes the point that family relations should never be sacrificed for material benefits. As Clark comes to realize that "family's everything,"[64] he informs Jende that he is moving back home to Arrington. Clark's decision to go home mirrors Jende's decision to return to Cameroon. Both have come to recognize the primacy of family over materialism and that one's happiness cannot be replaced by money. As Jende fittingly tells Clark: "I will miss America, but it will be good to live in my own country again. . . . I am no longer afraid of my country the way I used to be."[65] En route to the airport, Winston and Jende agree that the Cameroonian government "is our government and [Cameroon] is our country. How man go do? It's our country. We can never disown it."[66] At four in the morning of the day after they left America, the Jongas arrive at Douala International Airport in Cameroon. As they drive through the streets, having been picked up by relatives, Jende

---

61   Mbue, *Behold the Dreamers*, 352.

62   Mbue, *Behold the Dreamers*, 364.

63   Mbue, *Behold the Dreamers*, 368.

64   Mbue, *Behold the Dreamers*, 369.

65   Mbue, *Behold the Dreamers*, 373.

66   Mbue, *Behold the Dreamers*, 380.

observes "the red and white sign above the highway that said 'Welcome to Limbe, The Town of Friendship.'"[67]

The end of the novel, especially the question mark after "home," has provoked numerous responses concerning the specificity of the location and the possibility of locating where home actually is in view of Liomi's state of drowsy wakefulness. I read this in the context of continued liminality that, while exposing the challenges the returned migrant has to deal with, also demonstrates possibilities of a hybridized and successful future. Regardless of the perspective we bring to the end of the novel, the Jongas' decision to return home frees them from the horrific life of precarity that they were living in America and demonstrates, in Augusta Irele's conception, that in the face of current hostilities in the migratory country, it is important that migrants consider the possibility of returning to an alternative space or location.

---

67   Mbue, *Behold the Dreamers*, 381.

Part III

Return

Return is the third phase of the migration process. Given the precarity of life abroad, return becomes an alternative for the protagonists of *Ghana Must Go*, *Americanah*, and *So the Path Does Not Die*. In this section of the book, I pick up from the return of the Jonga family to Cameroon to explore three separate aspects of return, each in a different chapter.

Ghana Must Go focuses on the challenges to reintegration of the returned migrant in chapter 5. In chapter 6, I use *Americanah* to explore the construct of new hybridity in analyzing the possibilities of economic and social advancement of both the returned migrant and the homeland. In the final chapter, I posit an aesthetic of constructive liminality to explore the dual identities of returned migrants and the possibilities and challenges it offers them as they straddle two worlds. I use Pede Hollist's *So the Path Does Not Die* to examine this phase of the migration process.

Chapter 7 is unique in its exposition of the aesthetic of constructive liminality in the attempt of returned migrants to use their Western and Indigenous identities to their advantage. The construct is futuristic in its contemplation of liminality as a potential solution to the migrant problem of belonging. It postulates the in-between space, that is, the space that conflates Western and Indigenous identities, as a productive construct for negotiating geopolitical spaces and the benefits they accord the migrant. This space that allows for the intersections of geographical and cultural identities is considered the way forward for the returned migrants as they negotiate the complications of returning to a once familiar space that has undergone significant changes.

Chapter Five

Challenges to Reintegration

Ghana Must Go by Taiye Selasi begins the conversation on migrants' return to their homeland and the difficulties surrounding the process of reintegration. Kweku Sai's dismissal from Beth Israel Hospital provides the impetus for his return to Ghana, and the racism that underlies the incident is influential in his decision. Dismissed, blacklisted, and forcibly removed from the premises, Kweku returns to Ghana without informing his family, builds a house, marries another woman, and settles down until his death. The challenges to Kweku's return are highlighted in his abandoned relationship with his family and their struggles to reconcile. I argue that while Kweku's return and death provide an alternative to the racism in America, the move is not without its complications.

The critical reception of Selasi's novel has been enthusiastic. Conventionally received and critiqued in view of its connections to Afropolitanism, largely due to his seminal essay "Bye-Bye Babar," Aretha Phiri points out that Selasi "describes the aesthetic appeal and political agency of 'the newest generation of African emigrants,' whose embodied specificity and universality testify to the increasingly mobile and fluid, globalised character of Twenty-first century African subjectivities."[1] Several critics have drawn from this essay and Selasi's theorizations on mobilities and crossings, borders and boundaries, and their implications for identity, gender, race, and class to explore the experience of the Sai family in the novel—a mobile experience that constitutes journeys from Accra, Ghana, and Lagos, Nigeria, to New York, to Lagos, back to New York, and then to Accra. In this framework of spatial and temporal mobilities, writers have offered varied and at times contested readings of the novel. Phiri, as earlier mentioned, reads the novel as positing "a more nuanced and sophisticated appreciation of the African diaspora than is provided in [Selasi's] seminal essay . . . [arguing that] the novel articulates more complexly and illuminates more creatively the cultural and subjective anxiety associated with the negotiation of identitarian roots and routes."[2]

---

1   Phiri, "Lost in Translation," 144.
2   Phiri, "Lost in Translation," 144.

134 &❧ CHAPTER FIVE

Amy Rushton reads *Ghana Must Go* almost exclusively in terms of its depictions of different manifestations of home to explore the tensions between location and dislocation and the contemplation of return to an original space that carries a certain sense of cultural identity and belonging. While acknowledging Selasi's concern with mobilities and identities constructed out of such movements, Rushton argues that the novel does not frame "the African 'home' as a straightforward celebratory location, and the prospect of the return is one characterized by paradox, for it is an outcome both deeply desired and feared . . . [but] deploy[s] narrative strategies to dramatise and work through the anxiety of the home-coming for today's Afropolitans."[3] Rushton's article is crucial to my analysis of return as I argue that the paradox of return is both productive and restrictive and that it is in an understanding of both the limitations and possibilities to what can be achieved by the returned migrant that the benefits of returning to the country of origin can be fully discernible. The potential of return to both liberate and constrain reflects the complications of return and highlights the ambiguities of straddling a dual location and identity. I emphasize that when such an ambiguity is intentionally constructed, it leads to productive ends. I define this aesthetic of possibilities as both new hybridity and constructive liminality.

Chielozona Eze approaches the novel and its connections to Afropolitanism from a different angle. He argues that Afropolitanism "is an enunciation of the ideas of contamination, hybridity, hyperculturality and other postmodernist terms that disrupt essentialist and oppositional notions of African culture and identity" and gestures to "situate Afropolitanism within a larger philosophical tradition of cosmopolitanism and examine the moral implications of expanding the notion of African identity beyond the oppositional model."[4] Eze's article is influential in a discussion of African identity, new ways in which this construct can be viewed, revisited, or reevaluated, using new models of evaluation, as well as their implications for engaging "the complex nature of African identity in a somewhat dialectical form."[5] This perspective is important in understanding form and positionality in terms of identity and Afropolitans' relationship to the African continent. As he rightly notes, the concept of Afropolitanism forces us to think of ways we understand "culture, identity, and citizenship of countries."[6] The Sai family's affiliation with and habitation in Accra and Lagos provide a basis for understanding these relationships.

---

3   Rushton, "No Place Like Home," 45.
4   Eze, "Rethinking African Culture and Identity," 234.
5   Eze, "Rethinking African Culture and Identity," 235.
6   Eze, "Rethinking African Culture and Identity," 237.

CHALLENGES TO REINTEGRATION   **135**

Reading *Ghana Must Go* in the context of mobilities and identities has generated multiple responses and from different positions. While critics have produced numerous articles and have explored the novel in terms of migration, movement, travels, and journeys, Selasi, in an interview with Nicole Brittingham Furlonge, refrains from endorsing this conceptualization of her work:

> People say that there's a lot of motion in *Ghana Must Go*, but, it's funny, I don't actually really think that there is. I mean Kweku wants a scholarship and he leaves Ghana. He stays in one country on one side of it—like, between five states of it—for the next 30 years. In the way that anyone else would, he goes to college; he goes to med school; he gets a job. Those are the movements: from Pennsylvania to Baltimore to Boston, which I don't think that that's terribly much movement at all. Then everything goes burst and he goes back to where he started.[7]

Notwithstanding, as Dustin Crowley insists, one way to read Selasi's novel is through the lens of migration: "Through migrants Kweku Sai (from Ghana) and his wife Fola (from Nigeria), as well as their properly Afropolitan children (all born in the United States), the novel explores the desires, means, and consequences of being free from categorizations like nationalism, free to build homes, and identities in multiple places while striving to connect them together."[8]

In this chapter, I focus primarily on the lived experiences of the Sai family to argue that accomplishment of the dream does not exclude the migrant from racism. Kweku's dismissal in spite of his achievement of the dream indicates the possibility that living the dream back home is a better alternative to the racism in America, even though that move is not without complications. I use the Sai family as representative of the migrant experience of racism to foreground both the injustice meted out to the African migrant and the possibilities that come with reintegration upon return to the homeland.

The novel opens with the death of Kweku Sai after his return to Ghana sixteen years earlier. The circumstances that motivated his return have not been disclosed, but as the narrative unfolds, the reader is taken back in time to a course of events that records a history of academic and professional success against a backdrop of racism and prejudice and ends in unlawful dismissal and ultimately death. Closely tied to the plot is the exploded chronology narrative method that allows for a dual timeframe of past and present modes of narration, shifting configurations of two geographical landscapes—Accra and Boston—and in different time periods. The narrative method

---

7   Furlonge, "An Interview with Taiye Selasi," 535.
8   Crowley, "How Did They Come to This?," 128.

136 &♦ CHAPTER FIVE

accounts for the fragmented structure of the plot, which in part underscores its construction as a memory novel and its depiction of the stream of consciousness mode by which the mind operates. The fragmented structure of the plot reflects the traumatic memory of the characters. Kweku Sai's recollections are fragmented and indicative of his trauma. The fragmentation also supports the manner of his death—cardiac arrest that symbolizes a broken heart—with the brokenness reflected in the plot structure, that is, a fragmented narrative structure that also suggests a broken heart.

Later in the novel, we are introduced to a dilemma in Kweku's professional life. He has been dismissed from the hospital, but he doesn't have the courage to convey the information to his family. He drives aimlessly around the city and returns home in the evening. On one such day, he drives to the law offices of Kleinman & Kleinman, and we gather from his lawyer, Marty, that Kweku is fighting a wrongful dismissal lawsuit in court. Marty tells Kweku, "You've spent "hundreds . . . of thousands . . . of dollars . . . trying to fight this. They're not backing down, man. It's eating you alive."[9] From this conversation, Marty reveals the circumstances surrounding Kweku's dismissal from the hospital, and it becomes apparent that he is fighting an uphill battle against two monsters: capitalism, nicknamed the machine, and racism.

Kweku's experience in America demonstrates the negative consequences of being racial and ethnic other in a white-dominated society. Once reputed to be "general surgeon without equal, Ghanaian Carson," Kweku Sai was the inevitable choice to perform an emergency appendectomy on Jane "Ginny" Cabot, the wife of a donor to Beth Israel Hospital, where he worked.[10] It is a critical case of surgery, requiring the most skillful of hands. The narrative affirms: "The only reason Kweku had even attempted the appendectomy was because the Cabots had called the president of the hospital, a family friend, to suggest very politely that in light of their donation surely a last-ditch operation wasn't too much to ask? It wasn't. And they wanted the very best surgeon. The president found Kweku as he was leaving to go home."[11]

Two things are quite clear at this point: the operation was a last-ditch attempt to save a patient's life, and the professional credentials of the surgeon were unquestionable. However, when the operation turns out to be unsuccessful, the Cabots, "one of Boston's richest families, one of the hospital's biggest donors . . . had demanded that someone be held accountable."[12] Casting aside professional ethics, the hospital, fearing the loss of one of its biggest donors, decides "to fire a good surgeon to appease a strong family, to

---

9   Selasi, *Ghana Must Go*, 68.

10   Selasi, *Ghana Must Go*, 73.

11   Selasi, *Ghana Must Go*, 74.

12   Selasi, *Ghana Must Go*, 77.

CHALLENGES TO REINTEGRATION ❧ 137

say that he'd failed to 'account for the risks.'"[13] In spite of the fact that the hospital president had watched the surgical procedure himself, "Dr. Putnam 'Putty' Gardener—trusted Cabot family doctor . . . was insistent that the surgeon had (a) failed to appreciate and (b) failed to communicate the risks."[13] In one moment of capitalist greed and racism, Kweku Sai loses everything he has worked for. As Marty, his lawyer, notes of capitalism, "The machine was in control. And so he was in control who belonged to it."[14] And of Kweku's career, he says, "Then the machine turned against him, charged, swallowed him whole, mashed him up, and spat him out of some spout in the back."[15]

It was easy for Beth Israel Hospital to dismiss Kweku because of his ethnic identity. Even before he performed the operation, and despite his professional credentials, the Cabot family, based on the color of Kweku's skin, had already started questioning his training and effectiveness as a surgeon. The narrative records that "the Cabot family physician, smug, a general practitioner," asks of Kweku, "And where did you do your training?"[16] Kweku responds, "In the jungle, on beasts . . . Chimpanzees taught. Great instructors."[17] The racial prejudice is blatant and obvious. That one of his colleagues could question his credentials is in fact a contestation of the standards of the institution that recruited him in the first place. The whole thing turns into a conspiracy to make the African doctor the scapegoat for an inevitable death. Of their conspiracy to betray and destroy a colleague's career, Marty puts it bluntly, "Cause you're black. Right?"[18] Kweku Sai was not only wrongfully dismissed from his practice at Beth Israel; he was also blacklisted to work as a surgeon in the United States. As Marty summarizes the situation, "This is the end of the road."[19] In defeat, Kweku drives to the airport and departs for Ghana, never to return, and without a word to his family. Sixteen years later, the novel opens with his death. Lying on the floor of his lawn close to the garden, suffering from cardiac arrest, he fails to get help and eventually dies.

Kweku's wrongful dismissal foregrounds retention as a critical aspect of the American dream beyond its accomplishment. In this way, it explores what it means for the African migrant to succeed in America. Kweku's dismissal accentuates the point that success is predicated not only on the accomplishment of the dream but also on the improbability of its retention.

---

13 Selasi, *Ghana Must Go*, 77.
14 Selasi, *Ghana Must Go*, 69.
15 Selasi, *Ghana Must Go*, 69.
16 Selasi, *Ghana Must Go*, 74.
17 Selasi, *Ghana Must Go*, 74.
18 Selasi, *Ghana Must Go*, 76.
19 Selasi, *Ghana Must Go*, 71.

138 &♦ CHAPTER FIVE

That Kweku can be so unprofessionally dismissed signifies the fragility of the dream and the power of racism to exclude the outsider, even the best that society can produce. Kweku's experience suggests that the dream is not only difficult to achieve but also nearly impossible to sustain, given the ethnic identity of African migrants.

Kweku's situation brings to the fore the question of success. If his career and life are regarded as benchmarks for measuring success, then there are questions regarding success for the African migrant in America. His dismissal also raises questions about the future of the African migrant in this racially charged society. As Kweku suggests to Fola, the term "success" is nondescript and therefore incapable of defining meaning. When we witness his physical eviction from the hospital in the presence of his son, Kehinde, we are again reminded of the power of racism to destroy migrant lives. Lamenting her husband's death, Fola notes that Kweku's crime was that he had "dared to become. To escape would have sufficed. To be 'free,' if one wants swelling strings, to be 'human.' Beyond being 'citizen,' beyond being 'poor.' It was all he was after in the end, a human story, a way to be Kweku beyond being poor."[20] If migration cannot afford the migrant, even at this level of success, the courtesy to be respected, then its significance is questionable.

A more consequential aspect of Kweku's dismissal is the mental and psychological toll it takes on his family. The absence of the father and husband in the lives of Fola and the children, especially Taiwo, creates devastating outcomes for their lives. Beyond the financial constraints of a single parent raising four kids, the trauma of separation from their father amplifies the struggles of the family and heightens conflicts within it. The snowball effect of Kweku's dismissal is evident in Fola's decision to send the twins to Uncle Femi in Lagos, which results in the unfortunate abuse of Taiwo by Kehinde and, later, the scandalous affair with the dean of her division in law school. It also engenders Kehinde's reclusion from society, as well as Olu's distance from the family. The gradual deterioration of the family is a direct consequence of Kweku's dismissal and departure. The Sais will have to work very hard to redefine their relationships and to foster reconciliation through healing, repentance, and forgiveness. The narrative suggests possibilities of restoration through an exploration of symbols and images.

Precarity in the migrant's experience is not limited to Kweku. It is also manifested in Taiwo's psychological trauma after the abrupt departure of her father to Ghana. The trauma is evident in both her isolation and the longing for a father figure, a desire that leads to the scandalous affair with her dean. While Taiwo struggles with the trauma of separation, Sadie is troubled by her family's apparent lack of historical roots that can define cultural

---

20   Selasi, *Ghana Must Go*, 91.

CHALLENGES TO REINTEGRATION 139

identity. Of particular importance is this comparison she makes with the rich American family of Philae, her friend:

> Philae's family is *heavy*, a solid thing, weighted, perhaps by the money, an anchor of sorts? It holds them together, the wealth, Sadie sees this, it makes them invested in one solid thing and so *keeps* them together. . . . It isn't only that her family is poorer by contrast that makes Sadie cling to the Negropontes as she does. *It is that they are weightless, the Sais, scattered five-some, a family without gravity, completely unbound. With nothing as heavy as money beneath them, all pulling them down to the same piece of earth, a vertical axis, nor roots spreading out underneath them, with no living grand-parent, no history, a horizontal—they've floated, have scattered, drifting out-ward, or inward, barely noticing when someone has slipped off the grid.*[21] (emphasis added)

Sadie's reference to the absence of an anchor for the migrant family—an anchor that will keep them firmly rooted to their environment and collec-tively around it—is telling. She points out the absence of cultural and his-torical roots as frames for defining and grounding identity. She laments the absence of roots spreading out underneath them, the absence of any living grandparent as a repository of history. The emphasis on the absence of cul-ture, community, and history as frames of reference for children born to African migrant parents indicates their struggle with their cultural heritage.

The family's isolation is not Sadie's alone. In moments with Kweku, Olu had been troubled by this same feeling of fragility in the family. He frowns at the thought that both of his parents "were furiously tightlipped on the subject of who their own parents had been" and "didn't have photos, such as Olu found lining the stairs of the homes of his classmates in school, faded, framed and important, generations of family, at which he'd stand staring."[22] From this realization, he would "tour their homes aching with longing, for lineage, for a sense of having descended from faces in frames. That his fam-ily was thin in the backbench was troubling; it seemed to suggest they were faking it, false."[23] Olu's longing for a family with an ancestry, culture, and history that are visible and relatable is also Sadie's wish.

The dysfunction in the family is perhaps best reflected in the relationship between the twins, Taiwo and Kehinde. In some ways, this spirals into the tensions between Taiwo and Fola. At an early age, Taiwo had a disturbing suspicion that Fola preferred the male twin, Kehinde, to her. She ponders on the thought that Fola's letting go of Taiwo as Fola fell down the stairs while

---

21 Selasi, *Ghana Must Go*, 146–47.
22 Selasi, *Ghana Must Go*, 251.
23 Selasi, *Ghana Must Go*, 251.

holding on to Kehinde was not by accident. Taiwo sees this as a justification of her suspicion of her mother's preference for Kehinde. The fall suggests something on a broader scale—the separation and eventual fragmentation of the family. It leads to their departure for Lagos where they stay at the residence of Uncle Femi, Fola's brother. It is symbolically evident from the fall that Fola cannot take care of both children single-handedly and that she would need help to do so.

Unfortunately, the stay at Uncle Femi's turns out to be a disaster, for he is not only a drug dealer with a shady lifestyle; he is also immoral and criminal, especially after he goads Kehinde to have sexual intercourse with his twin sister. The trauma resulting from this incident is profound. The twins struggle to keep it a secret, and the psychological toll it takes on Taiwo is discernible in her outbursts of rage, while Kehinde uses art as therapy and a coping mechanism. Selasi describes Taiwo's anger as "the rage without name: that she sent them away, that she shipped them to Lagos when she should have known better, when she must have known somehow what would happen, who he was, her own brother, her own family. For the cost of tuition. The thought in the open. That mothers betray."[24]

Kweku's story highlights three important themes: the meanings of home, success, and return. The narrative affirms evidence of trauma stemming from his displacement and struggle for reintegration upon return. Kweku's circumstances in Boston and his return conflate identity with home, at least for migrants of his generation. Ghana will always be home to Kweku, and his identity is firmly rooted in that cultural space. While this might not be true for Olu, Kehinde, Taiwo, and Sadie, I argue that Ghana is better suited to them—despite the cultural adjustments and mental shifts that they would be required to make—than the challenges posed by their otherness in America. This perspective does not gloss over the fact that return has its limitations and setbacks. However, Sadie's experience with Ghanaian culture at the end of the novel suggests the possibility of cultural hybridity. In this way, it offers an alternative to their displacement and their integration into Ghanaian culture.

Notwithstanding, the plot of the novel makes explicit the difficulties to reintegration. Kweku's life in Ghana upon his return suggests that returned migrants might not even successfully reintegrate into their former society. The novel stresses that reintegration comes at a cost, perhaps at the cost of Kweku's life. His story validates the claim that return is fraught with indeterminacy, anchored in uncertainties and ambivalences. Kweku's death can be interpreted as a warning against return and could imply that the risks to reintegration are too high. Throughout the novel, however, Selasi explores the

---

24 Selasi, *Ghana Must Go*, 274.

juxtaposition of nuanced benefits and challenges to migration. Through the characters and roles of Kweku and Sadie, the reader understands that despite their displacements, the migrant character is still faced with possibilities in the process of migration, whether it be an integration into a new culture and space or the reintegration into a place that was once familiar. Sadie's perception of Ghana as mentioned suggests possibilities of cultural hybridity. It is important to note that this possibility comes after the death of Kweku. It is through Kweku's death that Sadie comes to embrace her body, a symbolic acceptance of her cultural heritage and ethnicity, and affirms her embrace of African culture. Her Black body eventually finds a place in an African space, unlike in white American spaces where that body is stigmatized and rejected.

Apart from Sadie's acceptance of Ghanaian culture, Kweku's relationship with Ama, the woman he marries upon his return to Ghana, shows possibilities for reconciliation. First, it ironically shows the emotional deficiencies with his family in the United States. Selasi notes that "he is gentle [to Ama] in a way that he wasn't with Fola. Not that he was brutish with Fola. But this is different. . . . The hours he worked were an expression of his affection, in direct proportion to keeping them well."[25] Second, it is in Ghana that we come to see Kweku's tender side on full display. Ama and Ghana offer him an alternative medium for the expression of his affection, and this is expressed in time spent with his family.

Selasi's use of symbols also suggests benefits to return. Kweku returns to Ghana and builds his life around his absent family even as he has deserted them. One such symbol is the house he constructed under the supervision of the Ghanaian builder, Lamptey. Several interpretations have been offered in relation to the symbolism of the house. Grace Musila reads the construction of the house as an indication of failure, as it replicates in her view the history of Kweku's father's abandonment of his family and his weak attempt to substitute family love with material design. She sets up the foundation for her argument in this way: "For Kweku Sai, his life's dream has been to bridge the gap between the life of his mother and the life of the US and its promise of success; and to be a different father to his children compared to his own father, who walked out on his family, leaving behind only his signature artistic gesture—a beautiful, rather eccentrically designed thatch hut."[26] Musila concludes: "That after abandoning his family in the US Kweku Sai returns to Ghana where he builds an equally eccentric house, at whose doorstep he dies of a heart attack, *is the heartbreaking irony at the center of the book*"[27] (emphasis added).

---

25 Selasi, *Ghana Must Go*, 46.

26 Musila, "Unoka's, Okonkwo's and Ezeulu's Grandsons," 94.

27 Musila, "Unoka's, Okonkwo's and Ezeulu's Grandsons," 94.

142 & CHAPTER FIVE

Viewed in terms of the replication of the action of the previous generation in the next, the basis of Musila's position in defining Kweku and Yosef in Dinaw Mengestu's *How to Read the Air* as grandsons of Unoka and Ezeulu, allows for too restrictive a frame to explore the layered and multifaceted meanings associated with the construction of such a complex symbol in the lives of not only Kweku but also that of his entire family who returned to Ghana after his death. I agree with Dustin Crowley that the "house, itself, then, acts as a physical embodiment of the cultural and relational bridge Kweku yearns for, a reflection of multiple places in one space, being 'at home' in multiple places simultaneously."[28] This interpretation is consistent with Crowley's earlier postulate: "All the characters yearn for what Kweku articulates early in the novel: a way to build a bridge 'between worlds,' to connect 'a modern thing entirely and a product of there, North America, snow, cow products' with 'an ancient thing, a product of here, hut, heat, raffia, West Africa.'"[29] This is the beginning of Selasi's articulation of the concept of the new hybridity, a hybridized identity consisting of an American design made manifest and revised in an African cultural space.

I read the symbolism of the house in connection to Kweku's return. First, his return provides the opportunity for the building of the house. It should be noted that the architectural design of the house was drawn by Kweku while he was in medical school in America. The house therefore has the imprints of American society and the life he aspires to live with his family. The house has room for all the family members and, as mentioned, a clear and symbolic reflection of the many rooms in his heart for each family member. This is why despite the advice of Lamptey, Kweku insists on keeping the design intact. He will not accept any alteration or modification to the design for that would imply a revision of his love for his family. However, the house is built by a Ghanaian contractor and in Ghana, not in the United States, where the design was initially conceptualized. If the construction of the house in Ghana is interpreted as the accomplishment of the dream, then it is crucial to the argument of return that the dream be fully experienced in the migrant's country of origin. The fact that the construction work is done by a Ghanaian suggests that, while the construction is conceptualized abroad, its implementation is to be done back home. This perspective allows for the transplanting of the design into the cultural context of Ghana and through the expertise of a local architect and engineer. In Kweku's situation, where racism prevents the full experience of his achievements, the symbolic implication of the house built in Ghana offers a more productive, and possibly a more guaranteed, way of implementing the dream. While the design

---

28   Crowley, "How Did They Come to This?," 131.
29   Crowley, "How Did They Come to This?," 130.

CHALLENGES TO REINTEGRATION 143

can be architecturally conceptualized abroad, its manifestation and impact are better experienced back home. In this way, the house depicts a cultural hybrid of the Western experience and its rootedness in Ghanaian culture. This is the new hybridity that offers the returned migrant cultural hybridity.

It is evident that Kweku's house is symbolic of his love for his family and the accomplishment of his version of the dream. The living room has ample space for all of his children, and each room represents a place in his heart for each of them. More importantly, within the courtyard in the middle of the house is a fountain. Inside the fountain is "the statue still standing, the 'mother of twins,' *iya-ibeji*, once a gift for his ex-wife Folasadé."[30] The symbolism is clear: he places Fola in the middle of his life, recognizes her position as mother of the twins, and places the statue in the fountain where its cleansing water will wash away the pain and guilt of the past. In fact, as the relationship with Ama unfolds, the narrative suggests that his love for Ama is an emotional projection of his love for Fola. He likes Ama because she looks like Fola and, through Ama, he reminisces on Fola's positive characteristics that he used to love and continues to love about her. Even before his death, he has made peace with Fola and himself.

Significantly, on the morning of his death, when he falls in the lawn and across the garden, Kweku realizes that he is going to die. He comes to this realization as he sees the "dewdrops on grass blades like diamonds flung freely from the pouch of some sprite-god who'd just happened by, stepping lightly and lithely through Kweku Sai's garden just moments before Kweku arrives there himself."[31] He admires the beauty around him and what he has built before he "stops on the threshold and stares at this, breathless, his shoulder against the sliding door, halfway slid open. He thinks to himself, with a pang in his chest, that the world is too beautiful sometimes."[32] Kweku feels the pain in his chest and has time to save himself by calling his wife for help. Instead, he uses his last minutes alive to admire the beauty around him and compares it to the beauty of his wife and children that he left in America. His death seems bleak at first, but upon close reading, Selasi notes that just before he dies, "he lies here facedown with a smile on his face."[33] Kweku dies a happy man, reconnected to his family through memory and expression of forgiveness, love, and reconciliation through the house and the garden. Importantly, at the end of the novel, Fola contemplates spreading Kweku's ashes in the ocean: "She had it in mind to toss his ash to the sea breeze, to let the man free, end at the beginning and

---

30 Selasi, *Ghana Must Go*, 9.
31 Selasi, *Ghana Must Go*, 8.
32 Selasi, *Ghana Must Go*, 9.
33 Selasi, *Ghana Must Go*, 92.

144   & CHAPTER FIVE

that. But now as she twists off the top, she can't do it. The idea of him scattered seems wrong in some way. *We've been scattered enough*, she thinks. Broken pots, fragments. *Keep him inside*, she thinks, *let him stay whole*"[34] (emphasis added). Fola comes to reconcile with Kweku and pledges to keep the family together through the symbolic ashes kept inside the jar. At this point, something crucial happens: she places the jar in the ocean expecting it to be washed away by the current, but it stays on the shoreline for a long time. Even in death, Kweku's ashes are reluctant to leave his home and the reunion with his family. He still longs to remain in Ghana and feels that the return to his homeland was worth it.

In addition, Kweku's return provides a pathway for healing; his death offers his family an incredibly meaningful interaction in a space and at a time that could not have been possible in America. And so, while Kweku is unable to return to Ghana with his family, he is able to bring them together both emotionally and physically in death. Sadie in particular embraces her Ghanaian ethnicity in ways that she would never have been able to in America. The children are in a situation where they are forced to interact with each other and to reflect on the past in previously unimaginable ways. In coming to Ghana, Kweku's family is in a better position to understand the choices he made and the reasons behind those choices. Just as he hides the physical effects of his work—by covering the callouses on his feet with the many slippers he keeps—Kweku hides his struggles to financially provide for his family after his dismissal from the hospital by unilaterally making the decision to return to Ghana. Leaving his family behind was a big blow to him and bringing them closer in death implies the creation of a legacy by which his children would come to understand his culture, their ancestry, and embrace it. Kweku's life demonstrates that return migration has its possibilities.

The reconciliation of the children is also a consequence of his return. In coming to Ghana, the children find themselves in a position where reconciliation is possible. Taiwo is back in a place, similar to Nigeria, that caused her so much pain and accounted for the rift between her and Kehinde, her twin brother. She has to forgive her brother and mother and allow them back into her life. The opportunity for mother and daughter to have an honest conversation at the end of the novel is indicative of the extension of grace and forgiveness to one another and signifies the transformative import of the situation. Both mother and daughter pledge to move forward after coming to terms with the pains of the past and the need to let go of them. As Taiwo pleads to Fola in her embrace of her mother, she repeats, "Don't let me go

---

34   Selasi, *Ghana Must Go*, 314.

CHALLENGES TO REINTEGRATION   145

yet, please don't let me go,"[35] a demonstration of their reconciliation and mutual forgiveness.

For Kehinde, the pain of living with the guilt that he hurt his sister is overwhelming: he was tricked by Uncle Femi into having sexual intercourse with her, despite his intention to save her from being assaulted by a drugged-up guard. In art, he finds a way of working through his trauma and lives in seclusion, away from his siblings, for a good part of his adult life. In Ghana, Kehinde witnesses firsthand the traumatic effect of the incident on Taiwo, and in a moment of closeness with each other while in bed, "He kisses her hands and he whispers, 'Forgive me.'"[36] Olu and his wife, Ling, also find themselves in a situation where they are forced to interact and address the sticking point in their marriage—the racism of Ling's father and its effect on Olu. At the end of the trip, Olu and Ling are in a much better frame of mind and have revised the basis on which their love and marriage is grounded: love for each other and their child.

Sadie's experience in Ghana is perhaps the most meaningful and therefore deserves particular critical attention. Her experience in America suggests her dissatisfaction with America's perception of otherness, especially the Black body. Her dissatisfaction illustrates a desire for authenticity and appreciation of her cultural identity. These are two elements of her life that she believes are critical to her sense of being human and her acceptance in the community. The place of the Black body in society and an understanding of the position in that place that it occupies are crucial to belonging. Accordingly, Sadie will be the most affected by exposure to a culture where the Black body and its significations are read in ways other than stigmatization. Cultural hybridization is open to Sadie, and the contrasting experience she receives in Ghana solidifies that desire.

When we meet Sadie in the narrative, she is clearly dissatisfied with her family's pretensions to happiness. She is weary of pretending to live as a family and pretending to enjoy Christmas. Sadie has come to realize that life in Boston is performative, an act of pretense that belies the reality of their circumstance as outsiders. She perceives the unsettling contradictions in her family's attempts to reconcile two seemingly conflicting cultures and comes to acknowledge the idea that "the beach and the sun and the boats smack of falseness, the truth in the open, that the whole thing's a sham, roasting chestnuts and sleigh bells, her greatest fear realized: she *doesn't* belong [emphasis added]. But isn't meant to. Not here."[37] It is evident that Sadie is insecure and angry over the circumstances surrounding the disruptions in

---

35   Selasi, *Ghana Must Go*, 292.

36   Selasi, *Ghana Must Go*, 309.

37   Selasi, *Ghana Must Go*, 158.

146 &❧ CHAPTER FIVE

her family, and she seeks an alternative in the family of her rich, American friend, Philae. We learn that Sadie "wants to be Philae. Rather, a part of Philae's family, of the Frick Negropontes, of their pictures on the wall along their stairs on the Cape, mother Sibby, sister Calli, father Andreas, of their photos on the Internet."[38] Further, she feels rejected by her own family for her closeness to white culture. Taiwo mocks her for speaking like Philae, "overusing *whatever* and *like*, or for dressing like Philae, monthly stipend permitting—by saying she, Sadie, secretly wants to be white."[39] Her confusion surrounding race and identity is revealed when Selasi states, "For all the hoopla about race, authentic blackness (which, as far as she's concerned, confuses identity and musical preference), it is obvious to Sadie that all of them carry this patina of whiteness. . . . They are ethnically heterogeneous and culturally homogeneous."[40]

As previously mentioned, compounding this sense of peripheral existence is Sadie's lack of appreciation of her body. She hates her body and is described in this way: "Her eyes are too small and her nose is too round and she hasn't got cheekbones like Taiwo or Philae, nor long slender limbs nor a clean chiseled jaw nor a dipping-in waist nor a jutting-out clavicle. She's five foot four, solid, not fat per se, stocky, pale milky-tea skin, number-four-colored hair, neither tall nor petite, with no edges, no angles; she looks like a doll, one she wouldn't have wanted."[41] The African features of her body are clearly depicted here, and in the context of a society where these features are sharply contrasted and, by implication, undervalued with the Caucasian bodily features of the white woman, Sadie feels the weight of exclusion. Her struggles with her body are her attempt to fit her bodily features into a schema that considers them outside the accepted standards of beauty.

In Ghana, she is introduced to the rhythms of African drumming and dance, and this provides the pathway for cultural hybridity and integration. Toward the end of the novel, Sadie watches a performance of an African dance. She sees it as beautiful, moving, and calming. She is fascinated by the choreography of the dance and its rhythmic quality, which seems to unify the dancers. At one point in the dance, a small chubby girl goes out to do a solo, and Sadie mentions that "she doesn't have the look of a dancer."[42] The reader immediately recognizes the cultural baggage that Sadie brings to Ghana. She is beginning to critique the body of the dancer through the Western images of beauty with which she is acquainted in the United States.

---

38 Selasi, *Ghana Must Go*, 146.
39 Selasi, *Ghana Must Go*, 145–46.
40 Selasi, *Ghana Must Go*, 146.
41 Selasi, *Ghana Must Go*, 265.
42 Selasi, *Ghana Must Go*, 267.

CHALLENGES TO REINTEGRATION   147

Her own insecurities about her body resurface. This is the first and potential barrier to Sadie's integration: the fear of trying to conform to a culture outside of whose norms she was raised and the anxiety of whether she will be accepted in that culture. Two things happen from this point: Sadie shows contempt for the dancer, but then she accepts the fact that the girl's body resembles her own. Sadie's struggle to make sense of the moment is reflected in her shifting perception of and attitude to the dancer. She then "considers the dancer with something like sadness, for both of them, a sadness made soft by acceptance."[43] At this point, Sadie has now conflated the identity of the dancer with her own bodily image and the sadness of exclusion she feels within her own family with what she assumed would be the sadness of the dancer over her supposed exclusion from the other dancers. However, as the girl begins to dance, Sadie notices that she dances beautifully, moving "in time to syncopation that only she hears."[44] The concept of syncopation is critically important here. The girl is not dancing in the same rhythm as the others. She dances to syncopation, to a different beat than the others. In that musical space she is comfortable, productive, beautiful, and accepted as part of the rhythm of the dance. The girl's syncopation is Sadie's as well. As an American of Ghanaian descent, she will dance to a different cultural syncopation but one that is nonetheless beautiful, productive, and meaningful for the collective rhythm of the dance. This is the syncopation of Sadie and the pathway to cultural hybridity and integration. Even though Sadie brings a different rhythm to the dance, it is a meaningful and productive one that is culturally enriching and liberating for dancers on both sides of the spectrum. Accordingly, when the drumming stops, the girl asks Sadie to dance. This is a symbolic initiation and an acceptance into the culture, a rite of passage into her Ghanaian ethnicity and ancestry.

Initially, Sadie is hesitant and misconstrues the girl's intentions. Sadie is also burdened by the psychological baggage regarding her body that she carries. With the encouragement of her siblings, who are "watching her with what looks like a mixture of worry and encouragement, their eyes and smiles wide, as if watching a baby trying to learn how to walk, ready to spring to their feet when she falls," Sadie accepts the girl's invitation and steps into the dance.[45] This is the first time she appreciates her body as something beautiful. The narrative describes her efforts in this way: "She is moving, not looking, afraid to stop moving, afraid to look up at the small cheering crowd, she is moving, she is sweating, she is crying . . . she is outside her body or in it, inside it, unaware of the exterior, unaware of the skin, unaware of the eyes,

---

43   Selasi, *Ghana Must Go*, 268.

44   Selasi, *Ghana Must Go*, 268,

45   Selasi, *Ghana Must Go*, 269.

148 ❧ CHAPTER FIVE

unaware of the onlookers, aware of the pounding, aware of the drum."[46] When the dance ends, Sadie is thrilled by the applause and recognition of the other dancers: "The children resume clapping and cheering in Ga, the chubby dancer, 'My Sees-tah!"[47] This is evidence symbolically of cultural baptism and rite of passage into Ghanaian culture. It shows Sadie's acceptance into the culture. The dance further solidifies the relationship between mother and daughter as Fola "leaps up from the bench to embrace [Sadie] as if she has just run a footrace and won."[48] Then, "Sadie, overcome by belated self-consciousness now that she's stopped and can feel warm eyes, lets her mother embrace her, her heart pounding wildly for, among other things, joy."[49]

Using spatial theory, I argue that Sadie has come to recognize the connections between body and space, between space and identity in terms of how space defines bodies. She recognizes that space has the potential to accept or reject bodies and their place in society. In this formulation, the Black body occupies a meaningful place in African cultural spaces, and the black Afropolitan body has the potential to reclaim its African identity and heritage. The Black body in this space is accepted as belonging to society, and this confirms its integration into the culture. Sadie bridges the cultural gap between the Afropolitans and their African heritage and, in so doing, indicates that hybridity is an attractive alternative to children of African descent in the diaspora. Instinctively, in her encounter with one of her aunts, the woman grabs Sadie by the hand and says, "'Ekua,' she repeats. 'Sister Ekua. It's you.'"[50] She is identified as the reincarnation of one of the elders in the clan. Sadie is neither alien nor stranger. She is a returned relative wholly welcomed into the tribe. Her blend of both identities affirms the blending of her experience in America and her African heritage to create a new hybridity that is meaningful to both Africans and peoples of African descent in the diaspora. As Fola intimates, she sees hope in the possibility of her children embracing their ancestry. She captures this belief in her statement, "We learned to love. Let them learn how to stay."[51]

Dustin Crowley sees the events surrounding the dance as Sadie's discovery of her body's place in the cultural matrices of the African environment, a moment of reconnecting with her father that ushers the much-needed resolution of conflicts in the family and engenders a move toward reconciliation.

---

46 Selasi, *Ghana Must Go*, 270.
47 Selasi, *Ghana Must Go*, 270.
48 Selasi, *Ghana Must Go*, 270.
49 Selasi, *Ghana Must Go*, 270.
50 Selasi, *Ghana Must Go*, 263.
51 Selasi, *Ghana Must Go*, 6.

In discovering this new image of her body and its place in the Ghanaian cultural setting, Crowley notes that "Sadie, who always felt that she lacked the family trait of attractiveness, meets relatives with whom she bears a striking resemblance, 'the same solid body she has.'"[52] More importantly, she discovers that the short and chubby body she has always hated is capable of dancing; it is "a stranger inside her that knows what to do, knows this music, these movements, this footwork, this rhythm," which gives her a sense of "joy," "triumph," and acceptance she has never before experienced."[53] The rejected black body in white American standards of beauty has found a home in black Ghanaian cultural space. As Phiri says along the lines of acceptance, "It is telling that the ritualised self-disciplined body is reinterpreted into the dancing, performing body, into an affirmative, even emancipatory cultural vehicle—of West African orientation."[54]

Fola's reconciliation with Taiwo is another aspect of the reintegration process. At the scene on the beach, Selasi suggests the reconciliation of mother and daughter. However, the trauma could not be erased: "She wants to make Taiwo stop crying. But can't. All she can do is stand weeping with Taiwo alone on this beach in the bearing down heat, knowing someone has damaged her children irreparably, unable to fix it. Able only to hold."[55] With Taiwo holding tightly on to her mother, gripping her waist, and crying, "Don't let me go yet, please don't let me go,"[56] Selasi highlights both the trauma and the possibility for reconciliation. Interestingly, Fola sees trauma as irreparably damaging. While this indicates her perception of the depth of the injury to her children, Selasi does not endorse this view of trauma because in the moment of reconciliation depicted here, she points out the path to healing. It is in the same context that Kehinde's art can be interpreted—a therapeutic mechanism of coping with the trauma but also a pathway to healing. The death of their father offers both of them the space and moment for reflection and introspection. From this reflection, the twins are able to extend grace, mercy, and forgiveness to each other. As Selasi points out, Kehinde, while staring at his sleeping sister, "sits on the bed by his sister. He smoothes down her dreadlocks, a tangle of snakes. He kisses her hands and he whispers, 'Forgive me.'"[57] In turn, Taiwo watches Kehinde as

---

52   Crowley, "How Did They Come to This?," 267.
53   Crowley, "How Did They Come to This?," 270.
54   Phiri, "Lost in Translation," 152.
55   Selasi, *Ghana Must Go*, 291.
56   Selasi, *Ghana Must Go*, 292.
57   Selasi, *Ghana Must Go*, 309.

150 ❧ CHAPTER FIVE

he is sleeping. She "stands there and stares at his face until she sees it, fifteen seconds and not longer. A smile in his sleep."[58]

Return is not devoid of complications. Each member of the Sai family struggles individually with distinct challenges upon arrival in Ghana, and Fola exhibits in unique ways some of the obstacles to reintegration into a once familiar but transformed culture. From the first days of her arrival in Ghana, tensions emerge between her and the servants in Kweku's household. To them, Fola realizes that "she is a woman, first; unmarried, worse; a Nigerian, worst; and fair-skinned. As suspicious persons go in Ghana, she might as well be a known terrorist."[59] The Ghanaians around her bristle at everything, from her accent to her habits of smoking and wearing shorts in public. An evident misconception of the norms and values of each side begins to play out:

> That she wanders around the garden in these shorts and a sun hat with cigarettes and clippers, snipping this, snipping that, hauling her catch into the kitchen, where she stands at the counter, not pounding yam, not shelling beans, but arranging flowers. It amuses her, always has, this disregard of Africans for flowers, the indifference of the abundantly blessed (or psychologically battered—the chronic self-loather who can't accept, even with evidence, that everything native to him, occurring in abundance, in excess, without effort, has value). They watch as research scientists observe a new species, a hybrid, herbivorous, likely harmless, maybe not.[60]

While this raises the possibility of exclusion from the members of the community, Fola takes intentional steps to build interpersonal bridges. This posture of intentionality is most evident in kindness to Ama at the end of the novel. She invites Ama not only to their home but into their grieving as well. Fola invites her to the celebration of Kweku's life, and Ama responds with the simple but profound gesture of returning Kweku's slippers. This exchange represents the potential for new levels of connection and harmony. By the end of the novel, Fola has not only achieved a deeper awareness of peace within herself but has also found hope in the possibility that her children might learn to adapt to both in the physical places they call home and in the security of relational stability. In the imaginative conversation she has with Kweku in the final pages of the novel, she tells him: "They're here. . . . I got what I wanted. You sent them all home. They're all here for Christmas."[61] In the final gesture of reconciliation and hope, "she picks up

---

58 Selasi, *Ghana Must Go*, 310.
59 Selasi, *Ghana Must Go*, 100.
60 Selasi, *Ghana Must Go*, 101.
61 Selasi, *Ghana Must Go*, 317.

CHALLENGES TO REINTEGRATION &❧ 151

his [Kweku's] slippers and brings them inside."[62] Through Fola's experience in Ghana, Selasi shows that returning to the homeland, ancestral or immediate, holds potential for both grief and hope. She demonstrates that reintegration can occur at several levels and need not be the same experience for every returned migrant. For Fola, reintegration is a consequence of the deliberate choices she made, in the gesture of compassion for Ama and the rejection of the potential for rivalry and conflict between them, made explicit in the symbolism of her acceptance of Kweku's slippers from Ama.

The title of the novel is a throwback to regional migration in Africa and the disastrous consequences that can result from it. While it places the theme of migration at the core of the novel, the title suggests that the complications of migration are not unique to the international dimension and that crossing regional borders within the African continent also has its implications. Selasi points out the expulsion of Ghanaians from Lagos in 1983 under "Ghana Must Go," which led to the "Nigerian government's summarily deporting two million Ghanaians" to begin life from scratch in Accra.[63] This expulsion and abrupt departure of Ghanaians in Lagos is used as a frame to explore the wrongful departure and dismissal of Kweku from Beth Israel Hospital and his abrupt departure from America, given the government's blacklisting of him and his professional practice. Whether in a regional or international context, the novel demonstrates that migration has the potential to leave deep traumatic scars in the lives of migrants, including their children born outside of the migrants' countries of origin. However, a return to the homeland, as tricky and unpredictable as it may seem, has the capacity, through cultural and social adjustments, for healing and reconciliation.

---

62   Selasi, *Ghana Must Go*, 318.
63   Selasi, *Ghana Must Go*, 237.

Chapter Six

The New Hybridity

Chimamanda Ngozi Adichie's *Americanah* continues the exploration of the complications of return to the migrant's homeland. The novel instantiates the possibilities that return migration affords both the returned migrants and the society to which they returned. The chapter predicates this possibility on the construct of the new hybridity that argues for a fusion of the migrant's experience abroad with the potential for transformation at home. I argue that when the worldliness of the returned migrant is combined with the transformative potential of the homeland, return is meaningful, even if complicated.

Americanah is crucial for my argument of return because it explores all three phases of the migration process—flight, arrival, and return. I focus on the otherness of the migrant to analyze the challenges to African migration as justification for return. This chapter has two main parts. In the first, I examine precarity as a necessary reason for return by analyzing the experiences of Ifemelu and Obinze in America and Nigeria, respectively. In the second, I assess their successes upon return through exploring the construct of the new hybridity, while also pointing out the challenges. Return makes possible the construction of a hybridized identity that is crucial to transforming individuals and society. I also include sections of the novel for examination where integration encounters obstacles and barriers.

The novel opens with Ifemelu's experiences as a resident writer on a fellowship at Princeton University in New Jersey. She is also an active blogger whose posts unveil controversial perspectives of life in America, especially relating to race, gender, and class. From the outset, Ifemelu focuses on the exclusion of the migrant. The alienation, amplified by and through simple everyday tasks like the braiding of hair, is one of the challenges African migrants must confront. The reader's first sense of the migrant's situation is noted in Ifemelu's train journey to Trenton in search of a salon that braids black hair. Maximilian Feldner notes the connections between hair as indicator of social identity and its racialization in the United States. Feldner asserts that hairstyle has serious implications for perception of the African migrant female, both in terms of its exotic attraction to society and its potential for exclusion.[1] Ifemelu comes to realize kinky hair can be perceived as unprofessional for employment. The association of hairstyle with racial and sexual implications has potential for both cultural erasure and cultural exclusion. In the early sections of the novel, it can be argued that the absence of such a salon in Princeton deepens the view that African migrants will have to contend with social exclusion in that city.

Ava Landry points out the link between racial identity and power and the role of racial categories in enhancing white hegemony. Describing the African immigrant as the "Ethnicized Other," she affirms that in "racialized societies such as the United States, superordinate races construct racial structures composed of relations, practices, and ideologies to create and maintain their differential possession of and access to material benefits."[2] She further elaborates on the relational and contingent status of whiteness and Blackness by noting that "the imposition of a perceived inferior racial identity on the African immigrant engenders complex implications of how African immigrants view themselves and are viewed by others when entering the United States."[3] As an ethnicized other, African migrants find their differences predicated on social dichotomies along ethnic lines. The migrant has to work toward understanding what it means to be Black in America.

Dina Yerima and Jana Fedtke also extend the conversation on hair, racial identity, and the aesthetics by which social standards are measured. Fedtke suggests that, through Ifemelu's blog posts, Adichie intentionally explores intersections between race, class, gender, and politics in the novel. Using the hair texture of African migrant women, she showcases how Western standards of beauty contribute to the othering of migrant women of color and foster their alienation in society. Racism is embedded in the construction of otherness, and beauty standards are one means of expressing this othering of Black people. In similar ways, Yerima examines the ever-imposing influence of beauty standards in Western culture and its relation to hair texture, skin color, and identity of non-Caucasian migrant women. She uses these social markers as a way of correlating "imperial aesthetics" to race and racism,[4] and calls attention to the struggles of others deemed outside or below those standards of beauty. Negotiating the implications of prejudiced notions of identity imposed on them is the burden of African women migrants in the diaspora.

The question of identity is thus crucial to the success of the African migrant in the diaspora. The notions of an ethnicized and racialized other

---

1   Feldner, *Narrating the New African Diaspora*, 188.

2   Landry, "Black Is Black Is Black?," 129.

3   Landry, "Black Is Black Is Black?," 129.

4   Fedtke, "'Racial Disorder Syndrome,'" 59–64.

154 ❧ CHAPTER SIX

make possible the relegation of Black people to the lower strata of the social order. Rose Sackeyfio recognizes the power of racial identity in the subjugation of the migrant when she notes: "Within a postmodern framework these ideas overshadow the realities of African migrant women today as expressed in the fiction of third-generation writers who create compelling works of diasporic expression that foregrounds perceptions of identity."[5] She asserts that "race, class, and gender mediate and reposition African women's experiences and those evolving realities confound self-definition from African cultural traditions in women's creative works."[6] Hence, *Americanah* is "a vivid rendering of the ways in which African immigrants are forced to negotiate the politics of race and identity as they encounter America's obsession with blackness as the legacy of slavery and distorted perceptions of 'racial other.'"[7]

Accordingly, on Ifemelu's rail journey to Trenton, she observes the social and geographical landscapes the train passes through and the social status of the passengers it reveals at every stop. While it links different geographical spaces, the train also unveils social and class disparities between people who board the train in the various sections of the city. The revelation is an indication of social, economic, and racial disparities. Ifemelu's experience deepens her sense of isolation, and it is evident that the exclusion triggers memories of home and nostalgia. She points out that the weight of the difficulties the migrant experiences is like "cement in the soul."[8] This constitutes disillusionment and creates a void that the migrant appears incapable of filling. Adichie describes Ifemelu's state of mind as "layer after layer of discontent [that] had settled on her" and compares her loneliness in America to "being content in a house but always sitting by the window and looking out."[9]

Ifemelu's discontent is typical of the experiences of migrants who, despite the comfort the country they migrate to offers, are always sitting by the window and looking out for something that's missing. The gaze outside the window is the yearning for the homeland, the longing to belong, a quality that the new environment, despite its very real comforts, cannot provide. The choice is between comfort and belonging, that is, between the need to be content with the comfort of the new home and the compelling desire to belong elsewhere. This relationship between the migrant and the host country becomes tenuous, as one will never be able to fulfill the expectations of the other.

---

5   Sackeyfio, *West African Women in the Diaspora*, 4.

6   Sackeyfio, *West African Women in the Diaspora*, 4.

7   Sackeyfio, *West African Women in the Diaspora*, 56.

8   Adichie, Americanah, 7.

9   Adichie, *Americanah*, 8–9.

Regarding return, it must be noted that *Americanah* follows the earlier literary tradition of West African migratory narratives of the returned been-tos to the continent after the completion of those studies, only to find they are no longer at ease with their homeland.[10] Ifemelu returns home to a barely recognizable Lagos, and her status as outsider is confirmed by her struggles to reintegrate into society. Feldner refers to this phase of disorientation as the "strange familiar" and highlights the confusion that comes with society's perception and expectations of the returned migrant.[11] The initial displacement of the returned migrant is part of the complications of return.

From the outset, Ifemelu's parents were apprehensive about her return. Adichie tells us of the response of Ifemelu's relatives and friends at the disclosure of her intentions to return: "Everyone she had told she was moving back seemed surprised, expecting an explanation, and when she said she was doing it because she wanted to, puzzled lines would appear on their foreheads."[12] At this point in the narrative, return is depicted as a struggle for reintegration into the home country. It is a question of whether, as Aunty Uju puts it, the migrant would be able to cope with the conditions back home. As Ifemelu notes, this view of the returned migrants is based on their perceived transformation in the West that seemingly conflicts with a narrative of continuing deteriorating circumstances at home. It is almost as if the migrants have changed so much that they have outgrown their native lands, and this transformation creates insurmountable challenges to reintegration upon return. The general impression is that "she was somehow irrevocably altered by America, had grown thorns on her skin."[13] The only redeeming aspect of her return is her parents' belief that since she now carries an American passport she has the ability to return to America whenever she chooses.

At the salon, Ifemelu watches as the braiding process unfolds. As she listens to the stories of the women, she is convinced of the rationality of her decision to return. Besides, as Ranyinudo, her schoolmate and friend in Lagos, has said: "Lagos is now full of American returnees, so you better come back and join them. Everyday you see them carrying a bottle of water as if they will die of heat if they are not drinking water every minute."[14] Ranyi's perspective is encouraging, but it also reveals that the returned

---

10   For a more detailed and comprehensive treatment of the been-tos in migratory narratives from West Africa, see William Lawson's *The Western Scar: The Theme of the Been-to in West African Fiction* (Athens: Ohio University Press, 1982).

11   Feldner, *Narrating the New African Diaspora*, 190.

12   Adichie, *Americanah*, 16.

13   Adichie, *Americanah*, 20.

14   Adichie, *Americanah*, 16.

156   ❧   CHAPTER SIX

migrant will have to go through a process of readjustment. Nonetheless, Ranyi points out that there has been a lot of progress back home, not only on the level of infrastructure but also in the lives of the people. Ranyi is now married, and Obinze, who had earlier returned from the United Kingdom, is also married and is living with his wife and daughter. He is now a wealthy real estate agent with tremendous influence in business circles. With money, a devoted wife, and a beautiful daughter, the implication is that Obinze is living the dream back home. Notwithstanding, Adichie does not gloss over the corruption in the country and its capacity to stifle growth and development. But even as she depicts the corruption, she also points out the progress that has been made. Such progress represents the possibilities for transformation of both migrants and society. Given the overlaps in the treatment of flight and the attention that I have already paid to this phase of migration in the other novels selected for study, I will focus on the experiences of Ifemelu and Obinze that necessitates return and the possibilities that come with that move.

The realities of life in Western societies are brought to light as early as Ifemelu's first impressions of New York City after she is picked up at the airport by Aunty Uju. The culture shock is profound and jarring in the reversal of her expectations of America. Her first impressions of New York City sharply contrast with the images of splendor she saw on American TV channels in Nigeria or in Obinze's romantic view of the United States obtained from reading fantasy novels. Ifemelu's shock at the spectacle of the boy urinating on one of the street corners en route from the airport is a clear indication that she has bought into a single story of America—the land of opportunities, abundance, and splendor. She never factored into her imagination the other America: that of dingy street corners where public urination is common. Later in the novel, as she struggles to seek employment and navigate the restrictions of the student visa while shouldering the unending pressure from home for financial assistance, she comes to realize the reality of life in the West, a reality predicated upon Western perceptions of otherness. The resulting depression is the experience of a host of characters examined in this book.

Augustine Nwanyanwu has examined the traumatic experiences of African migrants as they relate to social identity, racial otherness, and the failure of transculturalism to provide a basis for understanding difference. Exploring the relationship between the Caucasian American, African American, and African migrant, Nwanyanwu uses history, culture, and lived experiences to further conversations on the implications of otherness and Blackness and their role in shaping the American cultural landscape.[15] Adichie depicts the

---

15   Nwanyanwu, "Transculturation, Otherness, Exile, and Identity," 386–99.

THE NEW HYBRIDITY ❧ 157

struggles of her two main protagonists against this background of otherness at every phase of their journeys. Likewise, Karen Okigbo analyzes the traumatic experiences of African migrants as a consequence of race and racism in the migratory country. She examines Ifemelu's depression in the context of the racial stereotypes to which she is exposed and her struggle to make sense of the exclusion that comes with racial stratification in America.[16]

In this phase of the migrant's journey, Ifemelu has to deal with three fundamental issues: race and ethnicity, employment and work study, and the cost of living in America. From the outset, it is evident that Ifemelu had misunderstood the dynamics of life in America. In the same way that she had imagined the society as only "a cold place of wool and snow" and is not prepared for the sweltering heat of summer,[17] she is also not prepared for the shock of Aunty Uju living in a one-bedroom apartment in a rundown section of the city. Ifemelu is certainly astounded at the realization that, due to limited space, she will be sleeping on the floor. In disappointment, she understands that "this was glorious America at last, glorious America at last, and she had not expected to bed on the floor."[18] As she struggles to make sense of her new environment, she realizes that there is a bigger issue to contend with: race and racism in America. In Nigeria, race does not define people's existence. In America, she comes to recognize the racial categorization of people and the conflation of race and ethnicity with the humanity of the individual. She also realizes the socioeconomic limitations that living outside of the boundaries of accepted racial categories and configurations engenders. Categories such as Hispanics and Black carry social significance way beyond a people's origin to signify their place in the human spectrum and the social restrictions that come with belonging to the lower end of that spectrum. Racial positioning is linked to human essence. As she writes later in one of her blogs: "Hispanic means the frequent companions of American blacks in poverty rankings, Hispanic means a slight step above American blacks in the American race ladder."[19] To belong to or be placed in a certain racial category is to determine positionality—inside, outside, core, periphery—and the social and economic attractions that define those positions. Racial categories also embody stereotypes attached to them and determine human relationships. Such relationships can be characterized as other, different, scary, indolent, or disposable, each with its own precarity and vulnerability.

Similar to race, accent signifies much more than a linguistic marker of origin. Like Jojo Badu in *The Other Crucifix*, Ifemelu has to contend with the

---

16   Okigbo, "*Americanah* and *Ghana Must Go*," 444–48.
17   Adichie, *Americanah*, 127.
18   Adichie, *Americanah*, 130.
19   Adichie, *Americanah*, 129.

158 &❧ CHAPTER SIX

knowledge that speech patterns and pronunciation define a person's being and determine their position in society. Her encounter with Cristina Tomas, the receptionist at the front desk of the school, demonstrates racial otherness and the stereotypes associated with it. Tomes is so convinced of the limited mental capacities of international students that she has developed a strategic means of communicating with them—talking extremely slowly, pronouncing each word individually and with pauses in between. This, she believes, is the only way they can comprehend word usage in English. The prejudice is obvious—the outsider who is limited in mental ability to comprehend English but who also must be made aware of that limitation. The irony of the situation is that Ifemelu, like Jojo, comes from a former British colony where English is the second language. In making Ifemelu aware of her supposed limitation, Tomes is reinforcing the stereotype of their substandard education and implicitly questioning their admission into Western institutions, a similar perspective expressed in the *University Review* journal in *The Other Crucifix*.

Marlene Esplin examines the linguistic aspect of the migrant's experience in terms of the limits and possibilities of language use in society. Esplin demonstrates how linguistic flexibility can allow for a smoother transition and subsequent integration of migrant communities into the host country. Her argument is a reminder of the many borders that migrants from other parts of the world have to cross to integrate into Western societies.[20] Esplin stresses the transnational linguistic challenges migrants face and the pressure they feel to alter their linguistic identity. Jack Taylor also explores the intersections of language, race, and identity in the experience of African migrants abroad in both *Americanah* and *We Need New Names* to demonstrate their linguistic and social alienation.[21] This stereotype of otherness is a major cultural barrier the migrant has to transcend. Jojo Badu recognizes this in the op-ed published in the *University Review*. The connection between language and identity is noted, the reification of racial inferiority is evident, and its intersection with otherness is clear. The consequences are devastating to Ifemelu:

> Ifemelu shrank. In that strained, still second when her eyes met Cristina Tomas's before she took the forms, she shrank. She shrank like a dead leaf. She had spoken English all her life, led the debating society in secondary school, and always taught the American twang inchoate; she should not have caved and shrunk, but she did. And in the following weeks, as autumn's coolness descended, she began to practice an American accent.[22]

---

20 Esplin, "The Right Not to Translate," 73.
21 Taylor, "Language, Race, and Identity," 68–85.
22 Adichie, *Americanah*, 164.

The repetition of "shrank" in the excerpt points to the psychological toll stemming from the humiliation that Ifemelu faces. Tomas's refusal to recognize a different accent as normal is a deliberate strategy to point out to Ifemelu her otherness and humiliate her in the process. Given the connections to race, Tomas is using accent to reinforce racial superiority over the African.

Perhaps the most crucial aspect of race and ethnicity at this point in Ifemelu's journey is the social and cultural significance attached to hair in America. In the novel, hair texture and style indicate racial, regional, gender, and sexual identities. The African salon in Trenton is a space where racial identity is negotiated and affirmed, and hair texture becomes an ideological construct of identity. As previously mentioned, the journey to Trenton in search of an African salon reveals Ifemelu's status as an outsider in Princeton. The absence of salons that treat Black people's hair shows that Princeton excludes Black people from that space, socially and culturally. Thus displaced, or rendered out of place in that community, Ifemelu is forced to travel outside of that environment to a place where she feels accepted. Working with black hair points to the existence of a cultural space to which she has every potential of belonging. In the salon, she meets other migrants from sub-Saharan Africa, and in the ensuing conversations about life in America, she feels both a physical and psychological connection to that space. It is a place where the possibilities of reliving and reclaiming her Africanness can be realized. In this space, the conventional definition or standard of beauty as straight silky hair is replaced by the natural kinky or nappy hair. This replacement maps the path to the reclaiming of Ifemelu's cultural identity in America. The salon is a symbol of Black representation, and in its redefinition of beauty, it depicts possibilities for reinvention. As Ifemelu will demonstrate in her later blogs, the pride and value in being one's self through an embrace of cultural markers of identity like accent and hair texture are critical to her self-discovery and affirmation of her being.

Hair texture and style further illustrate racial identity and the limits to socioeconomic opportunities available to the migrant. Hairstyle will enhance or hinder career opportunities and, like one's accent, can be a barrier to achieving the dream. Ifemelu struggles with her appearance before the job interview; recognizing that the kinky hair could be perceived as unprofessional and therefore unacceptable in the workplace, she applies cosmetic products to her hair so it looks like a white woman's hair. This attempt at cultural transformation is indicative, first, of Ifemelu's desperation and, second and perhaps more importantly, the extent to which racial markers such as hair texture and accent can become insurmountable barriers to the migrant's progress. While it exposes the superficial nature of a society that values appearance over substance, it further indicates racial discrimination in

160 ᛒ CHAPTER SIX

the preference for the Caucasian over the Black woman's hair texture. The barriers that Ifemelu has to negotiate and the cultural boundaries she has to cross do not stem from an inability to accomplish the task at hand but rather come from the negative perceptions of her difference and America's racialization of those differences. Likewise, it is the racialization of Jojo's ethnic identity that almost precludes him from gainful employment at the completion of his studies.

The significance of racial identity to the migrant experience in America cannot go unnoticed. The identity crisis of Ginika, Ifemelu's friend from Nigeria, in America is another indication of the construction of racial identity in America and its significance. On first meeting Ginika in America a few years after their separation in Nigeria, Ifemelu is struck almost immediately by the change in her appearance. Her physical transformation into a slim, bony figure is stunning. Ginika has bought into the conventional standard of beauty in America of slim stature with straight hair. In a bid to avoid the stereotypes associated with her body, she adopts the image of the Caucasian woman. Feeling the need to transform her racial identity in order to fit in with society, she tells us that "now I say [I'm] biracial, and I'm supposed to be offended when somebody says [I'm] half-caste. I've met a lot of people here with white mothers and they are so full of issues, eh. I didn't know I was supposed to *have* issues until I came to America."[23] (Emphasis in the original.) Ginika comes to realize that being biracial in America is different than in Nigeria. Here, it is part of the othering process, an indication of the lukewarm disposition to interracial marriages in America. In desperation, Ifemelu transforms her hair to fit into the acceptable standard of straight hair.

Adichie makes it clear that race relations are not limited to interactions between Blacks and whites. She spends time exploring the relationships between Africans and African Americans in the novel. Similar to Benjamin Kwakye's exploration of the relationship between Jojo Badu and Norah Turner in *The Other Crucifix*, Adichie uses Ifemelu's relationship with her African American boyfriend, Blaine, to shed light on the divergent lived experiences of the two sets of people and the different perspectives they engender, regardless of a common ancestral heritage. Pede Hollist pursues a similar task in *So the Path Does Not Die* in his depiction of the Fina-Cammy and the Bayo-Aman relationships.

Adjusting to life in America is a huge task for Ifemelu. This process is made even more difficult by the perceptible changes in Aunty Uju and how migration is viewed by other African migrants like Bartholomew, her partner. The contrast between Aunty Uju's life in Nigeria and her current situation

---

23   Adichie, *Americanah*, 151.

in America is shocking. In America, Aunty Uju is under constant financial pressure to make ends meet. When she goes grocery shopping, she buys only goods on sale and others that come with perks such as "buy one, get one free," regardless of their quality. She is constantly on edge as she labors under the constraints of being a single parent while also striving to meet the needs of Bartholomew. Caught between traditional parenting and the modern American style of raising children, Aunty Uju acquiesces and reverts to the American style, raising Dike with the belief that these values are ideal for him. In this mindset, Ifemelu is told not speak pidgin or Yoruba to him, as these two languages will inhibit his acquisition of the English language. As Aunty Uju struggles to work three jobs, she loses her happiness and wears an abrasive personality. When she fails her medical exam, the effect is devastating. A gloom descends on her. Watching the slow disintegration of her aunt, Ifemelu cannot but contrast the present realities with how things seemed on the phone during her conversations with Aunty Uju. Ifemelu "has assumed, from Aunty Uju's calls home, that things were not too bad, although she realized now that Aunty Uju had always been vague, mentioning 'work' and 'exam' without details. . . . And she thought, watching her, how the old Aunty Uju would never have worn her hair in such scuffy braids. . . . *America had subdued her*"[24] (emphasis added). The contrast between the migrant's expectations and the reality of the situation upon arriving is arresting.

The ability of America to subdue the migrant and the resulting disillusionment are further demonstrated in the stories of the women at the African salon. From one story to the other, the women lament the amount of time they have spent in the country with little tangible evidence to show for it. Disappointment in love relationships, racism and exclusion, financial struggles, and a sense of loss run through the stories. The scene at the salon is reminiscent of that in Lagos, except that in this case, it is in a different country. Apart from that, the working conditions have not significantly changed.

If the story of the women at the salon and Aunty Uju's frustrations are reasons for reflection, Bartholomew adds to the picture of unrealized dreams. He is the symbol of the Americanah, particularly embodying its derogatory usage. He represents the African migrant or been-to who affects the lifestyle, speech patterns, and mannerisms of Americans in a bid to demonstrate what he sees as cultural refinement and a superior status. However, the joke is on him. Bartholomew's pretensions and overall characteristics serve as satirical commentary on the ridiculous attempt at cultural appropriation of supposed sophisticated Western standards and values. The irony exposes the gap between affectation and reality.

---

24   Adichie, *Americanah*, 135.

162   ❧   CHAPTER SIX

Bartholomew's depiction is worthy of comment. The narrative records: "Bartholomew wore khaki trousers pulled up high on his belly, and spoke with an American accent filled with holes, mangling words until they were impossible to understand. Ifemelu sensed, from his demeanor, a deprived rural upbringing that he tried to compensate for with his American affectation, his gonnas and wannas."[25] Later, Ifemelu defines him as an "exaggerated caricature" and notes that "he was one of those people who, in his village back home, would be called 'lost.' *He went to America and got lost*, his people would say. *He went to America and refused to come back*."[26] (Italics in the original.) Bartholomew is the epitome of pretentiousness and an indication of the frustrations that come with unfulfilled dreams. His pretensions, like those of Moki in *Blue White Red*, are deliberate and self-serving. Aunty Uju's efforts at belonging are based on affection and are debasing. Ifemelu is stunned by "the strange naïveté with which Aunty Uju had covered herself like a blanket. Sometimes, while having a conversation, it would occur to Ifemelu that Aunty Uju had deliberately left behind something of herself, something essential, in a distant and foreign place. Obinze said it was the exaggerated gratitude that came with immigrant insecurity."[27] Affectation and self-debasement expose Uju's struggles to belong. This struggle is not only Uju's but that of the other African characters as well. Hence, Bartholomew's affectation is also Ginika's—the conversion to an American lifestyle in order to conceal their cultural identity. Ginika's choice of food, clothing, and speech is also Bartholomew's "wannas" and "gonnas." The drive to embody the "cultural cues,"[28] as Ginika calls them, is reflective of the struggle to belong.

Ifemelu's search for employment marks a crucial stage in her journey. The agony of the wait, the overt racism confronted at job interviews, and the ignominy of the tasks she is asked to perform all point to the discrimination that migrants face abroad. Going through financial hardships, Ifemelu regularly consults newspapers for job ads. One such advertisement in the *City Paper* states: "*Strong Home Health Aide. Pays cash*."[29] (Italics in the original.) After questions about her accent and ability to lift a patient, Ifemelu is informed that the position is a live-in job and that the aide will be required to live in the house with the client, who will be in a separate bedroom, do three nights a week, and will "need to clean him up in the morning."[30]

---

25 Adichie, *Americanah*, 141–42.
26 Adichie, *Americanah*, 143.
27 Adichie, *Americanah*, 146–47.
28 Adichie, *Americanah*, 152.
29 Adichie, *Americanah*, 158.
30 Adichie, *Americanah*, 160.

THE NEW HYBRIDITY ❧ 163

The image of the BBCs (British Buttocks Cleaners) in Chikwava's *Harare North* is recalled, and once again, African migrants get the most demeaning jobs, those reserved for the undocumented. Even with this level of shame, Ifemelu is not considered fit for the job.

The next stop is a restaurant in the City Center where Wambui, Ifemelu's colleague from Uganda, works; Ifemelu applies as a waitress. In preparation for the job, she is advised by a colleague from Tanzania, Mwombeki, to delete her three years of university education in Nigeria as a way of boosting her chances. Despite her impressions that the interview went well and that she put on a good performance—wearing her nice shirt, smiling warmly, and shaking hands firmly—she is not offered the job. The manager calls to say that they had "decided to hire a more qualified person."[31] In desperation, she applies for a job in the *City Paper* ad that reads: "Female personal assistant for busy sports coach in Ardmore, communication and interpersonal skills required."[32] Upon arriving for an interview, the tennis coach says to her: "Look, you're not a kid. . . . I work so hard I can't sleep. I can't relax. I don't do drugs so I figured I need help to relax. You can give me a massage, help me relax, you know. I had somebody doing it before, but she's just moved to Pittsburgh. It's a great gig, at least she thought so. Helped her with a lot of her college debt."[33] In another instance, she "went to a gas station near Chestnut Street and a large Mexican man said, with his eyes on her chest, 'You're here for the attendant position? You can work for me in another way.' Then with a smile, the leer never leaving his eyes, he told her the job was taken."[34] On Ginika's recommendation, Ifemelu shows up for a conversation with Kimberly and her sister, Laura, in the hopes of getting a job as a babysitter. Under Laura's deep scrutiny and Kimberly's suffocating enthusiasm about Ifemelu's Black differences, she is happy to leave the house. Not surprisingly, she does not get the job, but Kimberly offers to "keep her in mind."[35] With the threat of default on her rent looming, Ifemelu thinks of working as an escort but decides against it. In defeat, she calls the sports coach and accepts the job. Work is to commence immediately. Before she leaves, she "shaved her underarms, dug out the lipstick she had not worn since the day she left Lagos."[36] When she arrives, the tennis coach requests that she keep him warm, adding that he will be touching her

---

31 Adichie, *Americanah*, 175.
32 Adichie, *Americanah*, 176.
33 Adichie, *Americanah*, 177.
34 Adichie, *Americanah*, 178.
35 Adichie, *Americanah*, 185.
36 Adichie, *Americanah*, 188.

164 &» CHAPTER SIX

a bit but nothing uncomfortable—just some human contact to keep him relaxed. Adichie describes the encounter as follows:

> There was, in his expression and tone, a complete assuredness; she felt defeated. How sordid it all was, that she was here with a stranger who already knew she would stay. He knew she would stay because she had come. She was already here, already tainted. She took off her shoes and climbed into his bed. She did not want to be here, did not want his active fingers between her legs, did not want his sigh-moans in her ear, and yet she felt her body rousing to a sickening wetness. Afterwards, she lay still, coiled and deadened.[37]

The excerpt is powerful in its exploration of the conflict between financial strain and the sordid path to its alleviation. The psychological battle is evident and the memory of the "sickening wetness" will haunt Ifemelu for a long time. The "coiled" and "deadened" position she assumes after the incident is her form of resistance, to put a distance between the act and her own self. As the events later demonstrate, she is deeply traumatized and spirals downward into depression. When Ginika suggests that she seek the services of a therapist, "Ifemelu kept her face to the window. She felt, again, that crushing desire to cry, and she took a deep breath, hoping it would pass. She wished she had told Ginika about the tennis coach . . . her self-loathing had hardened inside her. . . . The tears had come, she could not control them. Ginika stopped at a gas station, gave her a tissue, and waited for her sobs to die down before she started the car and drove to Kimberly's house."[38]

As Ifemelu struggles to find employment in spite of the repeated interviews she attends, it is evident that the unspoken racism is the reason for the rejections. Regardless of qualification and performance, her racial identity is the barrier to employment. Jojo Badu encounters the same problem in *The Other Crucifix* when, after graduating with a law degree from a reputable institution, the only job he can get is stacking hay at a farmyard. In *Americanah*, Ifemelu "applied to be a waitress, hostess, bartender, cashier, and then waited for job offers that never came, and for this she blamed herself. It had to be that she was not doing something right; and yet she did not know what it might be."[39] Racism pushes Ifemelu to internalize her rejection, and she suffers from depression. In the case of the protagonist in Chikwava's *Harare North*, he goes through a process of mental breakdown and insanity.

---

37 Adichie, *Americanah*, 189.
38 Adichie, *Americanah*, 195.
39 Adichie, *Americanah*, 161.

THE NEW HYBRIDITY   ❧   165

Apart from the struggle to secure employment, social relationships, particularly interracial love relationships, constitute another barrier to Ifemelu's success. It is at Kimberly's house and later in her relationships with Blaine and Curtis that she witnesses the impact of race on social relationships. Kimberly is a nice, well-meaning person, and kind. There is no mistaking the fact that she is empathetic to Ifemelu's situation. She gives Ifemelu a bonus when she eventually offers her the job as housemaid, invites her to stay at her home, even offers to make her old car available to her. Nevertheless, Kimberly has bought into the single story of Africa as a land of poverty and Africans as destitute. Even though she is sympathetic to Ifemelu's situation, she does so out of the conviction that people of Ifemelu's race and ethnicity are lost and can only be saved by a white humanitarian or charity giver. In the process, she reinforces the very stereotypes of Africa and Africans that she makes exaggerated efforts to avoid. First, she overcompensates in her lavish praise of Indigenous African values in her attempts to demonstrate her embrace of multiculturalism. In this frame of reference, she elevates every aspect of the life of the Other and romanticizes it. Kimberly describes Ifemelu's name as "beautiful" and loves "multicultural names because they have such wonderful meanings, from wonderful rich cultures."[40] She would say of a "quite ordinary-looking, but always black" woman, "I'm meeting my beautiful friend from graduate school."[41] Looking through a magazine, she describes the very dark skin of a plain model as "just stunning."[42] Exaggerated positions of acceptance of the Other creates the illusion that individual white acceptance of otherness is the solution to the problem of racism. It creates the false impression that racism can be solved by simply lavishing praise on difference. While this potentially highlights Kimberly's kind heart, it prevents society from recognizing and accepting the facts that the problem of racism is systemic and that simplistic individual overtures of acceptance are not only misleading but also a potential barrier to addressing the real problems. Unfortunately, Kimberly's position creates the conditions for racism to continue to prevail in society.

Kimberly unwittingly reveals and shockingly upholds the narrative of the white savior of the destitute African Other. In lauding her commitment to establishing charity missions in Malawi, a substitute for the entire African continent in her mind, she is reinforcing the single story of African poverty and dependence on Western aid for their livelihood. Kimberly notes that she and her husband, Don, are planning a trip to an orphanage in Malawi to help the foster children. As Don says to Ifemelu, "Well, we do our best but

---

40   Adichie, *Americanah*, 181.
41   Adichie, *Americanah*, 181.
42   Adichie, *Americanah*, 181.

166 ❧ CHAPTER SIX

we know very well that we're not messiahs."[43] The choice of "messiahs" is instructive. It recalls the use of the Bible by Western conservatives and evangelists as a support mechanism and justification of European imperialism in the jungles of Africa to rescue the savages and save their souls from perdition. The diction ascribes to white people the status of Christ and his role as savior of mankind. In Western racial epistemology, whiteness is elevated to the level of the Godhead, and white is the chosen race of people to save the world from the dangers of heathenism and primitivism. Kimberly's pity for the poor helpless orphans is an anointed one, sanctified by the God-given right that the Bible endorses and accords her. The effect on Ifemelu is devastating: "Kimberly's face had softened, her eyes misted over, and for a moment Ifemelu was sorry to have come from Africa, to be the reason that this beautiful woman, with her bleached teeth and bounteous hair, would have to dig deep to feel such pity, such hopelessness. She smiled brightly, hoping to make Kimberly feel better."[44] The sarcastic tone indicates that the act of pity achieves the opposite effect in Ifemelu because she redirects the pity to Kimberly and exposes her ignorance and misplaced sympathy. It is Kimberly who is the object of pity, as the excerpt demonstrates the consequences of blind ideological disposition and misdirected virtue. That said, Kimberly's intention in her demonstration of pity for the poor orphans is obvious: it is to undermine the values of the Other in ways that cause them to be ashamed of their identity and cultural heritage.

This image of the white savior is not restricted to Kimberly's perspective of white salvation alone. It is further demonstrated in the image of Africa as revealed in the speeches of the other guests at the party: "A couple spoke about their safari in Tanzania. 'We had a wonderful tour guide and we're now paying for his first daughter's education.' Two women spoke about their donations to a wonderful charity in Malawi that built wells, a wonderful orphanage in Botswana, a wonderful microfinance cooperative in Kenya. Ifemelu gazed at them. There was a certain luxury to charity that she could not identify with and did not have."[45] Another woman proudly declares that she is the "chair of the board of a charity in Ghana" that works with rural women.[46] The action reflects a certain sense of self-assuredness and depicts social hierarchies elevating the giver over the recipients and, by implication, justifying white superiority over other people. The conversation betrays a superficial interest in the lives of the Indigenous people and indicates that maintaining charities in Africa is all for show, a way to reinforce

---

43   Adichie, *Americanah*, 185.
44   Adichie, *Americanah*, 185.
45   Adichie, *Americanah*, 209.
46   Adichie, *Americanah*, 209.

social and economic status and to deliberately call attention to it. It is self-promoting and deceptive. This pretension is captured in Kimberly's husband, who "looked people in the eye not because he was interested in them but because he knew it made them feel that he was interested in them."[47] At best, donations to and work with the charities confirm how well-meaning people can reinforce stereotypes and ironically affirm the opposite of their intentions.

The gathering to celebrate Don's friend also brings out racism in America. At the party, a man echoes Kimberly's overcompensation of indigenous values when he says to Ifemelu, "You're so beautiful. . . . African women are gorgeous, especially Ethiopians."[48] The generalization is humorous, the basis for his claim of Ethiopian gorgeousness is never revealed, and his characterization of women exposes his ignorance of womanhood and beauty in Africa. More importantly, the focus of the conversation is on white charity missions and their rescue of Black people from poverty. The stereotype of Africa as the heart of darkness persists as the conversation centers on perspectives of the Other: "Horrible, what's going on in African countries,"[49] and "Some of the people we met had nothing, absolutely nothing, but they were so happy."[50] The economic and racial binary reinforces the stereotypical contrast between Western civilization and its safety, security, and abundance on the one hand and savagery, poverty, and destitution on the other. The flaw in this mode of thinking is the overgeneralization of these tropes to all Africa and Africans, as well as the seeming inability to recognize these same and sometimes worse human conditions in Western societies. The double standard stems from a deliberate intention to objectify, racialize, and dehumanize. The conversation is intentionally structured to call migrants into a recognition of their otherness and, in the process, reinforce Western superiority over them.

At other times, though, this flawed thinking stems from ignorance. Laura's stupidity and blind self-assurance accentuate this claim. She not only refers to Ifemelu as "sassy," a word that connotes an illegitimate attempt to step out of one's ascribed place in society; she also spends a lot of time on the internet looking up "so much information about Nigeria, asking [Ifemelu] about 419 scams, telling her how much money Nigerians in America sent back home every year."[51] Laura's attitude toward migrants reflects the hostility shown to other races, especially those considered lower on the American social ladder. Her resentment demonstrates the changing

---

47   Adichie, *Americanah*, 184.
48   Adichie, *Americanah*, 209.
49   Adichie, *Americanah*, 181.
50   Adichie, *Americanah*, 183.
51   Adichie, *Americanah*, 200–201.

168 &♦ CHAPTER SIX

perspective of the migrant and migration in America over the last ten years. The perception of the migrant as subhuman, destitute, and criminal—and who invades the calm safety and prosperity of the West to fleece it of its resources—has become the dominant narrative of the migrant. As Ifemelu notes of Laura's attitude to her, a microcosm of the larger society's view of migrants, "It was an aggressive, unaffectionate interest; strange indeed, to pay so much attention to something you did not like."[52]

This attitude of resentment for the migrant, especially those deemed to be successful, is reflected in the carpet cleaner who, upon opening the door to Kimberly's house, mistakes Ifemelu as the owner and immediately becomes hostile. Upon realizing his mistake, he promptly switches to a grin, relieved that the "universe was once again arranged as it should be."[53]

Ifemelu's relationship with Curtis provides another dimension to race relations and the barriers to success in her path. While Curtis playfully describes their attraction to each other as "love at first laugh," it is evident that American society sees the relationship very differently. The racism is clear. It is in the reference of Kimberly's daughter, Morgan, to the news of them dating as "disgusting" and in Don's disapproval because he "thought [Ifemelu] was attractive and interesting, and that Curt was attractive and interesting, but it did not occur to him to think of them both together, entangled in the delicate threads of romance."[54] And the racism is in Curtis's mother who sees Ifemelu as a gold digger and states: "I'm Republican, our whole family is. We are very anti-welfare, but we did very much support civil rights. I just want you to know the kind of Republicans we are."[55] What is surprising is Curtis's mother's encouragement of her son's sexual escapades with Indigenous women she is contemptuous of; that is, as long as he does not commit to a long-lasting relationship with them and "would, with time, settle down properly."[56] She fails to realize that if these girls are good enough for dating, they are also appropriate for marriage. Curtis's mother will support the sexual exploitation of the girls as long as they are disposed of in the end, when Curtis decides to "settle down" properly with a white woman.

Even Curtis himself is not immune to racist thinking. While he loves Ifemelu, his relationship with her is self-serving. He is more concerned with what he considers authentic culture than any consideration for her feelings. He prefers Ifemelu's natural air because of the proximity it offers him to racial difference. When she eventually transforms her image to that of the

---

52 Adichie, *Americanah*, 201.
53 Adichie, *Americanah*, 204–5.
54 Adichie, *Americanah*, 240.
55 Adichie, *Americanah*, 244.
56 Adichie, *Americanah*, 244.

THE NEW HYBRIDITY &❧ **169**

"white-girl swing,"[57] Curtis sees only the foundation of his loss—the exotic image of the Other—and glosses over Ifemelu's pain. And so he scolds Ifemelu, "Why do you have to do this? Your hair was gorgeous braided. And when you took out the braids the last time and just kind of let it be? It was even more gorgeous, so full and cool. . . . It's so fucking *wrong* that you have to do this"[58] (italics in the original). Curtis's anger is centered on the wrongheadedness of Ifemelu's decision to destroy the gorgeous exotic beauty of her natural hair. For Curtis this is a symbolic act of severance from the evidence of his acceptance of other cultures and differences. The repetition of "gorgeous" eerily reminds us of Kimberly's pretensions and self-promoting acts of exaggerated acceptance of multiculturalism.

Perhaps more disturbing is Curtis's ignorance about the extent of animosity directed at interracial relationships. His naïveté prevents him from understanding the complexity of racial prejudice, and so he cannot fathom or relate to the depth of the lived experiences of Ifemelu. Her perspective will always strike him as rash, exaggerated, or misplaced. He not only doesn't have the experience to understand what it means to be Other but also lacks the cultural tools to do so. Curtis is either ignorant of the meaning of white privilege or consciously downplays it. He cannot recognize that his ability to accomplish whatever he wants with the snapping of his fingers is contrary to the experience of millions of people like Ifemelu struggling against prejudice in society. He fails to see the inequities in society that allow him to process a green card application and change someone's residency status in an instant, something that often takes migrants decades to accomplish. And so, while his intentions may even be genuine, he fails to see how his privilege as a white man and conservative Republican amplifies the struggles of the less privileged like Ifemelu living in the margins. Curtis's assistance reminds Ifemelu of her exclusion and deepens the pain of her struggles to succeed. It makes her more aware of the barriers to her dreams and the unfairness in a society in which this system of inequalities is racialized.

If Curtis is not immune to racist thinking, neither is Blaine. In spite of the promise their relationship initially holds, it breaks down over differences in character and perceptions of life. Blaine is cold and distant. He lives in the world of books, of abstract theories, and applies his theorizations to his life uncritically. Superimposing his ideologies upon the real world, he forces Ifemelu to live in that world too. He is self-righteous and judgmental. More revealing is the fact that he can be unforgiving, is completely blind to his own shortcomings, and uses his intellectual accomplishments as an excuse to punish Ifemelu in what he sees as her deviation from the norm. In addition

---

57   Adichie, *Americanah*, 251.

58   Adichie, *Americanah*, 252.

170 & CHAPTER SIX

to Blaine's pride, his sister's rude behavior is a contributing factor to the breakup of their relationship. In the end, the racism in Dike's school and his attempted suicide are the last straw in Ifemelu's efforts at acculturation. When Dike is framed for a crime he did not commit, one that leads to his overdose on Tylenol, Ifemelu decides to return to Nigeria.

The struggle of the characters to succeed abroad is not limited to those in America. Obinze's experience in England is no different from Ifemelu's, and this indicates that racial prejudice is typified not by a specific geographical space but, rather, by a system that structures humans on the basis of skin color and determines how they will be treated and the opportunities open to them according to the system of classification. When we first meet Obinze, he is a happy young man from a wealthy family, going through his undergraduate education at the University of Nigeria, Nsukka. His mother is a professor in the academy, and his relationship with his girlfriend, Ifemelu, is blossoming. However, from the outset, the narrative makes it clear that Obinze is obsessed with the idea of America and the American dream: the principles of liberty, freedom, and the pursuit of happiness enshrined in the Declaration of Independence. As for many aspiring African students, Jojo Badu in *The Other Crucifix*, Darling in *We Need New Names*, and Neni in *Behold the Dreamers*, America is the ideal for the pursuit of education. Obinze's fascination goes beyond educational pursuit. He loves America, believes in its ideals, and longs to be a part of society. As a teenager, he devoted time to reading American history, literature, and culture. He constantly engages with American values through popular culture and media. However, his belief in America is first shaken the American embassy rejects his application for a student visa over Western fear of the rise of global terrorism against America.

With the deteriorating socioeconomic conditions back home, he is advised by his mother to find a job and reapply for the student visa later. Adichie tells us, "His job applications yielded nothing. He traveled to Lagos and to Port Harcourt and to Abuja to take assessment tests, which he found easy, and he attended interviews, answering questions fluidly, but then a long empty silence would follow. Some friends were getting jobs, people who did not have his second-class upper degree and could not speak as well as he did."[59] The reader is again reminded of the reason why Africans flee their homelands. The corruption in government circles is stifling. Opportunities are available not on the basis of merit but on being well connected to the system. Inequalities are rife, and the frustration is palpable. And so, when his mother avails him of the opportunity to be her research assistant at a conference in England that she will be attending, Obinze jumps at the chance of

---

59   Adichie, *Americanah*, 289.

THE NEW HYBRIDITY 🙿 171

getting a six-month visa and leaving the shores of Nigeria. He ends up staying in England for three years.

In England, Obinze experiences what it means to live as an undocumented migrant abroad. With the expiration of his residency status, he has to deal with unemployment, racism, and the social exclusion that comes with it. As he has overstayed his visa, he can only be employed in menial jobs for which employers are prepared to risk circumventing the immigration approval process for migrant workers. In this situation, he is vulnerable and open to exploitation. Given his residency status, he gets a job cleaning toilets in an estate agent's office building in London. He approaches his new job fully cognizant of the humiliation. His description of the "mound of shit on the toilet lid, solid, tapering, centered as though it had been carefully arranged and the exact spot had been measured,"[60] highlights the dehumanizing nature of the job. With the increase in antimigrant rhetoric in the UK and the threats it poses to his safety, Obinze recognizes the need for permanent residency as one aspect of the solution to his immigration status. Thus, at the expiration of his visa, he resorts to a fake marriage with a teenager of Angolan descent, Cleotilde, in order to secure his residency papers. The sham marriage is presented as a survival strategy, a consequence of the restrictive and discriminatory immigration laws in England. Nevertheless, it constitutes a felony, and the guilty parties are liable to deportation if they are not British or EU citizens. In some cases, migrants have been incarcerated and then deported. Unfortunately for Obinze, he is arrested by immigration police on the day of the wedding, apparently from a tip by Vincent, another Nigerian migrant in London, for overstaying his student visa and is taken to the police station. The scene is humiliating:

> A policeman clamped handcuffs around his wrists. He felt himself watching the scene from far away, watching himself walk to the police car outside, and sink into the too-soft seat in the back. . . . It was he who felt the heaviness of the handcuffs during the drive to the police station, who silently handed over his watch and his belt, and his wallet, and watched the policeman take his phone and switch it off. Nicholas's large trousers were slipping down his hips.[61]

The immigration police later inform him that the government has a strong case against him and that he will be deported to Nigeria. The ignominy of deportation is registered in the description of the process as removal, and as Adichie describes the effect: "That word made Obinze feel inanimate. A

---

60 Adichie, *Americanah*, 292–93.
61 Adichie, *Americanah*, 344.

172 &❧ CHAPTER SIX

thing to be removed. A thing without breath and mind. A thing."[62] The objectification and dehumanization inherent in the process are conveyed, and they reflect the changing perspective of the migrant and of migration. The spectacle that is made of the deportee adds to the picture of dehumanization. He is put in chains and literally paraded across the lounges of Manchester Airport like a common criminal. Obinze is led into a waiting room at the airport where three other African migrants have been held and are awaiting deportation. The agony of the deportees is conveyed: "He was led into a room, bunk beds pushed forlornly against the walls. Three men were already there. One, from Djibouti, said little, lying and staring at the ceiling as though retracing the journey of how he had ended up at a holding facility in Manchester Airport. Two were Nigerian. The younger sat upon his up on his bed eternally cracking his fingers. The older paced the small room and would not stop talking."[63] The trauma is powerfully depicted: from the silence of the migrant from Djibouti to the endless chatter of the older Nigerian. The scene can be likened to the deportation of Massala-Massala together with other migrants from Africa in *Blue White Red*.

Obinze's psychological trauma is also discernible. His mother will meet him upon arrival at the international airport in Lagos. In the meantime, he is transported to Dover, a former prison, where he awaits a flight to Nigeria in a small cell. He describes the experience as "surreal, to be driven past the electronic gates, the high walls, the wires" and remarks that he "felt suffocated in that cell, let out only to exercise and to eat, food that brought to mind a bowl of boiled worms."[64] One morning, he joined "two women and five men, all handcuffed, all bound for Nigeria, and they were marched, at Heathrow Airport, through security and immigration and onto the plane, while other passengers stared. They were seated at the very back, in the last row of seats, closest to the toilet."[65] The next day, they arrived in Lagos, and as the plane "began its descent into Lagos, a flight attendant stood above them and said loudly, 'You cannot leave. An immigration officer will come to take charge of you.' Her face tight with disgust, as though they were all criminals bringing shame on upright Nigerians like her."[66] After going through immigration and completing the arrival forms, the uniformed officer asks Obinze, "So do you have anything for the boys?,"[67] a grim reminder of the bribery and corruption that warrants departure of migrants and a

---

62 Adichie, *Americanah*, 345.

63 Adichie, *Americanah*, 346.

64 Adichie, *Americanah*, 349.

65 Adichie, *Americanah*, 348–49.

66 Adichie, *Americanah*, 350.

67 Adichie, *Americanah*, 350.

THE NEW HYBRIDITY   ❧   173

stark recognition of the challenges to return that lie ahead. The hurdles are encountered on day one and at the first port of call or entrance into the country: the airport.

Ifemelu's return journey to Nigeria is not as dramatic or humiliating as that of Obinze. Managing a thriving blog that quickly becomes an advertising platform with many followers, invitations to speak on race and diversity, travel opportunities as a speaker in multicultural workshops and talks, and money to purchase a small condominium, Ifemelu is doing way better than Obinze was doing in England. Despite these achievements, and with the breakup of her relationship with Curtis, Ifemelu returns home.

The return of the two main protagonists to their homeland has received much critical commentary. Dustin Crowley advances that *Americanah* proposes a more positive perspective on what it means to return through exploring the barriers associated with immigration and undercuts the idealization of America and the American dream.[68] While Chike Mgbeadichie focuses on three economic models of entrepreneurship, apprenticeship, and vocation and their adoption as critical to the transformation of the homeland,[69] Helen Cousins and Pauline Dodgson-Katiyo focus on alienation and belonging as catalysts for understanding isolation in the migratory country and the decision to return home.[70] Julia Iromuanya also foregrounds racial identity as hairstyle in exploring exclusion and makes the case for reclaiming cultural identity in the context of the migrant's return home.[71] Adichie depicts several incidents in *Americanah* that support these perspectives of return.

Upon arriving, Ifemelu is caught between the nostalgia of reconnecting with her homeland and the challenges of reintegration. Adichie remarks that, at first, she was assaulted by Lagos. She has to deal with the congestion, homicide, flooding, crowded buses, blackouts, sprawling wares on roadsides—a way of life that she had gradually drifted away from during her stay in America. Reintegration will involve a reencounter and reengagement with some of the negative experiences prior to departure. It is a return to memories that returned migrants, in some cases, would be happy to obliterate from their minds. However, if return is to be meaningful, returned migrants will have to deal with the realities of the present, confront unhappy memories of the past, and carve out a future. They have to engage with the changes that have taken place in both the society and the people. Ifemelu must deal with a society that is now strangely familiar and confront the new discourse that now defines people's aspirations and moral values. There have

---

68   Crowley, "How Did They Come to This?," 125.

69   Mgbeadichie, "Beyond Storytelling," 119–35.

70   Cousins and Dodgson-Katiyo, "Editorial," 163–83.

71   Iromuanya, "Are We all Feminists?," 163–83.

174 ❧ CHAPTER SIX

been changes to both infrastructure and to people's mindsets. People not only see things differently but also see themselves and the returned migrant in a different light as well. The returned migrants are Americanah, and society's expectations of them are high. There is also the changed lifestyle of Lagosians, and this is epitomized in Ranyinudo's new perspective on life. She adores the materialism of Lagos and aspires to the life of the wealthy and privileged. Fixated on marriage and the supposedly elevated status that marriage to a rich man could accord her, she daydreams of attractive suitors and expensive engagement ceremonies and weddings and speaks of potential relationships with rich men who are in the oil industry, managing local and international offices. She has no scruples dating married men so long as they can meet her material demands. Material acquisitions are the new benchmark for socioeconomic advancement. In her friends' worldview, the success of a wedding or importance of a person's life is measured by their connections to wealthy people or those in authority. Priya notes, "It shows you're connected. It shows prestige,"[72] and Ranyi says such connections "show levels, serious levels."[73] Her view of marriage is framed around a fascinating logic of love: "You do not marry the man you love. You marry the man who can best maintain you."[74] The returned migrant will have to navigate this new mindset upon return. Ifemelu's realization of this change in her countrymen hit her forcefully. People had not only changed but so too had their preferences and priorities. She observes, "People changed, sometimes they changed too much."[75] The subject of marriage and material wealth is the dominant discourse while moral and ethical considerations have taken a back seat. However, she is quick to recognize that, in spite of the veneer of success, many of her friends like Tochi are mired by "a great personal unhappiness."[76]

Adjusting to these changes will be a challenge. This is clearly discernible in her reunion with her friends. Ifemelu tells us, "There was, also, a strained nostalgia in those reunions, some in Ranyinudo's flat, some in hers, some in restaurants, because she struggled to find, in these adult women, some remnants from her past that were often no longer there."[77] Even as Ifemelu recognizes the changes in her friends, it is equally important to point out that she has also changed and that change is visible to her friends too. After all, she is Americanah, and she brings a certain sense of difference back to Nigeria.

---

72 Adichie, *Americanah*, 492.
73 Adichie, *Americanah*, 492.
74 Adichie, *Americanah*, 492.
75 Adichie, *Americanah*, 491.
76 Adichie, *Americanah*, 491.
77 Adichie, *Americanah*, 490.

THE NEW HYBRIDITY ❧ 175

In spite of the obvious challenges, return offers many positive possibilities to both the migrant and society. The nostalgia of returning is a good place to start. At her first visit to Ranyi's home, Ifemelu reflects on the words of the gateman who welcomed her back home to Nigeria: "She thanked him, and in the gray of the evening darkness, the air burdened with smells, she ached with an almost unbearable emotion that she could not name. *It was nostalgic and melancholy, a beautiful sadness for the things she had missed and the things she would never know*"[78] (emphasis added). And so, later, while watching TV, Adichie describes her musing in a state of quiet disbelief: "She had done it. She had come back. She turned the TV on and searched for the Nigerian channels."[79] There is the recognition of emotions at the crossroads of nostalgia and melancholy, but the dominant impression is one of relief at returning home. This is the beginning of the process of reintegration, and the search for local channels registers the intentionality of the process.

Return also offers the migrant the invaluable opportunity of reunion with family. Upon her return, Ifemelu "spent weekends with her parents, in the old flat, happy simply to sit and look at the walls that had witnessed her childhood; only when she began to eat her mother's stew, an oil layer floating on top of the pureed tomatoes, did she realize how much she had missed it."[80] The connection to family fills the void in Ifemelu's life and helps quell the depression of isolation she felt in America. She is realizing that spiritual connectedness, especially with family, cannot be replaced with material comfort. The connection to home is unique, spiritual, and grounded in history, culture, and identity.

Using the construct of the "worldliness of the migrant," I explore the possibilities in the return. I define this as the experience acquired abroad that the migrants bring to their homelands. I argue that, in the fusion of the experiences of both the returned migrant and those in the homeland, a new hybridity is constructed, and in that fusion, return will be meaningful and reintegration made possible. Feldner affirms that "Ifemelu's position [as] in-between not only allows for her contrapuntal awareness, but also makes her an example of Homi Bhabha's notion of hybridity."[81] It is the transfer of knowledge and skills, for instance, in Ifemelu's blogging to her editorial work for *Zoe* magazine. The education acquired from Princeton University and the experience in managing a digital platform prepare her for the editorial work of the magazine. Her influence through popular culture is a major canvas for transforming society. Worldliness is the space where the migrant's

---

78 Adichie, *Americanah*, 478.
79 Adichie, *Americanah*, 479.
80 Adichie, *Americanah*, 489.
81 Feldner, *Narrating the New African Diaspora*, 193.

experience converges with those in the homeland and creates possibilities for reformulation, synthesis, and cultural hybridity. Ifemelu's work as editor offers her a new lens to see the changing trends and values in society and an opportunity to evaluate them against her own. The writing accords both individual and society a space for reciprocity and mutual engagement with possibilities for transformation and the formulation of a new hybridized path for the future. The space is both affirming and challenging: different perspectives are expressed; unrealistic expectations, bias, and arrogance are exposed; snobbery, contempt, and affectation are condemned; and collective responsibility and unity are affirmed. As with all social spaces there are bound to be conflicting perspectives and differences of opinion. What worldliness offers individual society is not the absence of conflicts but, rather, the opportunity to work through them with honesty and sincerity, intentionality and open-mindedness in order to come up with solutions and pathways for the future. I hypothesize that this construct could be about new directions, a modification of the present, a contestation of the old, but also a validation of the present. Given its complexity, it will require time, patience, and grace to work through and unpack layers of differences, assumptions, and expectations on both sides of the divide. This task of engagement should not take away the significance of the process and the possibilities it offers both the returned migrant and those in the homeland.

Challenges to this process of engagement are revealed in the novel in the tensions at the workplace between returned migrants and citizens and in the meetings of the returned migrants at the Nigerpolitan Club. The tensions between Doris and Zemaye in the office of *Zoe* magazine expose the biases, wrong assumptions, and false expectations that both the returned migrant and those in the homeland have for each other. The resentment stems primarily from misconceptions of each other, and the struggle to prove the superiority of each other's view undermines unity and collective responsibility. Notions of self and other have to be constantly negotiated, and differences in perspectives have to be resolved to ensure productivity. If the workspace is perceived as a metaphor for Nigeria, then the workers are the instrument of societal transformation, and so the importance of mutual responsibility cannot be overstated. The insider-outsider dynamic has to be resolved, and the biases associated with the been-tos and the assumed superiority complex they bring to the homeland have to be addressed. In essence, how the homeland receives its returned migrants and how the returned migrants see and relate to those in the homeland are both crucial to meaningful coexistence and societal transformation. Doris's superiority complex and Zemaye's contempt for her American lifestyle are both limiting and counterproductive. What is evident in the resulting stalemate between the two is the need for the creation of a hybridized culture that recognizes

THE NEW HYBRIDITY &• **177**

the differences on both sides; while it poses a dialectic, it is one that can be transcended for meaningful coexistence.

The Nigerpolitan Club is a vivid illustration of how not to handle the return to the homeland. Doris describes the club as "just a bunch of people who have recently moved back, some from England, but mostly from the U.S.? Really low key, just like sharing experiences and networking?"[82] While the intentions behind the creation of the club might be good, the practical reality is that it creates social hierarchies and reinforces a superiority complex of returned migrants that reflects the snobbery of the been-tos of the late 1960s. Thus, initially conceived as a space to revisit their experiences abroad with the intention of finding a path to a smooth transition to the homeland, the club becomes a place for endless denigration of the home country. The display of self-righteousness, the uninformed conclusions reached about everyday incidents, and the unfair comparisons to Western societies are all indicative of an attempt at elevation above the homeland. The been-tos' contempt for their own country is noted in Adichie's assessment of them as "the sanctified, the returnees, back home with an extra gleaming layer," who were soon "laughing and listing the things they missed about America."[83] In some ways, the conversation implies that returned migrants bring with them a slice of the lifestyle of the countries in which they have lived abroad. Upon returning home, they would have to negotiate the differences with their pre-departure lifestyle. This is a challenge the returned migrants must confront and overcome. They cannot continue to have the sort of high expectations associated with their lifestyle abroad, as such expectations in Nigeria will be unrealistic and misplaced. The returnee who misses a "decent vegetarian place" to eat ought to be reminded of Nigerian cuisine and the eating habits of his or her people.[84] Another returnee expresses delight at "this new place that opened on Akin Adesola. . . . The brunch is really good. They have the kinds of things we can eat."[85] It is vain and misleading to convey the impression that the transformation abroad is so extreme that returned migrants can no longer eat the food they grew up eating. Adichie is suggesting that this kind of attitude impedes reintegration and undermines the benefits of returning.

In other instances at the club, a returned migrant refers to Nollywood as being "so offensive to my intelligence" because the "products are just bad," even though, as Ifemelu notes, "Hollywood makes equally bad movies."[86]

---

82 Adichie, *Americanah*, 499.
83 Adichie, *Americanah*, 502.
84 Adichie, *Americanah*, 502.
85 Adichie, *Americanah*, 503.
86 Adichie, *Americanah*, 584.

178 ❧ CHAPTER SIX

Another complains that "the industry is regressive. . . . The films are more misogynistic than the society,"[87] while another is looking for a place where he can listen to "classical music."[88] However, not all returned migrants think this way. Ifemelu refers to this mentality as "really a kind of snobbery," and Obinze confirms that it is "secretly feeling that your taste is superior."[89] He goes on to reveal the truth about America and the American dream when he says, "[America]'s wonderful but it's not heaven. . . . The best thing about America is that it gives you space. I like that. *I like that you buy into the dream, it's a lie but you buy into it and that's all that matters*"[90] (emphasis added). Obinze realizes what Jende comes to recognize in *Behold the Dreamers*: the elusivity of the dream and the very high possibility of failing to accomplish it because, in most cases, it is contrary to the realities of the migrant's experience. The dream is not accessible to everyone, not even to all Americans. At the same time, even when it is accomplished, it comes at a huge cost, both to those like him who struggle to achieve it and to those who achieve it, like Clark Edwards, and struggle to keep it. Obinze and Jende might be advocating the fact that, while the dream can be pursued abroad, it is best lived in the migrant's homeland. Obinze and Jende returned to a life of success, fulfillment, and happiness they would never have accomplished in the West.

Ifemelu's controversial reunion with Obinze and the subsequent divorce of Kosi, Obinze's wife, needs some critical attention. I must state that even though the moral and ethical considerations regarding reunion and divorce are legitimate, they are beyond the scope of this monograph. Rather than focus on what was obtained and how it was done, I focus on what could have been lost between them. I contend that Adichie's purpose, which substantiates my argument of return, is to demonstrate the disruptions that migration brings to the lives of ordinary people. I focus on the beauty of a love relationship that could never have come to fruition had they not taken the risk and returned home. The reunion is a validation of the cost of migration; the rekindled love is a reminder of what could have been lost over time and distance, rather than an ethical indictment of the process by which the love was rekindled. As Adichie describes Ifemelu's feelings: "The pain of his absence did not decrease with time; it seemed instead to sink in deeper each day, to rouse in her even clearer memories. *Still, she was at peace: to be home, to be writing her blog, to have discovered Lagos again. She had, finally, spun herself fully into being*"[91] (emphasis added). The realization of the spiritual and psy-

---

87   Adichie, *Americanah*, 504.
88   Adichie, *Americanah*, 505.
89   Adichie, *Americanah*, 535.
90   Adichie, *Americanah*, 536.
91   Adichie, *Americanah*, 586.

THE NEW HYBRIDITY   179

chological anchor of the homeland best exemplifies the merits of returning home to the been-to. In the return of the two main protagonists to Nigeria, Adichie communicates her message of return. The situation is ambivalent: the returned migrant has a cross to bear, a sacrifice to make, and adjustments to undergo in order to transition to a society that was once familiar but is now very different. There is a cost to return. It is hard work to reintegrate, time consuming to understand the changes, and painful to make the adjustments. However, there are possibilities for great rewards that staying abroad would never accord the migrant. The benefits to both individual and society are great, at times immeasurable, as in the stability, fulfillment, and peace of mind at being home but also exciting in the rediscovery of self and the contributions one can make to the future of one's homeland.

Chapter Seven

Constructive Liminality

Pede Hollist's *So the Path Does Not Die* is the culmination of the migration process. The novel accomplishes two distinct objectives in this chapter: first, it extends the conversation on the theory of the new hybridity in *Americanah* in the previous chapter. It uses the hyphenated identity of Dimusu-Celeste, the child born to Cammy and Finaba, to explore this construct. I use Sten Moslund's concept of a globalized society as context to situate this hypothesis.

Second, the novel introduces the concept of constructive liminality as a pathway to navigating dual identities in the migrant's homeland. I posit an aesthetic of liminality to examine returned migrants with dual nationalities trying to make sense of the demands of the in-between space this identity offers them. Liminality as a framework to explore the possibilities to return migration posits that the migration process has not come to an end. Rather, it creates a space where the process for reconciling cultural opposites can be enacted. By its duality, the space allows for an embrace of Indigenous identity while also retaining some indications of Western acculturation as symbolized by the American passport. Constructive liminality posits that this brand of returned migrants occupies a liminal space that is both productive and ambivalent, an opposition with possibilities for a synthesis. Finaba can still embrace her Sierra Leonean identity while also keeping her American passport. Dimusu-Celeste can reclaim her African ancestry while still keeping her Caribbean one. This ability to reconcile seemingly opposing identities creates the context for understanding the benefits that a liminal framework to theorizing return provides.

In the introduction to *Migration Literature and Hybridity: The Different Speeds of Transcultural Change*, Sten Moslund defines contemporary globalized society in this way:

> So, our age is supposed to be an age of unparalleled mobility, migration and border crossings. Reading the literature of globalisation, the whole world appears to be on the move. It is the grand spectacle of the virtual surge of people flowing across the surface of the globe: refugees, exiles, expatriates, international vagrants, guest workers, immigrants, globetrotting travelers

and package tourists, wanderers of all kinds crisscrossing the planet and all its natural, ethnic, cultural, social and linguistic borders.[1]

Border crossings have accounted for a critical phenomenon in migration narratives: the construction of the hybrid and its representation in migration literature. Critical attention to hybridity in literature is not new. It has a long tradition and has been represented in myriad ways in the past decades. I do not intend to rehash the literary history and critical conversation surrounding hybridity and its representation in migration narratives. Instead, I put forward a theorization of a new hybridity that offers new grounds and methodologies for a synthesis of migrants' experiences in the diaspora with those in the homeland. I offer this aesthetics of fusion not as a blueprint for addressing the potential for transcendence that return offers but, rather, as a way of acknowledging its variegated structure and the multiple pathways that can be constructed. One such pathway, as discussed in chapter 6, is the hyphenated identity that synthesizes the worldliness of migrants and the transformations in the homeland during their absence to create a hybrid of experiences that draws from the past but in new ways and recalibrated forms to ascertain a different future. This hybridity is also symbolically represented in the return of three sets of people with immediate and ancestral ties to the continent and the synthesis of their experiences with what they encounter upon return: the African migrant, the Caribbean of African descent, and the African American. The new hybridity is further revealed in the character and role of the girl born to Cammy and Finaba, a fusion of history and culture and of past and present. Although born in America, she will grow up in Sierra Leone and will have the advantage of being initiated into the ways of the tribe. At the same time, she also has American citizenship by virtue of her birth. This allows her to straddle both worlds and to accomplish the best of both.

Dimusu-Celeste's hyphenated identity is also that of her parents and symbolizes this new brand of returned migrants to the continent. By virtue of their dual nationalities, they are in a position to not only blend different cultural experiences but also to traverse both worlds. Ifemelu and Finaba represent this brand of returned migrants. It is in the confluence of their dual identity that pathways for nation building can be formulated. The new hybridity is the product of a hybridization process that departs from dichotomizing the experience of migrants and putting them into sets of binaries. This aesthetic of identity emphasizes a blend of opposites, rather than a dichotomy of differences. In Moslund's view, hybridity has roots in Bhabha's conception of the third space. As he says of Bhabha: "'The

---

1   Moslund, *Migration Literature and Hybridity*, 1–2.

182 &❧ CHAPTER SEVEN

truest eye' belongs not to people who are rooted in one national identity or another, but to the migrants' 'double vision.'"[2]

To date, Hollist's *So the Path Does Not Die* is the most thorough exposition of the complications of returning to the homeland. Deeply contemplative and reflective, the novel examines various aspects of return pertaining to both its limitations and its possibilities. I situate Hollist's text as a sequel to *Americanah* and begin my analysis with the returned migrants trying to make sense of the changes that occurred in their home countries and the adjustments they will have to make. Finaba, Cammy, Finaba's friend, Aman; and her boyfriend, Bayo; represent this phase of the migration process.

The prologue to the novel offers a framework to explore migration and return. It does so in the context of community values and one's connectedness to it. Musudugu is a rural setting that thrives on communal living. Requiring a space for women in which "darkness must never cover a man,"[3] the community relies on its traditional norms and values for its existence. The wisdom of the gods was a critical determinant of progress. One particular aspect of community emphasized in the prologue is connectedness to the traditions of the tribe, which must never be severed, and the path toward it must always be kept open. Rites of passage and rituals that ensure connectedness include female circumcision, and the prologue emphasizes the need for cultural preservation. The rules that govern society ought to be maintained, and the inhabitants of Musudugu need to follow the path of traditional norms for harmony and continuity in the tribe. As the prologue notes, "When you do not follow the path, you will end up lost in the bush."[4] This requirement for direction is also based on the understanding that "life is about seeing yourself as a part of others and being ready to share in their plan."[5] It is in recognition of this sense of connectedness to community through adherence to traditional norms that "villagers sit under the tree according to the shade it casts."[6] Into this seemingly stable and cohesive community come two elements of change: modernity and migration. The birth of Kumba Kargbo heralds the onset of change in the community. A symbol of change, Kumba professes that the women in the community "must learn new ways," and she begins to challenge the decision of the Virgin Girl, the daughter of Atala the supreme, that "darkness must never

---

2   Moslund, *Migration Literature and Hybridity*, 70.
3   Hollist, *So the Path Does Not Die*, v.
4   Hollist, *So the Path Does Not Die*, iv.
5   Hollist, *So the Path Does Not Die*, v.
6   Hollist, *So the Path Does Not Die*, v.

CONSTRUCTIVE LIMINALITY ❧ 183

cover a man in Musudugu."[7] In addition, she initiates the first instance of migration in the community by journeying to a distant land.

The prologue operates on two levels: the authoritative discourse of the voice of Baramusu that emphasizes traditional identity and community values and the internally persuasive discourse that interrogates the traditional and gestures to modernity by postulating individual judgment, societal reform, and migration. Mikhail Bakhtin's analysis of discourse in *The Dialogic Imagination* is useful in analyzing both levels of discourse and their implications for the theme of migration and return. In the chapter "Discourse on the Novel," Bakhtin makes a distinction between the authoritative discourse and the internally persuasive discourse. I apply Bakhtin's construct to analyze the dual voice in the prologue and to make the case for Baramusu's argument against migration.[8] Baramusu's emphasis on the traditional values of the community constitutes the authoritative or dominant discourse in the prologue. In her address to Kumba, she provides a critical frame to read migration: "Our lives today are the harvest left to us by women like you who refused to see what is at their feet but instead looked to the horizon. The ways of white people only bring trouble. . . . A wise woman walks through the high grass where the elephant has already trod, so she does not get soaked with dew. So the path does not die, do not follow footprints in the sand."[9] Baramusu urges a refocusing on what the homeland has to offer instead of the compulsion to look to the horizon for answers. She cautions against acquiring "the ways of white people," a lifestyle that could mainly be accomplished through migration to foreign lands and at the cost to traditional values. She emphasizes that it is wise to preserve culture and tradition, and she reveres the path to such preservation.

Migration threatens to upset this traditional model, and Baramusu's argument, drawn from her authority as custodian of traditional values, is that even if the horizon is good and offers an alternative to the rope, the path should never be allowed to die simply because of the attractions of the horizon. Cultural values and one's connections to them are life-giving and must never be severed. As Sophia Akhuemokhan asserts, through the structural devices of repetition and originality, reinforcement and revelation, and in using Gionanni Vico's theory of the cycles of human history, that the thesis of not cutting the rope is the *cantus firmus*, the "fixed song" that underlies the independent melodies. Here, the myth of Musudugu and its message of cultural proximity are literary extensions of the *fafei* and the *cantus firmus*,

---

7   Hollist, *So the Path Does Not Die*, v.

8   Bakhtin, *The Dialogic Imagination*, 342.

9   Hollist, *So the Path Does Not Die*, 3.

184 ❧ CHAPTER SEVEN

respectively.[10] Hence, the advice "do not cut the rope" for both "the big and little ropes work together to protect the farm from the birds" supports Akhuemokhan's argument.[11] I affirm that Finaba is the one sent by the ancestors to "show our people the way because we have strayed from the path."[12]

There is another level of discourse discernible in the prologue, an internally persuasive discourse by a seemingly unknown speaker or voice. This voice reconfigures home and return in new and interesting ways that interrogate Baramusu's conception of ancestry and tradition. The theorizations of the unknown voice provide a platform on which Baramusu's conceptions are constantly tested. It is as if the author, while listening to Baramusu, is internally weighing her views and the implications for his themes. The operation of both discourses conveys the complexity of the theme and the multiperspectivism that would be required to unpack it. In this regard, "do not cut the rope" is both authoritative and internally persuasive for it brings into focus the point of intersection of two narratives that are both parallel and connected.

The prologue tells us that Kumba "left to find out why darkness should not cover a man in Musudugu and why women should continue to follow the ways of the Virgin Girl."[13] Kumba's movement from her homeland, the first instance of migration in the novel, sets the context for analyzing modern-day migration in the work. The question it poses for readers is this: What does migration do to the homeland and the traditional foundations on which it is built? Two things become clear in Kumba's decision to leave. First, it accentuates the danger of Kumba cutting the rope, straying from the path, and breaking the connections to traditions that define her. In this interpretation of Kumba's migration, I suggest that migration is conceptualized as a movement that cuts migrants from the rope of their roots, ancestry, traditions, and identity. This is the authoritative discourse that Baramusu brings to the novel. She sees travel as a violation of the rules that constitute traditional norms and values, an undermining of the authority of the elders, and a devaluation of the wisdom of the gods. Baramusu's discourse underscores the view that migration is a deviation from the path, a cutting of the rope, and a possible loss of direction. It is a movement that is potentially not worth taking.

There is also a sense in which Kumba's departure further accentuates this discourse for it could be interpreted as pushing the boundaries of knowledge and inquiry. This view then privileges contentment with the homeland and

---

10 Akhuemokhan, "The Backward Glance," 124.

11 Hollist, *So the Path Does Not Die*, 5.

12 Hollist, *So the Path Does Not Die*, 4.

13 Hollist, *So the Path Does Not Die*, v.

CONSTRUCTIVE LIMINALITY ❧ **185**

not the gesture to the horizon, regardless of its promises. Kumba is searching for knowledge, for answers that will calm the restless spirit in her soul. She sees the journey outward as the means to gain this knowledge. Her travels could be interpreted as an ironic reference to the grass being greener on the other side and that answers to the migrant's questions lie elsewhere. This preference for the horizon as against the homeland is brought into question. In fact, the prologue even interrogates the validity of the knowledge that the migrant accomplishes outside of home. Kumba notes upon return: "I have much knowledge yet I feel lost."[14]

The second aspect in Kumba's migration is the return of the migrant. The prologue emphasizes the consequences of migration in both its physical and psychological manifestations. As Kumba embarks on her travels, she acquires much knowledge, but ironically the knowledge makes her too big for Musudugu upon her return. She cannot remember where she comes from or who she is. Time and distance have taken a toll on identity to the point of cultural amnesia, if not erasure. Migration not only uproots the migrants but further detribalizes them and makes them appear as misfits who must struggle to reintegrate into society upon return. The prologue also makes it clear that the process of readjustment is critical to continuity for, if not handled properly, it can lead to destruction of the community.

From this point, the prologue theorizes home and migration. This constitutes the internally persuasive discourse of the unknown voice underlying the authoritative discourse of Baramusu. The voice notes that "true knowledge lies deep within the self" and that return should be reconfigured to be "not [a] *return* home, but [to] be *at* home."[15] (Italics in original) A couple of interpretations are possible from this theorization of return. First, return interrogates the concept of home as a physical place to which the migrant makes a backward journey after acquiring knowledge. In this perspective, (cultural) identity is not tied to a specific geographical location from which movement to and away from affects identity and knowledge of self. H. Oby Okolocha similarly acknowledges and explores this perspective of home. Using Said's assertions on exile, Okolocha argues that home is not a physical location but is rather a psychological construct that promotes an understanding of self, and extends into a cultural attitude of "sharing that self with others.'"[16] However, the traditional perspective that is the dominant voice of Baramusu seems to suggest otherwise: that home is the community from whose apron strings the members should never sever themselves. Her

---

14   Hollist, *So the Path Does Not Die*, v.
15   Hollist, *So the Path Does Not Die*, v.
16   Okolocha, "Negotiating, Race, Identity, and Homecoming," 101.

186   ✖️   CHAPTER SEVEN

perspective validates the view that the further travelers go from home, the less they know about themselves and the values of the community they hail from.

The unknown voice suggests otherwise—that the traveler does not return home as in a geographical space but rather the traveler is at home wherever he or she is. The implication here is that home obtains more in the spiritual than in the physical realm because it is about self-realization, regardless of physical connections to a geographic location. The prologue's theorization is a nod to Afropolitanism in its suggestion of a certain fluidity in the conception of African identity as not defined by a specific location or its norms and values. The prologue asserts, "Home is not a place, like a village. To be at home means knowing one's self and sharing that self with others."[17] This construction of identity interrogates Baramusu's conception of the significance of roots and heritage in self-definition. As the prologue notes, migration is about the search for the self, and that knowledge of self is not rooted to a specific physical place. Migration is about knowing and understanding the self, and that knowledge of self brings forth fulfillment and satisfaction. It is the knowledge of self that puts individuals at home with themselves, their society, and purposes in life.

Having established this interpretive framework, it is important to explore how the journeys of the characters—three sets of people with ancestral ties to the continent of Africa: African migrants in the diaspora, African Americans, and the Caribbean—illustrate the perspectives of migration expressed in the prologue. From the outset, it must be stated that Finaba's journey to America and her eventual return home to Sierra Leone fit the traditional model and authoritative discourse that Baramusu represents and articulates in the novel. The journey to America echoes Kumba Kargbo's journey to the horizon in search of knowledge and her eventual return to Musudugu. Her experiences in the West constitute the basis of knowledge that the prologue describes, and her return to her homeland suggests a validation of home as a construct of a physical place and connections to its values. They indicate the rope has not been cut, and the path to its preservation has been maintained. Finaba's return can be read as justification of the need to preserve the path to tradition.

Hollist provides incidents in the novel that expose the limitations to migration. These incidents foreshadow Finaba's disillusionment in America and her return to Sierra Leone. Finaba's journey to Freetown with her parents provides the second instance of migration in the novel. Fleeing the persecution that stems from the abortive initiation of Finaba, the family arrives in Freetown to start life anew. The journey is conceived as an alternative to the impending ostracism in the village of Talaba. Amadu, Finaba's father,

---

17   Hollist, *So the Path Does Not Die*, vi.

justifies departure in the metaphor of the bed a sleeper lies too long in: "Even a comfortable bed hurts when you stay in it for too long."[18] The expectations for a new beginning are high, and as Amadu contemplates, "Freetown is a big place. You will make many new friends and grow to be princess."[19]

The family's journey to Freetown parallels and prefigures her journey to America later in the novel. In this way, it echoes the migrant's belief in the foundation of the American dream and its contextualization of the values of liberty, freedom, and pursuit of happiness in the Declaration of Independence. As Amadu notes, "*Here*, we can do whatever we want. . . . Here, you can choose your paths like them. . . . No one will make you feel like an outsider because you're not an initiate. *Here*, you'll be the same as those girls. *Here*, you belong"[20] (italics in the original). The echoes of the American dream are unmistakable in Amadu's expectations; the promise of equality, belonging, and becoming are indicative of the reasons for departure. However, like the dream, Freetown promises much more than it can deliver, and within a short time, the gap between expectations and outcomes becomes fully evident in their lives. This reversal of expectation is a dominant trope in the migrant's journey abroad. It will provide the impetus for Finaba's return to her homeland. The narrative asserts that "Freetown took away as quickly as it gave. A little less than a year after their arrival, Amadu died of tetanus poisoning."[21] If Finaba's journey to Freetown is a mirror image of her journey abroad, then similar elements of alterity and precarity dominate the migrant's experiences. The move to Freetown exposes the family's vulnerabilities and the challenges they must overcome. Financial hardships, tribal discrimination, and physical abuse define their experience in Freetown. Finaba's sufferings are epitomized in the abuses she receives from Pa Heddle, who became her guardian in Freetown, the ostracism of her college mates for belonging to a minority tribe, and the sexual abuse from Kizzy, a teaching assistant at Crowther College. These experiences mirror the struggles she later undergoes in America where the marginalization stems from racial and ethnic differences, rather than from tribal discrimination. While America does provide something more substantial than Freetown by way of achievement, it nevertheless conveys the same message—the struggle of the outsider to belong in a hostile and unwelcoming society.

The mirror image is one of displacement and the disillusionment that comes with it. In Freetown as in America, "Fina learned quickly to appreciate the virtues of restraint and deference among children who were

---

18 Hollist, *So the Path Does Not Die*, 14.
19 Hollist, *So the Path Does Not Die*, 14.
20 Hollist, *So the Path Does Not Die*, 16.
21 Hollist, *So the Path Does Not Die*, 17.

188 ᛞ CHAPTER SEVEN

accustomed to having their needs and whims gratified."[22] The vulnerability of the adopted child is much like the precarity of the migrant. There is also susceptibility to violence and danger. Freetown is not Amadu's expected bastion of refuge, love, and acceptance, and belonging. In Finaba's abuse, the image of the mother surfaces to shed light on her exclusion. This image was first noticed in Ade, Pa Heddle's son, tearing up the photo of Finaba's mother. This suggests the destruction of the homeland, the motherland, from where she hails. Ade is symbolically ripping up the migrant's connections to their motherland. In another instance, after Pa Heddle beats Finaba, she goes to the bathroom, shuts the door, and lies down on the floor: "She pulled her knees into her chest and curled her shoulders and head into them, fetus-like."[23] The reference to the fetal position is symbolic—a desire for the mother's protection and a longing for a return to the embrace of the motherland. Right from the initial migration to Freetown, Hollist has prefigured Finaba's precarious situation in America, subtly suggested a nostalgia for the homeland, and introduced the topic of return. The references to the photographic depiction and emotional longings for reconnection to the mother(land), is a structural device that replicates Finaba's migratory experiences in the West and provides a narrative for return to her birth land.

The journey to Freetown also unveils the country's historical connections and the significance of its founding. Freetown, founded as the Province of Freedom for the return of the Black Poor emancipated slaves in Liverpool following the abolition of slavery by Lord Mansfield in 1772, is historically and culturally a nation of refugees and migrants. It was a place of refuge for the freed slaves from England and the Recaptives from the west coast of Africa. Sierra Leone is a "physical and psychic sanctuary" for displaced people to "start their new life."[24] The condition of Finaba's family recalls the plight of the freed slaves: "They had brought with them nothing, but a few hundred leones and the clothes on their backs."[25] Again, like America, Sierra Leone was founded as a safe haven for immigrants, people fleeing persecution, and refugees. Finaba's experiences parallel that of the Puritans who moved from England and arrived in the New World fleeing persecution. Sierra Leone's history, in this regard, is similar to that of America's, as both can be considered nations of migrants. Yet, there is the denial of freedom and liberty to both the later-arriving migrants and those with a different tribal identity in America and Sierra Leone, respectively, which those that

---

22   Hollist, *So the Path Does Not Die*, 20.
23   Hollist, *So the Path Does Not Die*, 28.
24   Hollist, *So the Path Does Not Die*, 15.
25   Hollist, *So the Path Does Not Die*, 15.

CONSTRUCTIVE LIMINALITY 189

arrived earlier benefited from. This denial illustrates the barriers to achieving the dream for the characters in the novels selected for study.

Finaba's journey to Kono is another instance of internal migration. The journey is important for two main reasons. First, it brings her into contact with Meredith Frank, the American who works for the Christian mission. Their friendship will pave the way for Finaba's departure for America. Second, Finaba's interactions with Meredith present another view of the migrant's homeland. Meredith is American but has adopted Sierra Leone as home and sees herself as Sierra Leonean. The daughter of missionary parents in Sierra Leone, she tells us that she "never stopped dreaming of returning to Sierra Leone."[26] For Meredith, the dream is not about staying in America; it is about returning to Sierra Leone, which is, ironically, Finaba's birth land she is fleeing from. She tells Finaba, "I am American by birth and passport, but, you know, deep inside, Sierra Leone is my home."[27] Meredith sees Sierra Leone through a different lens. Her presence is an indication that the journey to the West is not everything; it ironically reveals Westerners' preference for the migrant's homeland.

In the migratory spaces of Freetown and America, Finaba will learn to "endure the pain, sacrifice a little of the body and [hope that] much will be gained."[28] This is the hope of every character whose dreams have not been realized. It is the dilemma of Jojo in *The Other Crucifix*, of Darling in *We Need New Names*, and of Obinze and Ifemelu in *Americanah*.

It is in Finaba's experience in America that the African migrant's return is fully depicted. This decision is the consequence of a long process of introspection for Finaba. She is the outsider who is constantly reminded of her inferior cultural background. Impeded by the many barriers to progress, she recognizes the many hurdles that she will have to overcome. The never-ending requests for assistance from home also complicate her situation. In addition, the consequences of the abortive initiation and the unresolved past continue to dominate her thoughts. She is unable to resolve the past and recalls being treated as an outside "other" in Sierra Leone because she belonged to the Fula ethnic group. At the same time, she sees her exclusion in America as a mirror image of the social isolation she encountered in Sierra Leone, only that in America, the exclusion stems from race and not ethnicity. She then sees her migration to America as both a failed attempt at belonging and a replication of the cycle of alienation. Sophia Akhuemokhan has examined this process of replication of the

---

26   Hollist, *So the Path Does Not Die*, 53.

27   Hollist, *So the Path Does Not Die*, 54.

28   Hollist, *So the Path Does Not Die*, 29.

190 ❧ CHAPTER SEVEN

cycle of alternatives in her theory of repetition and revelation and demonstrates its connection to the argument of return:

> Repetition accordingly communicates the twin paradoxes to be scrutinized here: that of repetition/originality and of backward/forward movement. Technically speaking, repetition is singularly suited to the author's thematic purpose because each instance of it—in action, event, language or scenarios—is a return in disguise, and return is what he is pressing for. Hollist is persuaded that there are areas in which African migrants need to return, to look backward and retrace their steps. Repetition and return are in this sense synonymous.[29]

As Finaba meditates on this situation, she recognizes a critical aspect of the puzzle—that her life in America has been made more complex and unsatisfying because she cut ties to her culture and traditions. She notes: "But why am I surprised. Baramusu said I should never cut the rope and that alone I was just an animal. Did I listen? No! I have spent most of my time living alone, cut off from or running away from my people. And, today, I just tried to cut the rope by trying to marry Cammy."[30] This is the beginning of Finaba's realization that returning to the homeland is not only a question of reconnecting to her culture; it is also her heart and soul and the defining aspect of her identity. Becoming is a function of returning to the source of that identity characterized by a reintegration into the ways of the tribe. "Cutting the rope," in this case, or running away from one's origins, is therefore counterproductive as it undermines self-fulfillment. It is from this perspective that she sees her marriage to Cammy as an attempt to "cut the rope" because it will make her stay abroad rather than return home to Sierra Leone. Finaba's disillusionment stems from cutting the ties to her roots, culture, and identity. Eventually, she decides to return home. In their conversation after the abortive marriage, she tells Aman, "I have only one home and that's Sierra Leone! . . . Haven't you heard people say there's no place like home? That's where I belong right now."[31] Questioned by Aman about the security of the country after the atrocities of the civil war, Finaba replies that "several million people still live, eat, and sleep in my war-torn country. If they can survive, so can I."[32]

Finaba's decision to return raises multiple questions about home. For Finaba, return becomes all the more important as she will be going back to the legacies of a brutal ten-year civil war. She presents home as a place

---

29 Akhuemokhan, "The Backward Glance," 125.

30 Hollist, *So the Path Does Not Die*, 153.

31 Hollist, *So the Path Does Not Die*, 158.

32 Hollist, *So the Path Does Not Die*, 158.

CONSTRUCTIVE LIMINALITY & 191

of comfort and happiness, regardless of the economic status of the country. Return is depicted as an act of love of one's country that transcends socioeconomic considerations. Home is "the place you feel comfortable no matter whether you live in a mansion with climate control or a windowless hut sitting on the equator."[33]

The decision to return is also conceptualized in terms of the contrast between comfort and happiness. Finaba realizes that she would potentially miss the comfortable life she lives in America upon returning to Sierra Leone, and she is aware that return could pose similar problems with integration that she faces in America. Nevertheless, the difference between these two sets of problems is the happiness that the returned migrant experiences upon return, which is absent in America. The novel's plot supports the argument that happiness is not a function of material wealth or comfort but rather a state of mind. Happiness is achieved with or without material wealth. Clark Edwards in *Behold the Dreamers* epitomizes the unhappiness of the wealthy and the dysfunction that comes with materialism. Jende in *Behold the Dreamers* interrogates the meaning of happiness if individuals can never be accepted in the society in which they live. Similarly, Kweku Sai in *Ghana Must Go* raises the question of what it means to succeed professionally in the West, and whether happiness and belonging are achievable if the color of one's skin can lead to wrongful dismissal and blacklisting from jobs. Finaba emphasizes her preference for happiness over material comfort when she states, "Millions of people live everyday with inconveniences [back home]. Are they any less happy? My life here is much more convenient than it would ever be at home, yet I don't feel fulfilled. Something is missing."[34] The missing piece is happiness and, as Finaba asks, a question that every migrant must ask themselves, "What is comfort without happiness?"[35] The novel suggests that if self-fulfillment is the objective of migration, then comfort without happiness amplifies the migrant's discomfort even with material and professional accomplishments.

Return is also depicted as a construct of belonging. This perspective stems from America's refusal to accept the otherness of the migrant. Finaba's assumption that professional or material success would open the door to belonging is thwarted by the realities of racism and social exclusion she faces in America. She comes to realize, like Ifemelu, the reality that no migrant, regardless of professional and material success, is immune from racism and its systemic policies of marginalization. In fact, there seems to be a never-ending desire to remind migrants of their otherness and status as an outsider.

---

33 Hollist, *So the Path Does Not Die*, 160.
34 Hollist, *So the Path Does Not Die*, 172.
35 Hollist, *So the Path Does Not Die*, 172.

192 ❧ CHAPTER SEVEN

It is in the struggle to belong that Jende in *Behold the Dreamers* comes to realize that he will never be accepted as American or be seen as an embodiment of its values. As Finaba rightly states, "The real question is what do I connect with here. . . ? Not much. I thought I would find myself here and enjoy being free of what confines and defines."[36]

With the struggle to belong comes a criticism of the American dream. Finaba criticizes the notion of the dream as a pathway to the recognition and acceptance of the migrant. On the contrary, the plots of the novels selected for study demonstrate that even at its accomplishment, the migrant is not free from racial prejudice and social inequities. She tells us, "I need to get on the path to return home. . . . What dream? I only have nightmares. *Ar Taya*, . . . I'm tired. I live in permanent anxiety, continually second-guessing people's motives. Did she say that, do that, because I'm black, because I'm African? Was I hired, not hired, promoted, not promoted because I'm a woman, a foreigner?"[37] Hollist's use of the local vernacular, *Ar Taya*, the Krio expression for exasperation, registers the depth of Finaba's frustrations and disappointment. The linguistic and cultural implications are that the individual has reached the breaking point, and it is now time for action.

In accordance with the above, returning home illustrates nostalgia for the homeland. It is in the recognition and longing for something that is missing in the life of Finaba that she expresses her longing in this way: "I wish I could go back to my village and sit in the shade of the baobab tree. I want to hear the mosquito whine in my ear. Then, I'll slap at it, miss, and give myself an ear ache."[38] She adds, "I want to smell *ogiri* . . . and catch the birds flutter away. . . . I wish I had been able to say goodbye to my mother, and Baramusu. . . . I want to be sure she loves me. . . . Most of all, I wish I had got to know my father more."[39] These expressions of longing that are sometimes fraught with pain demonstrate the desire to return. Nostalgia promotes agency and makes possible a resolution of the unresolved past. Finaba tells us: "Circumcision, belonging, society. Not FGM, but my point is that my family has never been back to Talaba, and we have never made amends for my father's action. Now's a good time for me to go and set things straight."[40] Finaba's agency is predicated on nostalgia, and her aspirations are rooted in a specific location. Her sense of identity is tied to Sierra Leone.

As in *Americanah*, return in *So the Path Does Not Die* is depicted as complicated. One aspect of return that has been cited as a drawback is the idea that

---

36 Hollist, *So the Path Does Not Die*, 161.
37 Hollist, *So the Path Does Not Die*, 161–62.
38 Hollist, *So the Path Does Not Die*, 171.
39 Hollist, *So the Path Does Not Die*, 171.
40 Hollist, *So the Path Does Not Die*, 171.

apologists of return are romanticizing a nostalgic past of their home country that no longer exists and, therefore, cannot be reclaimed. Supporters of this view, like Aman and, to a lesser degree, Kizzy, hold this view of return. One crucial question that Aman asks Finaba as she is contemplating return is whether she has considered the possibility of being unable to find her grandmother upon returning to Sierra Leone. Aman's question is crucial to understanding the sacrifices and adjustments that the returned migrants will be called upon to make. To imagine the home country as the same one that they left behind is shortsighted. In the same way, to imagine the returned migrant as the same person who left the homeland is misleading. Both the homeland and the returned migrant have been transformed in a number of ways. The objective of the returned migrants is not to re-create the past or relive the old homestead: it is rather to draw from their experiences abroad to contribute to the new and transformed society they will experience upon arrival. Indeed, the old order has passed away. Hollist stresses this in the fact that Baramusu cannot be found and Talaba's life has been ruined. The question here is whether the returned migrants can work with what they encounter upon return. Even though Baramusu may be gone, the novel suggests that in her place is Mama Yegbe who, though not exactly Baramusu, can perform the same functions she did. Baramusu and Mama Yegbe represent two different versions of Sierra Leone: Baramusu is the Sierra Leone the migrant left, and Mama Yegbe is the version she will encounter upon return. Both look familiar and different at the same time. The important issue is not one of exact representation but rather of similarity of function. Returning to the rope—that is, the cultural ties that bind the migrant to their homeland— is not a reconnection to the old ways that Baramusu extolled in the prologue; it is the connection to the new values that Mama Yegbe represents. And this is why Mama Yegbe is qualified to perform the naming ceremony of Dimusu-Celeste, the child born to Finaba and Cammy. Mama Yegbe is still the symbolic custodian of traditional values and a representation of the wisdom of and connection to the world of the ancestors, regardless of the changes. In a scene that recalls the naming ceremony of Elewa's daughter in Chinua Achebe's *Anthills of the Savannah*, Mama Yegbe performs the traditional rites that will fully anchor Dimusu-Celeste to her roots, as well as those of her parents. Beatrice notes: "There was an Old Testament prophet who named his son *The-remnant-shall-return*. They must have lived in times like this. We have a different metaphor, though; we have our own version of hope that springs eternal. We shall call this child AMAECHINA: May-the-path-never-close."[41] Of critical importance here is the recognition that the excerpt is based on return and progress. The naming of the child is a return

---

41   Hollist, *So the Path Does Not Die*, 206.

194 &❧ CHAPTER SEVEN

to the values of the tribe. Importantly, this act of return is the foundation for hope and continuity. The implication is that for both tradition and society to meaningfully intersect, return is a critical part of the process. The migrant's return is critical to society's hope for continuity because it ensures that the path to continuity is never closed.

One challenge to return is the mental disposition of the returned migrant. This is critical for a smooth transition and reintegration into the homeland. Cammy epitomizes this perspective in his realization that, upon return, returned migrants might just realize that they have outgrown their homeland. They have been so transformed in their thinking that the structures they encounter upon return are incompatible with their new ways of seeing and could even threaten their contributions to society. And so, while intent may be good, the structures back home must be flexible enough and willing to accommodate different ideas, new systems, and unfamiliar models of development. In the absence of such flexibility, the returned migrant is frustrated. Cammy's disillusionment on his return to Trinidad is a case in point. His skepticism is legitimate and validates the claim that return is complex. While I recognize this line of reasoning, I disagree with its logic. I contest Cammy's view that "back home is a memory, a canvas of good times stitched together to cope with the present realities."[42] I disagree that "all of this talk of going back reflects our unwillingness to accept our new home."[43] On the contrary, I agree with Finaba that "you never outgrow your home, not if it meant something to you."[44] I also agree that it is "the smell of the marketplace, the sound of the church bells, or the call to prayers of the Muezzin. *It is the world that you recognize and understand*"[45] (emphasis added). It is on the basis of this recognition and understanding that the metaphor of the rope is both crucial to self but integral to understanding that self and its place in the context of human existence. That sense of self is tied to a place and as Kizzy, another migrant from Sierra Leone, tells Cammy, "Ah want to be more than Trinidadian, American, or Nigerian—more than even a black man. I want to be bigger than one place and one culture!"[46] Identity and self-fulfillment are tied to place. Kizzy asks Cammy, "So what are you if you're not Trinandadian, American, or black? I love America but there's still a part of me back home."[47] Kizzy's conception of identity and

---

42   Hollist, *So the Path Does Not Die*, 213.
43   Hollist, *So the Path Does Not Die*, 213.
44   Hollist, *So the Path Does Not Die*, 213.
45   Hollist, *So the Path Does Not Die*, 213.
46   Hollist, *So the Path Does Not Die*, 213.
47   Hollist, *So the Path Does Not Die*, 213.

geography interrogates Cammy's conception of identity as unrestricted to a specific culture and location.

One aspect of return that both Kizzy and Cammy agree on is the motive for return. They cite the quest for personal material aggrandizement as the motive for many Africans in the diaspora. Cammy insinuates that the apologists for return "don't want to go back to help make things better. [They] want to go back to make themselves rich."[48] Likewise, Kizzy notes that "it's all about money."[49] Again, Cammy's and Kizzy's concerns are legitimate. Bayo's experience in Nigeria suggests that the corruption back home is simply overwhelming. In addition, the system is politicized, and returned migrants who find themselves on the wrong side of the political spectrum have faced recriminations from politicians.

Finaba's and Bayo's experiences upon return also add to their nuanced depictions. Finaba's perspective hinges on the need to contribute to national development through collaborative endeavors with responsible partners back home. Her focus on Mawaf's rehabilitation depicts Finaba's commitment to addressing the trauma of the child soldiers who participated in Sierra Leone's brutal civil war. Mawaf's trauma, as former child soldier, is also the trauma of the nation, and Finaba's commitment to rehabilitation indicates that there is work to be done back home and that it is imperative for diasporan Africans to contribute to this needed work of rebuilding. The condition of living in the resettlement and rehabilitation centers unveils the enormous amount of work that lies ahead in the rebuilding of both individuals and society. Finaba tells the party at Kizzy's house: "These are the very reasons why I must go back. If I'm not willing to stand up for women and work for change, who will? Besides, aren't there things you'd like to see change in your country, or even here? *Should we abandon our countries because they have problems?* For me, going back is about finding where I belong"[50] (emphasis added). Finaba's perspective indicates that return is not only necessary but also imperative. Return is imperative not because the individual *has* to go back but because it is *good* to do so. The benefits that come with return are fully depicted in Mawaf's transformation. If the bruised body and traumatized soul of Mawaf is a template to read the battered body politic, then Finaba's contribution to Mawaf's rehabilitation could not have been more crucial. Finaba's work with Mawaf indicates that opportunities for transformation are extant.

Mawaf's encounter with Finaba deserves some comment before bringing this chapter to a close. Earlier I suggested a connection between Mawaf's

---

48   Hollist, *So the Path Does Not Die*, 211.

49   Hollist, *So the Path Does Not Die*, 211.

50   Hollist, *So the Path Does Not Die*, 212.

196 &❧ CHAPTER SEVEN

body and the body politic of Sierra Leone. Mawaf serves as a template for reading both the atrocities of the past and the challenges to rehabilitation in the future. She is at the intersection of past destruction and future hope. A clear understanding of the symbolism that Mawaf represents for the future of Sierra Leone is crucial to the success of the migrant's aspirations upon returning home. In her relationship with Mawaf, Finaba remarks that she is committed "to give her and others like her a semblance of normal life."[51] Read as a metaphor for Sierra Leone, the implications are that there is work to be done to bring the country back to the normalcy it enjoyed before the mayhem. Mawaf symbolizes the extent of psychological trauma the nation endured and the extent of rehabilitation that it will require to accomplish the normalcy Finaba expects. One warning sign in this process is the tendency for relapse: in Mawaf's case, it is her desire to go back to her abuser and relive the carnage. Mawaf, like Sierra Leone, poses a challenge to the returned migrant. She is a symbol of the negative transformation that occurred, the extent of the physical and psychological burden the country bears, and the sheer amount of rehabilitation that has to be done. Finaba and the partners of international organizations assure the reader that, though the work is daunting, it is not insurmountable.

One thing that Mawaf's rehabilitation requires is a good understanding of her situation and of her complicated identity as both perpetrator and victim. It is important to fully understand this complexity if Mawaf is to receive the kind of help she needs for a positive rehabilitation. It is not clear that the returned migrant fully comprehends this complexity or is fully equipped to handle it. The message here is that good intentions are certainly important, but they must be balanced with a realistic understanding of the task at hand and what is required to succeed at it. In the scene where Mawaf walks away from Finaba, Finaba recognizes the challenge that lies with the task of rehabilitation. She sits in her chair *"transfixed by a desire to do something and knowledge that she did not fully understand what she was dealing with or what to do if she did"*[52] (emphasis added). In this situation, the hope lies in the possibility for collaboration with Svetlana and Sidibe Kakay, a UN worker and local businessman, respectively, as well as the concerted efforts of the returned migrant with those of the local inhabitants, including international partners like NGOs. If Mawaf is the future, then there is hope. It is a daunting task, but we are reminded that in helping Mawaf rebuild her life, Finaba is also symbolically rebuilding the broken walls of her own life and breaking down the borders and fences erected between herself and her homeland over time. The process of rehabilitation is thus double-edged. As

---

51   Hollist, *So the Path Does Not Die*, 248.

52   Hollist, *So the Path Does Not Die*, 251.

CONSTRUCTIVE LIMINALITY ❧ 197

Baramusu emphasizes in the prologue, "You survive best when you can give strength to others and draw some from them when you need it. . . . Life is when people work together."[53]

Bayo's perspective on return closely aligns with Finaba's. On returning to America, Bayo professes his love for Aman by offering marriage and a return to Nigeria. Aman's hesitation underscores the uncertainties of migration. There is always the sense of indeterminacy that comes with traveling to an unknown place. It is unsettling and can even be disorienting. But, as Bayo notes, this should not impede return to the homeland, for the same conditions were present at the migrants' departure for America. However, to dismiss Aman's questions as trivial misses the complexity of return. The novel, like *Behold the Dreamers*, suggests that return should not be a spontaneous or impulsive decision born out of a humanitarian, philanthropic, or romanticized view of the homeland. It calls for careful planning and thinking. Bayo's argument, however, is that this need for careful planning should not take away motivation or agency. He reminds us of the need to give back to one's community and the sacrifice it will require to do so. He emphasizes, "I *have* to give something back to those traders, farmers, and laborers [my sponsors]. I *have* to return to the nest"[54] (emphasis in the original). The italicization of the verb "have" demonstrates the fact that the act, the principle of giving back, is an imperative. Bayo sums up his view of migration as follows: "A bird that does not leave its nest to find food for fear it might lose its way back home will surely starve to death. The food it finds for flying into the unknown is what gave it the nourishment and strength to find its way home."[55] The implication is that the sojourners must always find their way back home. He tells Finaba that "things are bad back home. A few live like royalty. The rest do with little or nothing. I want to do my little bit to change things. I can't just turn my back on my country."[56] The case for return cannot be made more forcefully. Bayo's experiences in Nigeria are nuanced, and while they reveal the need for societal transformation, they also highlight the collective effort it will take to address corruption in society. His stance against bribery is one that every migrant will be required to take. He refuses to bribe the worker at the NEPA station, despite the threat of his wedding celebrations being disrupted: "We've got to stop this kind of thing. . . . We'll only be able to change this country when we either hold somebody

---

53 Hollist, *So the Path Does Not Die*, 6.
54 Hollist, *So the Path Does Not Die*, 204.
55 Hollist, *So the Path Does Not Die*, 203.
56 Hollist, *So the Path Does Not Die*, 205.

198 ❧ CHAPTER SEVEN

accountable or forgo something we want."[57] Return will be challenging, but with the right disposition and determination, it will be meaningful.

Aman's encounter with return is also not without its challenges. Regardless of the changes that have occurred in the continent in the four hundred years since the forced migration of African Americans, Aman still predicates her identity on the authentic past, the Africa of the ancient kingdoms. Cammy cautions that Aman's view might be unrealistic since the Africa she sees as representing the authentic past no longer exists. Aman defends her viewpoint: "Even if I have no past to recover, at least I now know where it once existed."[58] Notwithstanding, she references the DNA test that shows she is from Yoruba stock in Nigeria. In tracing her ancestry to a specific tribe and place in Africa, Aman recovers her identity, culture, and history. As she tells Cammy, "This points me to a specific people, culture, and place. I belong somewhere. I am no longer defined just by my color."[59] Aman's celebration of her Africanness indicates a coming of age, a deep desire to embrace ancestry, and a willingness to contest the narrative of the dark continent by which African Americans have been defined.

I would like to put forward my theory of constructive liminality by expanding on this idea earlier introduced in this chapter. At the end of *So the Path Does Not Die*, the narrative hints that return is a function of how the returned migrant straddles both the migratory country and the homeland. It is a construct that requires a synthesis of two seemingly opposing cultural spaces and articulates hybridity rather than singularity. The possibility of living in this dual space is represented primarily by Cammy and Dimusu-Celeste. Cammy's journey to Sierra Leone after Aman's marriage illustrates this duality of return. In his conversation with Finaba about the possibility of moving to Sierra Leone, he says, "Love is like a diamond. Rough and ugly when you first find it. But if you work on it, clean and polish it, its beauty will shine through."[60] He adds, "How about if we alternate visits at first, take turns washing and cleaning this rough diamond?"[61] Cammy's metaphor of return is fascinating. Moving back to the homeland is like encountering a beautiful but rough diamond. It is a precious commodity, but it requires a lot of work to bring out its full value. There is promise but there is also the need for strategy. Alternating visits between the homeland and the migratory country is one such strategy. The notion of the returned migrant straddling two spaces supports the argument of constructive liminality as

---

57 Hollist, *So the Path Does Not Die*, 278.
58 Hollist, *So the Path Does Not Die*, 214.
59 Hollist, *So the Path Does Not Die*, 213.
60 Hollist, *So the Path Does Not Die*, 277.
61 Hollist, *So the Path Does Not Die*, 277.

a deliberate choice of the in-between through a synthesis of both spaces, rather than a singularity of one. Constructive liminality is the product of the new hybridity that attempts at reconciling the values inherent in both the Western and the Indigenous. As Finaba confesses, it is necessary as a pathway to the future, especially the future of Dimusu-Celeste. It is critical that she maintains dual citizenship if she is to benefit from the traditions and values of her ancestry but also from "all the advantages of being American."[62] The dual citizenship of the returned migrant is another way to frame the duality of the hybridized process and the in-between of constructive liminality. Cammy assures Finaba that this position is simply a matter of a strategic response to the changing dynamics of life. It does not imply that Cammy is not appreciative of his ancestral ties to Sierra Leone. On the contrary, and as Finaba tells us at his departure from Lungi, "he knew he would come back, for this was a path he could not let die."[63] This liminal framework of return is also suggested by Adichie at the end of *Americanah*, where Ifemelu takes comfort in the fact that she carries an American passport and can return to America if need be.

Another unique contribution I make to the conversation on African migration in the diaspora is on the return of the African American and the Caribbean to their ancestral home. Bayo returns home to Nigeria and takes Aman with him. The marriage, celebrated in Nigeria, has Cammy, his son, Glen Gibson, Finaba, and Mawaf in attendance. Aman's journey to Nigeria and Cammy's travel to Sierra Leone foreground the conversation of homecoming for African Americans and Caribbeans. Their journey can symbolize the reversed Middle Passage and is based on a voluntary rather than forced migration. I suggest that while returning to the continent is homegoing for Bayo and Finaba, it is a homecoming for Cammy and Aman. Both depict a reconnection to Africa but with a slight distinction: for the African it is more of a physical reconnection, while for the African American and Caribbean, it is both a physical and spiritual reconnection. My theory of liminality implies that the migration process has not come to an end. Rather, it has created a new way of thinking about identity and belonging in geographical and cultural spaces previously perceived as problematic, as instantiated in Ama Ata Aidoo's *Dilemma of a Ghost* and Loraine Hansberry's *A Raisin in the Sun*.[64] These plays center more on the chal-

---

62   Hollist, *So the Path Does Not Die*, 277.

63   Hollist, *So the Path Does Not Die*, 280.

64   Ama Ata Aidoo's *Dilemma of a Ghost* and Loraine Hansberry's *A Raisin in the Sun* dramatize the initial optimism of African Americans to return to their ancestral homeland and the disillusionment upon arrival. The conflict between lived experiences in the West and expectations, on the one hand, and the realities of life in Africa and the disappointment, on the other, is the focus of the

200 &• CHAPTER SEVEN

lenges of peoples of African descent returning to their ancestral homeland than on the possibilities such a move offers.

As earlier introduced, the hyphenated identity of Dimusu-Celeste is crucial to understanding the nuances of constructive liminality. The naming ceremony is critical to understanding this concept. As Mama Yegbe notes, "To name is to be given a destiny."[65] Here, to give a name to a child is for all to be made aware of the destiny of the child blessed with the task of keeping the path open. Figuratively, the naming of the child is a reminder that Sierra Leone needs its own name, a new name, this time a hyphenated name that captures the essence of past and present, traditional and modern. This liminal position will enable her to design a new pathway and propel her into a new destiny. In Hollist's conception of that path, there is the promise of a hybridized future for Sierra Leone, a future that rests on revising the old path for the future. The future is not a return to the past for, in fact, that past hardly exists. It is rather the hybridization of a modified past with a transformed present. It is the synthesis of Mama Yegbe and Finaba, the hybrid of cultures in the Caribbean and the American born in her ancestral Sierra Leone. The reader notes that "Mama Yegbe and Fina found in each other, a surrogate daughter and grandmother."[66] This is the relationship between the returned migrant and the home country they will be returning to—both are surrogates, alike but subtly different. Finaba has returned to the rope, but it is not the same rope she left. In place of Baramusu, she meets Mama Yegbe. The indications are that the content of the rope metaphor has changed. However, character and function remain the same. Mama Yegbe, like Baramusu, is a cultural symbol and can therefore perform the task of naming Finaba's daughter. The essence of the rope metaphor may have changed, but the function remains the same. Returned migrants might not find Baramusu upon their return home, in much the same way as Finaba did not find her village of Talaba existing upon return. However, they will meet Mama Yegbe. And so, the question is not whether returned migrants encounter Baramusu upon return. It is rather whether they recognize the similar function that Mama Yegbe can perform and their willingness to work with what she has to offer. It is here that hope for the future lies.

Dimusu-Celeste concretizes that hope for the future. Samuel Kamara points out the symbolic significance of the birth of Dimusu-Celeste and the way her birth retells the Musudugu myth in the context of Hollist's thematization on cultural identity, female liberation, home, and return:

---

literature of this period. Eulalie and Beneatha represent a return to an African past that no longer exists and struggle to integrate into the society.

65   Hollist, *So the Path Does Not Die*, 239.

66   Hollist, *So the Path Does Not Die*, 249.

CONSTRUCTIVE LIMINALITY 🙿 201

Quite significantly, the child's naming ceremony is performed by Yegbe, the reincarnation of Baramusu, and the African component of her name suggests the rebirth of Finaba's dead sister, Dimusu. By this name, Dimusu-Celeste also becomes a *Denkileni*, and a storyteller. . . . But, Dimusu-Celeste's brand of storytelling significantly deviates from that of her traditional predecessors. She does not merely reiterate traditional narratives, or even reproduce traditional knowledge; instead, she retells those narratives and undermines their ideological underpinnings that hold our subjectivities captive.[67]

In retelling the story in this way, as Kamara contends, "Dimusu-Celeste highlights a significant feature of cultural myths as texts that can be revisited, retold, and rewritten."[68] I argue that it is in the process of retelling and reconfiguration of myths that the new pathways to nation building are constructed. It is a process of hybridization that calls for a synthesis of recalibrated knowledge of past and present. In this way, old norms of endogeneity and sexism are reconfigured, myths are recalibrated, and society's image redeemed. Pathways to the future are realized when, as Kamara adds, society recognizes that culture is "a human construct, an inherited text whose narrative strands are reflective, not only of the way human reality is structured in specific time, but also how power structures within cultures shape those realities."[69] The reconfiguration of these texts in the present cultural and temporal landscapes in the migrant's homeland is the burden of return.

Clearly, then, the dual identity of Dimusu-Celeste is the future of Sierra Leone. If African migrants in the diaspora are to return and make meaningful contributions to their homeland, they have to intentionally combine two identities and successfully navigate the liminal space that this affords them. For the African American and the Caribbean, it is a blend of Western experiences and their cultural heritage. The Dimusu in her name represents her African heritage, while the Celeste is the Caribbean. The hyphen between the two is the meeting point, a liminal space that is nevertheless a synthesis of the African and Caribbean identity and culture. The fact that the hybridized symbol is a baby is also significant. It heralds a new beginning, an opportunity to start afresh, and a new direction that embraces both the possibilities as well as the limitations of the new pathway.

---

67 Kamara, "Enduring Paths, Crossroads and Intersections," 20.
68 Kamara, "Enduring Paths, Crossroads and Intersections," 20.
69 Kamara, "Enduring Paths, Crossroads and Intersections," 21.

Conclusion

In the introduction to this book, I note that the tragic deaths of Yaguine Koita and Fode Tounkara provided the impetus for writing. This incident was particularly instructive to my conception of the dangers of African migration because it exposes the risks that migrants are willing to take simply to improve their lives. The tragedy further sheds light on the conditions at home that make such a choice for departure a possibility.

My main argument in the book is that, given the psychological depression, precarity, and death that stem from racial prejudice shown to African migrants in the diaspora, return to the homeland is a better alternative, even if such a move is complicated. I explore the migrant experience in three phases—flight, arrival, and departure—using nine novels from both Anglophone and Francophone African literature in three countries abroad: America, England, and France. Part 1 uses *We Need New Names*, *Open City*, and *The Other Crucifix* to expose the frustrations that come with unrealized dreams; part 2 uses *Blue White Red*, *Harare North*, and *Behold the Dreamers* to explore the precarity of life abroad; and in part 3, I use *Ghana Must Go*, *Americanah*, and *So the Path Does Not Die* to argue for return despite its complications.

The characters whose experiences I have examined are all motivated by dreams of socioeconomic advancement abroad. The American dream and its promise of liberty, freedom, and equality is the motivating factor for Jojo in *The Other Crucifix*, Julius in *Open City*, Darling in *We Need New Names*, Finaba in *So the Path Does Not Die*, Kweku in *Ghana Must Go*, Jende in *Behold the Dreamers*, and Ifemelu in *Americanah*. As my analysis shows that these characters, when confronted with the realities of social alienation and exclusion that come with racial prejudice, eventually understand that the barriers to the realization of the dream are varied and, in many cases, insurmountable. They realize that their optimism is misplaced and that the dream is not accessible to all migrants. Even for those who have succeeded, as Kweku in *Ghana Must Go*, Ifemelu in *Americanah*, and Finaba in *So the Path Does Not Die*, the realities of migrant life for the African do not stop upon achieving an education or with a change of social status. Life for the African migrant is defined by racial hierarchies, and unfortunately, Africans occupy the lower stratum of this hierarchy. Given the unending struggle to make sense of their situations, they eventually made the difficult decision

CONCLUSION ❧ 203

to return home. I explore in detail the suffering of the characters in the sections labeled "Flight" and "Arrival" while pointing out their experience with precarity and alterity based on the racial othering of Africans. The book concludes with a justification for return predicated on the aesthetics of new hybridity and constructive liminality.

Historical evidence of the Black man's struggle for both liberation and integration in a free society during Reconstruction, Jim Crow, and the Civil Rights Movement suggests that the optimism of the African to succeed in America either ignores historical evidence or was misplaced. The history of Black people in America from slavery through Reconstruction to the Civil Rights Movement has been one endless struggle for acceptance. Racial prejudice attests to the role of race in shaping the destiny of Black people. I posit that not only do the African characters in these novels face this historical prejudice but also that their racial exclusion is further compounded by their ethnic identity. Farouq, the African of Arab descent, faced racial and ethnic bias in Brussels. Massala-Massala had a similar experience in Paris, and Ifemelu and Obinze were not exempt from these experiences in New Jersey and London. I argue that historical and literary evidence of the suffering of Blacks in the diaspora validates my thesis of return. The assumption of material prosperity and freedom that initiates flight is misconstrued. What this book has clearly unveiled is the precarity of life for illegal African migrants in the diaspora that comes at tremendous cost. The unnamed character in *Harare North* comes to a recognition of the vulnerability and exploitation associated with migrant life as he pushes his mind and body to extremes in order to succeed and drives himself insane in the process: walking the streets of London, half-naked and with an empty cardboard suitcase on his head.

Carol Anderson, Kate Masur, and Thomas C. Holt provide historical evidence that offers a different perspective on the experience of people of color, particularly African Americans, that can be used to critique the aspirations of African migrants and their motivations for departure. Carol Anderson in *One Person, No Vote* points out the criminalization of Blackness through mass incarceration and other state and federal legislatures geared toward the disenfranchisement of Black people and the violent state measures adopted to suppress Black rebellion in moments of resistance.[1]

Kate Masur, in the preface to *Until Justice Be Done: America's First Civil Rights Movement, from the Revolution to Reconstruction*, elaborates on the antimigration laws, with specific reference to Connecticut's Gradual Emancipation Act and the Anti-Black Laws in Ohio, to argue that white America's attitude to Black migration (and Blackness) has fundamentally remained unchanged since the eighteenth century. Details of state and

---

1   Anderson, *One Person, No Vote*, 94.

204 ❧ CONCLUSION

federal legislatures that contest and reverse internal migration of Black people and prevent the growth of the class of "New Negroes" (as Masur describes them) give a clear indication of America's refusal to acknowledge Black bodies on the same level of equality, freedom, and dignity as theirs.[2] Masur further uses the Law of the Free Womb to demonstrate how state legislatures work to undermine and subvert equality of all people, one of the pillars of the American Declaration of Independence. It is an unfortunate paradox then that the motivation for departure for many of the characters in these novels is the freedom and equality that American society has not only denied Black people but has also been working earnestly to subvert. It is not too far-fetched to say that freed people who are still in bondage illustrate that Black bodies might never find a place in white America.

I am drawn to the arguments in these historical works, especially their depiction of racial prejudice, to argue that historically Black bodies do not belong to white America and that currently they are still struggling for representation in white spaces. Details of atrocities as state-sponsored lynching, political intimidation, racial terrorism, segregation, mass incarceration, police brutality, and killings of Black men suggest a history of Black dispossession and destruction that denies equal opportunities for Black socioeconomic advancement. The barriers to material success for Black bodies in America are layered and include racial, ethnic, and legal barriers. It is not only difficult for the Black body to succeed; it is also particularly hard to do so if that body is African and illegal.

I return to the poetry of Langston Hughes to argue that America has not lived up to its promises and that the Black migrant experience has largely been one of otherness, inequality, and oppression. His poem "Let America Be America Again" laments America's failure to live up to its ideals.[3] Hughes cites in the opening section his wishes for America to "be the dream it used to be" and alludes to the "pioneer on the plain/Seeking a home where he himself is free." He expresses his deep desire for America to live up to its promises, a land where dreams are said to come to fruition, where love, liberty, and freedom reign supreme; because for black people America has "never been [a place of] equality . . . / Not freedom in 'this homeland of the free.'"

I draw from the spirit of Hughes's poem to argue that return is a better alternative to the precarity of illegal migrant life in the West. While I recognize the complications involved in this move, I also realize, as the experiences of these characters reflect, that the cost of continued suffering can be quite high. For some migrants, it comes at the cost of their minds and bodies,

2   Masur, *Until Justice Be Done*, xvi.
3   Rampersad, ed., *The Poems: 1921–1940*, 131.

CONCLUSION ❧ 205

even their lives. Hughes's poem is emphatic in its depiction of the social alienation, denial of equal opportunity, and depression that comes with racial exclusion. These bleak conditions undermine the chances of Black bodies accomplishing the dream in America.

In my analysis of the historical evidence of migration in America, I retain the argument that return is not new to migrants from West Africa. It was the basis for the founding of Sierra Leone and Liberia. Return is historically constructed and artistically supported and justified. Thomas C. Holt argues that the first wave of return of the freed slaves was a form of forced removal and that the founding of the overseas settlements of freed slaves in Liberia and Sierra Leone was racially motivated. Holt's perspective contests the notion of philanthropist and Christian evangelism usually advanced as reasons for the establishment of these societies. He further points out that some of the freed slaves even rebelled against the idea of resettlement in Africa.[4] I view this perspective on the resettlement as further indication of the long-standing attitude of resentment American society has against people of color. Historical evidence suggests that to migrate to America, especially from West Africa, is to ignore the lessons of history. As the novels selected for study have abundantly shown, the chances for the illegal African migrant to succeed in the West are becoming alarmingly slim, if not nonexistent.

To conclude, I emphasize that, in the face of racial prejudice and the precarity of migrant life for the African characters in the diaspora, return is a better alternative, despite its complications. The suffering of the characters goes beyond legal status, and as Delphine Fongang has attested, regardless of the migrant's immigration status, "the struggle for cultural inclusion is constant."[5] And so I agree with her that "migrants with legal status have the slight edge in the sense that they can freely participate in economic opportunities; however, the shared notion of being racialized subjects limits their social and class mobility. Some migrants can only move up the economic ladder to a certain extent that hardly fulfills the envisioned desire of economic independence and empowerment."[6] Hence, "although migrants strive to live better lives in the West, many end up at the margins of society. *There are always singular stories of success and affluence enjoyed by some migrants, but the diasporic condition of the plurality of others remains pathetic*"[7] (emphasis added).

I validate Fongang's claim that "although migrants like Africans labor to create a life for themselves in the diaspora, the spaces they occupy are

---

4   Holt, *Children of Fire*, 224–25.
5   Fongang, "Cosmopolitan Dilemma," 30.
6   Fongang, "Cosmopolitan Dilemma," 30.
7   Fongang, "Cosmopolitan Dilemma," 30.

206 ❧ CONCLUSION

structurally exclusive, making it harder for them to belong as global citizens of the world. It is doubly hard for undocumented migrants who contribute to labor markets and economies, but remain in the shadows blanketed by their irregular or illegal status."[8] My analysis of the lives of Jende and Neni in *Behold the Dreamers* and the unnamed narrator in *Harare North* validates Fongang's assertion that "although the diaspora might be economically empowering to some migrants, it remains a space for continuous struggle by many facing marginality in society."[9] Hence, although "there are individual stories of self-definition and empowerment . . . it is safe to say that the diasporic experience remains for many a constant struggle for cultural inclusion and economic fulfillment."[10] For the great majority of these characters, departure and lived experience "did not result in automatic economic independence and cultural integration."[11] Life in the West for many remains "a constant struggle for adaptability and economic survival . . . characterized by fragmentation and traumatic alienations," as it is "becoming harder and harder to enjoy economic empowerment and cultural inclusion, leaving some migrants estranged and alienated in metropolitan spaces."[12]

Emmanuel Akyeampong, while acknowledging that migration offers a space for self-discovery and the possibility of accomplishing the dream, leading to a triumphant return to the homeland, laments that "many Africans abroad struggle to accomplish this feat of a successful return, and for many who discover to their chagrin that Western streets are not paved with gold, longing for home or nostalgia becomes an even more powerful memory and emotion."[13] The case for return cannot be better presented.

I reiterate, as *Ghana Must Go, Americanah,* and *So the Path Does Not Die* show, that return is not free of challenges. While Obinze and Ifemelu achieve economic success and socioeconomic advancement in Nigeria, Kweku dies upon his return to Ghana. Cammy recognizes the depths of emotional fulfillment that return to the homeland can provide, but he also points out the over-glamorization of the process and the rude shock of corruption and incompetence that await the returned migrant. While I recognize the challenges to return, I also point out the potential for creating a new hybridity that return offers as a basis for individual and societal transformation. I end with a theorization of an aesthetic of constructive liminality by which the returned migrant with a British or American passport assumes a dual identity

---

8   Fongang, "Cosmopolitan Dilemma," 29.
9   Fongang, "Cosmopolitan Dilemma," 27.
10   Fongang, "Cosmopolitan Dilemma," 27.
11   Fongang, "Cosmopolitan Dilemma," 28.
12   Fongang, "Cosmopolitan Dilemma," 28.
13   Akyeampong, "Africans in the Diaspora," 187.

and straddles both societies—the birth land and the adopted homeland. Even though this puts them in a state of continued liminality, it is intentional and constructive to combine the best of both worlds and ensure their creative potential. This is the perspective of the female protagonists Ifemelu in *Americanah* and Finaba in *So the Path Does Not Die* as a possible pathway for the future of African societies and the African migrant. It allows for a return home while keeping the doors to the adopted country open.

Bibliography

Achebe, Chinua. *Anthills of the Savannah*. New York: Anchor Press, 1988.

Achebe, Chinua. *A Man of the People*. New York: Anchor Books, 1989.

Adelakun, Abimbola, and Toyin Falola, eds. *Art, Creativity, and Politics in Africa and the Diaspora*. African Histories and Modernities. Cham, Switzerland: Springer Nature, 2018.

Adichie, Chimamanda Ngozi. *Americanah*. New York: Alfred A. Knopf, 2013.

Adichie, Chimamanda Ngozi. *Half of a Yellow Sun*. New York: Anchor Books, 2007.

Afolayan, Bosede Funke. "Politics of Migration: Dreams, Illusions, and Reality in Okey Ndibe's *Foreign Gods, Inc.* and NoViolet Bulawayo's *We Need New Names*." In *The Postcolonial Subject in Transit: Migration, Borders, and Subjectivity in Contemporary African Diaspora Literature*, edited by Delphine Fongang. Lanham, MD: Lexington Books, 2018.

Aidoo, Ama Ata. *The Dilemma of a Ghost; Anowa: Two Plays*. Burnt Mill, Harlow, Essex, England: Longman, 1987.

Akhuemokhan, Sophia. "'The Backward Glance': Repetition & Return in Pede Hollist's *So the Path Does Not Die*." *Diaspora & Returns in Fiction* African Literature Today, 34, edited by edited by Ernest N. Emenyǫnu, Helen Cousins, and Pauline Dodgson-Katiyo, 123–42. Woodbridge, Suffolk: James Curry, 2016.

Akyeampong, Emmanuel Kwaku. "Africans in the Diaspora: The Diaspora and Africa." *African Affairs: The Journal of the Royal African Society* 99, no. 395 (April 2000): 183-215.

Anderson, Carol. *One Person, No Vote: How Voter Suppression Is Destroying Our Democracy*. New York: Bloomsbury Publishing, 2018.

Armah, Ayi Kwei. *The Beautyful Ones Are Not Yet Born*. African Writers Series. Oxford: Heinemann, 1988.

Armah, Ayi Kwei. *Fragments: A Novel*. Popenguine, Senegal: Per Ankh, 2006.

Arnett, James, and Angela Wright. "Paul's Letter to the Congolese: Allegory, Optimism, and Universality in Alain Mabanckou's *Blue White Red*." *Genre* 50, no. 2 (July 2017): 239–65.

Arthur, John A. *African Diaspora Identities: Negotiating Culture in Transnational Migration*. Lanham, MD: Lexington Books, 2012.

210 ❧ BIBLIOGRAPHY

Arthur, John A., Joseph Takougang, and Thomas Owusu, eds. *Africans in Global Migration: Searching for Promised Lands*. Lanham, MD: Lexington Books, 2012.

Aspinall, Peter J., and Martha J Chinouya. *The African Diaspora Population in Britain: Migrant Identities and Experiences*. London: Palgrave Macmillan, 2016.

Beah, Ishmael. *A Long Way Gone: Memoirs of a Boy Soldier*. New York: Farrar, Straus and Giroux, 2007.

Bakhtin, Mikhail. *The Dialogic Imagination: Four Essays*. Edited by Michael Holquist. Translated by Caryl Emerson. University of Texas Press Slavic Series, No. 1. Austin: University of Texas Press, 1981.

Bhabha, Homi K. *The Location of Culture*. London: Routledge, 1994.

Borsa, Joan. "Towards a Politics of Location: Rethinking Marginality." *Canadian Woman Studies* 11, no. 1 (1990): 36–39.

Bulawayo, NoViolet. *We Need New Names*. Vintage Classics. London: Vintage, 2021.

Carter, Donald. *Navigating the African diaspora: the anthropology of invisibility*. Minneapolis: University of Minnesota Press, 2010.

Chikwava, Brian. *Harare North*. London: Vintage Books, 2010.

Cobo Pinero, Maria Rocio. "NoViolet Bulawayo's *We Need New Names* (2013): Mobilities and the Afropolitan Picaresque." *Journal of Postcolonial Writing* 55 (February 2019): 472–85.

Cole, Teju. *Open City: A Novel*. New York: Random House, 2011.

Cooper, Brenda. *A New Generation of African Writers: Migration, Material Culture & Language*. Woodbridge, Suffolk: James Currey, 2013.

Cousins, Helen. "Editorial: Leaving Home/Returning Home: Migration & Contemporary African Literature." In *Diaspora & Returns in Fiction*. African Literature Today, 34, edited by Ernest N. Emenyonu, Helen Cousins, and Pauline Dodgson-Katiyo, 1–11. Woodbridge, Suffolk: James Curry, 2016.

Crowley, Dustin. "How Did They Come to This? Afropolitanism, Migration, and Displacement." *Research in African Literatures* 49, no. 2 (2018): 125.

Diome, Fatou. *Le Ventre de L'Atlantique*. Paris: Éditions Anne Carrière, 2003.

Edwards, Kirsten T. "Incidents in the Life of Kirsten T. Edwards: A Personal Examination of the Academic In-Between Space." In *Learning from the Lived Experiences of Graduate Student Writers*, edited by Shannon Madden, Michele Eodice, Kirsten T. Edwards, and Alexandria Lockett, 52–72. Denver: University Press of Colorado, 2020.

Emenyonu, Ernest N., Helen Cousins, and Pauline Dodgson-Katiyo, eds. *Diaspora & Returns in Fiction*. African Literature Today, 34. Woodbridge, Suffolk: James Curry, 2016.

BIBLIOGRAPHY ❧ 211

Esplin, Marlene. "The Right Not to Translate: The Linguistic Stakes of Immigration in Chimamanda Ngozi Adichie's *Americanah*." *Research in African Literatures* 49, no. 2 (July 2018): 73.

Eze, Chielozona. "Rethinking African Culture and Identity: The Afropolitan Model." In *Afropolitanism: Reboot*, edited by Carli Coetzee, 4–17. London: Routledge, 2017.

Falola, Toyin, Niyi Afolabi, and Adérónké Adésolá Adésànyà. *Migrations and Creative Expressions in Africa and the African Diaspora*. Durham, NC: Carolina Academic Press, 2008.

Falola, Toyin. *The African Diaspora: Slavery, Modernity, and Globalization*. New York: University of Rochester Press, 2013.

Fedtke, Jana. "'Racial Disorder Syndrome': Observations on Racism in Chimamanda Ngozi Adichie's *Americanah*." *South Central Review* 38, no. 3 (2021): 59–64.

Feldner, Maximilian. *Narrating the New African Diaspora: 21st Century Nigerian Literature in Context*. African Histories and Modernities. Cham, Switzerland: Palgrave Macmillan, 2019.

Fongang, Delphine. "Cosmopolitan Dilemma: Diasporic Subjectivity and Postcolonial Liminality in Teju Cole 's *Open City*." *Research in African Literatures* 48, no. 4 (January 2017): 138.

Fongang, Delphine. "Inescapable Predicament: Migration and Diasporic Identity in Brian Chikwava's *Harare North*." In *The Postcolonial Subject in Transit: Migration, Borders, and Subjectivity in Contemporary African Diaspora Literature*, edited by Delphine Fongang. Lanham, MD: Lexington Books, 2018.

Fongang, Delphine, ed. *Postcolonial Subject in Transit: Migration, Borders, and Subjectivity in Contemporary African Diaspora Literature*. Lanham, MD: Lexington Books, 2018.

Foster, Christopher Ian. *Conscripts of Migration: Neoliberal Globalization, Nationalism, and the Literature of New African Diasporas*. Jackson, MS: University Press of Mississippi, 2020.

Furlonge, Nicole. "An Interview with Taiye Selasi." *Callaloo* 36, no. 3 (June 2013): 531–39.

Gikandi, Simon. "On Afropolitanism." In *Negotiating Afropolitanism: Essays on Borders and Spaces in Contemporary African Literature and Folklore*. Wawrzinek, Jennifer, and J. K. S. Makokha, 9–11. Amsterdam: Rodopi, 2011.

Gueye, Marame. "Fatou Diome's Le Ventre de l'Atlantique: Reconfiguring Local Discourses of Emigration." *Journal of African Literature Association* 14, no. 3 (2020): 472–85.

212 &❧ BIBLIOGRAPHY

Hall, Stuart. "The Local and Global: Globalization and Ethnicity." In *Culture, Globalization and the World-System: Contemporary Condition for the Representation of Identity*, edited by Anthony D. King, 19–39. Minneapolis, MN: University of Minnesota Press, 1977.

Hansberry, Lorraine. *A Raisin in the Sun*. New York: Vintage Books, 1994.

Hartwiger, Alexander Greer. "The Postcolonial Flâneur: *Open City* and the Urban Palimpsest." *Postcolonial Text* 11, no. 1 (2016): 1–17.

Hollist, Pede. *So the Path Does Not Die*. London: Jacaranda, 2016.

Holt, Thomas C. *Children of Fire: A History of African Americans*. New York: Farrar, Straus and Giroux, 2013.

Iheka, Cajetan Nwabueze, and Jack Taylor, eds. "Introduction: The Migration Turn in African Cultural Productions." In *African Migration Narratives: Politics, Race, and Space. Rochester Studies.*" Rochester, NY: University of Rochester Press, 2018.

Iheka, Cajetan Nwabueze, and Jack Taylor, eds. *African Migration Narratives: Politics, Race, and Space*. Rochester, NY: University of Rochester Press, 2018.

Irele, Augusta Atinuke. "Dystopian Dissonance: Migration, and Alienation in Imbolo Mbue's *Behold the Dreamers*." In *Literature of Indigeneity, Migration, and Trauma*, edited by Kate Rose. New York: Routledge, 2020.

Iromuanya, Julie. "Are We all Feminists? The Global Black Hair Industry and Marketplace in Chimamanda Ngozi Adichie's *Americanah*." *Meridians Feminism Race Transnationalism* 16, no. 1 (September 2018): 163–83.

Iyer, Nalini. "No Place to Call Home: Citizenship and Belonging in M. G. Vassaji's *The In-Between World of Vikram Lall*." In *Negotiating Afropolitanism: Essays on Borders and Spaces in Contemporary African Literature and Folklore*, edited by Jennifer Wawrzinek and J. K. S. Makokha, 9–11. Amsterdam: Rodopi, 2011.

Kamara, Samuel. "Enduring Paths, Crossroads and Intersections: Path-breaking Knowledges in Pede Hollist's *So the Path Does Not Die*." *Research in Sierra Leone Studies: Weave* 3, no. 1 (2015): 1–24.

Kane, Abdoulaye, and Todd H. Leedy, eds. *African Migrations: Patterns and Perspectives*. Bloomington: Indiana University Press, 2013.

Kirsch, Gesa E., and Joy S. Ritchie. "Beyond the Personal: Theorizing a Politics of Location in Composition Research." *College Composition and Communication* 46, no. 1(1995): 7.

Kral, Francoise. *Critical Identities in Contemporary Anglophone Disaporic Literature*. New York: Palgrave Macmillan, 2009.

Krishnan, Madhu. "Postcoloniality, Spatiality and Cosmopolitanism in the *Open City*." *Textual Practice* 29, no. 4 (February 2015): 675–96.

Krishnan, Madhu. "Reading Space, Subjectivity, and Form in the 21st Century Narrative of Return." In *The Contemporary African Migration Narrative: Politics, Race, Space, and Representation.* Edited by Cajetan Iheka and Jack Taylor, 143–59. Rochester, NY: University of Rochester Press, 2018.

Kwakye, Benjamin. *The Other Crucifix.* Banbury, UK: Ayebia Clarke Publishing, 2010.

Landry, Ava. "Black Is Black Is Black? African Immigrant Acculturation in Chimamanda Ngozi Adichie's *Americanah* and Yaa Gyasi's *Homegoing.*" *MELUS* 4, no. 3 (November 2018): 127–47.

Lawson, William. "The Western Scar: The Theme of the Been-To in West African Fiction." PhD diss., Ohio University, 1984.

Leigh, Raiford, and Heike Raphael-Hernandez, eds. *Migrating the Black Body: The African Diaspora and Visual Culture.* Seattle: University of Washington Press, 2017.

Long, Lynellyn D., and Ellen Oxfeld, eds. *Coming Home? Refugees, Migrants, and Those Who Stayed Behind.* Philadelphia: University of Pennsylvania Press, 2017.

Mabanckou, Alain. *Blue White Red: A Novel.* Translated by Alison Dundy. Bloomington: Indiana University Press, 2013.

Marsico, Giuseppina. "The 'Non-cuttable' Space in Between: Context, Boundaries and Their Natural Fluidity." *Journal of Integrated Psychology and Behavioral Science* 45, no. 2 (June 2011): 185–93.

Masur, Kate. *Until Justice Be Done: America's First Civil Rights Movement, from the Revolution to Reconstruction.* New York: W. W. Norton & Company, 2021.

Maver, Igor. "Teju Cole's Nigeria and the Open Cities of New York and Brussels." *Acta Neophilologica* 46, nos. 1–2 (December 2013): 3–11.

Mbue, Imbolo. *Behold the Dreamers: A Novel.* New York: Random House, 2016.

Mgbeadichie, Chike. "Beyond Storytelling: Conceptualizing Economic Principles in Chimamanda Adichie's *Americanah.*" *African Literatures* 52, no. 2 (2021): 119–35.

Moji, Polo Belina. "New Names, Translational Subjectivities: (Dis)location and (Re)naming in NoViolet Bulawayo's *We Need New Names.*" *Journal of African Cultural Studies* 27, no. 2 (January 2015): 181–90.

Moslund, Sten Pultz. *Migration Literature and Hybridity: The Different Speeds of Transcultural Change.* Basingstoke: Palgrave Macmillan, 2010.

Musila, Grace. "Unoka's, Okonkwo's and Ezeulu's Grandsons in Taiye Selasi's *Ghana Must Go* and Dinaw Mengestu's *How to Read the Air.*" In *Chinua Achebe's Legacy: Illuminations from Africa,* edited by James Ogude. Pretoria, South Africa: Africa Institute of South Africa, 2015.

Neumann, Birgit, and Yvonne Kappel. "Music and Latency in Teju Cole's *Open City*: Presences of the Past." *Ariel: A Review of International English Literature* 50, no. 1 (2019): 31–62.

Nnaemeka, Obioma. "Re-imagining the Diaspora: History, Responsibility, and Commitment in an Age of Globalization." *Dialectical Anthropology* 31 (2007): 127–41.

Nnaemeka, Obioma, and Jennifer Thornton Springer. *Unveiling Gender, Race & Diaspora*. Trenton, New Jersey: Africa World Press, 2016.

Njoya, Wandia. "Lark Mirror: African Culture, Masculinity, and Migration to France in Alain Mabanckou's *Bleu Blanc Rouge*." *Comparative Literature Studies: Literature and Theories of Africa* 46, no. 2 (January 2009): 338–59.

Nyman, Jopi. *Displacement, Memory, and Travel in Contemporary Migrant Writing*. Leiden: Brill / Rodopi, 2017.

Nyongesa, Andrew. *Cultural Hybridity and Fixity: Strategies of Resistance in Migration Literatures*. Oxford: Mwanaka Media and Publishing, 2018.

Nwanyanwu, Augustine. "Transculturalism, Otherness, Exile, and Identity in Chimamanda Ngozi Adichie's *Americanah*." *Matatu* 49, no. 2 (December 2017): 386–99.

Ogude, James, ed. *Chinua Achebe's Legacy: Illuminations from Africa*. Pretoria, South Africa: Africa Institute of South Africa, 2016.

Okigbo, Karen "*Americanah* and *Ghana Must Go*: Two Tales of the Assimilation Experiences of African Immigrants." Sociological Forum 32, no. 2 (June 2017): 444-448.Okolocha, H. Oby. "Negotiating Race, Identity and Homecoming in Chimamanda Ngozi Adichie's *Americanah* and Pede Hollist's *So the Path Does Not Die*." In *Diaspora & Returns in Fiction*, African Literature Today 34, edited by Ernest N. Emenyonu, Helen Cousins, and Pauline Dodgson-Katiyo, 143–63. Woodbridge, UK: James Curry, 2016.

Okpewho, Isidore, Carole Boyce Davies, and Ali A. Mazrui, eds. *The African Diaspora: African Origins and New World Identities*. Bloomington and Indianapolis: Indiana University Press, 2001.

Oniwe, Bernard Ayo. "Cosmopolitan Conversation and Challenge in Teju Cole's *Open City*." *Ufahamu: A Journal of African Studies* 39, no. 1 (2016): 43–65.

Phiri, Aretha. "Lost in Translation: Re-reading the Contemporary Afrodiasporic Condition in Taiye Selasi's *Ghana Must Go*." *European Journal of English Studies* 21, no. 2 (May 2017): 144–58.

Rampersad, Arnold, ed. *The Poems: 1921-1940 (Collected Works of Langston Hughes*, vol. 1). Columbia, MO: University of Missouri, 2001.

Rampersad, Arnold, ed. *The Poems: 1951-1967 (Collected Works of Langston Hughes*, vol. 3). Columbia, MO: University of Missouri, 2001.

BIBLIOGRAPHY 👪 **215**

Rose, Kate, ed. *Displaced: Literature of Indigeneity, Migration, and Trauma.* Routledge Studies in Contemporary Literature. New York: Routledge, 2021.

Rushton, Amy. "No Place Like Home: The Anxiety of Return in Taiye Selasi's *Ghana Must Go* and Yvonne Adhiambo Owuor's *Dust.*" *Etudes anglaises* 70, no. 1 (2017): 45–62.

Sackeyfio, Rose A. *West African Women in the Diaspora: Narratives of Other Spaces, Other Selves.* Abingdon, Oxon; New York: Routledge, 2023.

Said, Edward W. *Orientalism.* New York: Pantheon Books, 1978.

Schmidt-Haberkamp, Barbara, Marion Gymnich, and Klaus P Schneider, eds. *Representing Poverty and Precarity in a Postcolonial World.* edited by Cross/Cultures, Volume 25. Leiden: Brill, 2021.

Selasi, Taiye. *Ghana Must Go.* Toronto: Penguin, 2014.

Shillington, Kevin. *History of Africa.* New York: Macmillan, 1989.

Taylor, Jack. "Language, Race, and Identity in Adichie's *Americanah* and Bulowayo's *We Need New Names.*" Research in African Literatures 50 (2019): 68–85.

Terkenli, Theano S. "Home as a Region." *Geographical Review* 85, no. 3 (July 1995): 324.

Thomas, Dominic. "African Migration and African Dandys." In *Black France: Colonialism, Immigration, and Transnationalism.* Bloomington: Indiana University Press, 2007.

Thomas, Dominic. "The Global Mediterranean: Literature and Migration." *Yale French Studies* (January 2011): 140–53.

Thomas, Dominic. "The World of Alain Mabanckou." *World Literature Today* 90, no. 5 (September–October 2016): 68.

Traseira, Maria Jesus Cabarcos. "Between Diasporic Identity and Agency: Versions of the Pastoral in Gunah's Pilgrim's Way and Mohjoub's Navigation of a Rainmaker." In *Negotiating Afropolitanism: Essays on Borders and Spaces in Contemporary African Literature and Folklore,* edited by Jennifer Wawrzinek and J. K. S. Makokha. Amsterdam: Rodopi, 2011.

Uwakweh, Pauline Ada. *Women Writers of the New African Diaspora: Transnational Negotiations and Female Agency.* New York: Routledge, 2023.

Vermeulen, Pieter. "Flights of Memory: Teju Cole's *Open City* and the Limits of Aesthetic Cosmopolitanism." *Journal of Modern Literature* 37, no. 1 (Fall 2013): 40.

Walker, J. "Bringing the Wisdom of Wall Street to Limbe: Precarity and (American) Dream Narratives in Imbolo Mbue's *Behold the Dreamers.*" In *Representing Poverty and Precarity in a Postcolonial World,* edited by Barbara Schmidt-Haberkamp, Marion Gymnich, and Klaus P. Schneider. Boston: Brill, 2022.

BIBLIOGRAPHY

Walsh, John Patrick. "Mapping Afropea: The Translation of Black Paris in the Fiction of Alain Mabanckou." In *Francophone Afropean Literatures: Francophone Postcolonial Studies* edited by Nicki Hitchcott and Dominic Thomas. Liverpool: University of Liverpool Press, 2014.

Wawrzinek, Jennifer, and J. K. S. Makokha, eds. *Negotiating Afropolitanism: Essays on Borders and Spaces in Contemporary African Literature and Folklore*, 146. Amsterdam: Rodopi, 2011.

Yerima, Dina. "Regimentation or Hybridity? Western Beauty Practices by Black Women in Adichie's *Americanah*." *Journal of Black Studies* 48, no 7 (October 2017): 639–50.

Yitah, Helen, and Michael P. K. Okyerefo. "Migration, Cultural Memory and Identity in Benjamin Kwakye's *The Other Crucifix*." In *Diaspora & Returns in Fiction, African Literature Today* 34, edited by Ernest N. Emenyonu, Helen Cousins, and Pauline Dodgson-Katiyo. Woodbridge, UK: James Currey, 2016.

Zembe, Christopher Roy. *Zimbabwean Communities in Britain: Imperial and Post-Colonial Identities and Legacies*. Cham: Palgrave Macmillan, 2018.

Index

acculturation, 2, 7, 12, 180
Adichie, Chimamanda Ngozi, 2, 7, 8
aesthetics of fusion, 181; identity, 181;
 representation, 9
Afolayan, Bosede, 24–25, 37, 39
African diaspora literature, 1, 4, 6, 9
African diaspora women writers, 8
African migration, 4, 9; migrant
 experience, 3, 7–8, 18
Afropolitanism, 9–10, 12–13, 15–16,
 133–34, 186
Akhuemokhan, Sophia, 183–84, 189
Akyeampong, Emmanuel, 206
alterity, 1, 6, 9, 12
American accent, 68; blacks, 36, 157;
 citizen, 70, 72; cultural landscape,
 156; Declaration of Independence,
 50, 61–62, 170, 187, 204; dream,
 24, 45, 60, 109, 113, 116–17,
 119, 126, 129, 170, 173, 187,
 192, 202; Folk Art Museum, 52;
 passport, 112, 199, 206
Americanah, 161, 174
Anderson, Carol, 203
anthropology of invisibility, 9
Arnett, James, 93
assimilation, 35

Bakhtin, Mikhail, 181
Been-tos, 5, 58–59
belonging, 7, 9, 11, 13, 16–17, 59,
 191
Bhabha, Homi, 49, 52, 175, 181
border crossings, 9, 181
Borsa, Joan, 17

British Buttocks Cleaners, 99, 103,
 163
Bulawayo, NoViolet, 23, 26, 33, 37

Cancel, Robert, 9
capitalism, 117, 119, 137
capitalist system, 18, 116–17, 119,
 122, 125
Carter, Donald, 9
Chikwava, Brian, 33, 37, 94
Christ's crucifixion, 61
constructive liminality, 6, 16, 130–31,
 134, 180, 198–99
Cole, Teju, 22, 32, 45, 49, 51
Cooper, Brenda, 11
cosmopolitan ideology, 57
Cousins, Helen, 7, 173
Crow, Jim, 3, 203
Crowley, Dustin, 135, 142, 148, 173
cultural alienation, 61; barriers, 1;
 criticism, 8; erasure, 72, 153;
 heritage, 72, 139; hybridity,
 10–11, 140, 143, 176; identity,
 70, 173, 200; impunity, 14;
 integration, 15, 65, 69; memory,
 60; stereotypes, 67; stigma, 67
culture shock, 51, 56, 90

Davies, Carol Boyce, 9
discourse authoritative, 183–84;
 internally persuasive, 183–85;
 praxis, 9
Diome, Fatou, 6, 13
disillusionment, 18–19, 24, 28, 41,
 54, 76, 78, 89, 90, 187

218   INDEX

dislocation, 5
displacement, 7, 9–10, 28, 54, 60, 140
Dodgson-Katiyo, Pauline, 7, 173

Esplin, Marlene, 158
ethnic discrimination, 73
ethnocentrism, 8
emancipation, 3
exclusion, 59, 108, 146, 153, 161
Eze, Chielozona, 134

Falola, Toyin, 8
Fedtke, Jana, 153
Feldner, Maximilian, 7, 152, 155
Fongang, Delphine, 51, 108, 205
Foster, Christopher, 8

Ghanaian culture, 16
Ghanaian ethnicity, 144
Gikandi, Simon, 9, 13, 15
globalization, 8–9, 51
Gueye, Marame, 13–14

Hartwiger, Alexander, 46–48
history, 47, marginalized, 49, 51, 53, 127
Hollist, Pede, 16, 160, 180, 182, 186, 192–93, 200
Holt, Thomas C., 203, 205
home, 12–14, 16, 59, 125, 130, 152, 179, 186, 188–89, 191, 200, 207
Hughes, Langston, 3, 204–5
hyperculturality, 134

identity: African, 68, 134, 186;
American, 68; Caribbean, 209;
cultural, 139; diasporic, 8;
ethnic, 4, 7, 68; formation, 9–10;
Ghanaian, 26, 71; hybridized, 142, 152; hyphenated, 180–81, 200;
racial, 4, 7; traditional markers, 10
ideological construct, 8
Iheka, Cajetan, 11–12

illegal migrants, 18, 40, 76–77, 101, 126
illegal migration, 77, 82
immigration system, 109, 113–14
integration, 8, 10–12, 17, 35, 140, 148
Irele, Augusta Atinuke, 111
Iromuanya, Julia, 173
Islamophobia, 55
Iyer, Nalini, 13, 15

Kane, Abdoulaye, 7
Kappel, Yvonne, 53
Kamara, Samuel, 200–201
Koita, Yaguine, 79, 200
Krishnan, Madhu, 12, 46
Kwakye, Benjamin, 3, 22, 57–59, 65, 160

Landry, Ava, 2, 66, 153
Lawson, William, 5
Leedy, Todd, 7
linguistic fragmentation, 8

Mabanckou, Alain, 6, 77, 81
marginality, 51–52
Marisco, Guiseppina, 16
Masur, Kate, 200
Maver, Igor, 53
Mediterranean Sea, 1, 79
memory, 41, 77
Mbembe, Achille, 15
Mbue, Imbolo, 8, 25, 109–11, 113, 115
Mgbeadichie, Chike, 173
Middle Passage, 51, 199
migration: African, 55; bird, 49;
human, 54; internal, 189;
international, 5, 151; regional, 32, 151
Moji, Polo Belina, 24, 26, 37
MoneyGram, 41
Moslund, Sten P., 9, 11, 180–81

multiculturalism, 165, 169
Musila, Grace, 16, 141–42

narratives of war, 5
Native American genocide, 52, 55
nativism, 14, 55
naturalization, 70, 72
nepotism, 4
Neumann, Brigit, 53
new hybridity, 6, 9, 131, 134, 143, 152, 175, 180–81
Njoya, Wandia, 80–81
Nkrumah, Kwame, 39, 69
Nnaemeka, Obioma, 9
Nollywood, 177
nostalgia, 9, 14, 34–35, 41–44, 115, 175, 192
NPFL, 53, 55
Nwanyanwu, Augustine, 156
Nyman, Jopi, 9
Nyongesa, Andrew, 10

Obama, Barack, 112
Okigbo, Karen, 157
Okpewho, Isidore, 9
Okolocha, Oby H., 185
Okyerefo, Michael, 9
Oniwe, Bernard Ayo, 57
Orientalism, 55–56
Other, 62, 69, 166–67; African, 165; ethnicized, 2, 56, 62; racialized, 2, 56; victimized, 56

palimpsest, 47
Phiri, Aretha, 133
Pinera, Maria Roco Cobo, 24–25
postcolonial flaneur, 45
post-independence disillusionment, 4
postmodernism, 134
precarity, 6, 9, 12, 24, 76, 90, 98, 130, 131
Promised Land, 61
Province of Freedom, 188

psychological breakdown, 8; connotations, 14; consequences, 3; damage, 3; dependence, 90; depression, 1, 3, 18–19, 22, 76, 109; displacement, 60; toll, 138, 140; torture, 77, 121; turmoil, 64; trauma, 39, 95, 108, 125, 138, 172, 196

reintegration, 9, 19, 58, 131, 141, 151, 173
racial difference, 55–56; discrimination, 6, 55; identity, 64, 66, 153, 160, 164; inferiority, 66; prejudice, 22, 137, 169, 204; profiling, 78; superiority, 38
racism, 1, 3, 8, 34, 36, 38, 44, 53, 61, 63–64, 73, 133, 135, 145, 153, 161–62, 164–65, 168, 191
reconciliation, 143–44, 148–51
residency permanent, 72; undocumented, 76, 97
return, 7, 9, 43–44, 59, 69, 128, 175, 179, 191, 195, 198; argument for, 8, 18, 67; complications of, 69, 76, 150, 152; dilemma of, 35; hermeneutic of, 3, 9; motivation for, 73; possibility of, 11, 24
returned migrant, 6, 9, 131, 181, 193, 200
right-wing nationalism, 55
rootedness, 5, 10, 14
Rushton, Amy, 134

Sackeyfio, Rose, 154
Sahara Desert, 1, 54
Selasi, Taiye, 12, 15, 133, 141
social alienation, 79
spatial constructions, 7; geography, 7, 17; theory, 148
spatiality, 12
Springer, Jennifer Thornton, 9
standard English, 63

220 ❧ INDEX

syncopation, 147

Taylor, Jack, 11–12, 38, 158
Terkenli, Theano S., 13–14
Thomas, Dominic, 78–79
Tounkara, Fode, 79, 200
transcultural fluidity, 10
transculturalism, 156
trauma, 5, 28–30, 34, 51, 119, 135, 140, 172

unrealized dreams, 45
Uwakweh, Pauline, 8

Vermeulen, Pieter, 53
Vico, Gionanni, 183
violence, 5, 30, 33, 51, 53, 109

Walmart, 42
Walker, Julian, 126
Walsh, John Patrick, 88
Western Union, 41
whiteness, 64, 153
worldliness of the migrant, 175, 181
World Trade Center, 52
Wright, Angela, 93

xenophobia, 8, 55

Yitah, Helen, 59–60
Yerima, Dina, 153

ZANU-PF, 98
Zembe, Christopher, 7

Printed in the United States
by Baker & Taylor Publisher Services